CISTERCIAN FATHERS SERIES: NUMBER SIXTY-NINE

GW00685625

Sky-blue is the Sapphire, Crimson the Rose

Stillpoint of Desire in John of Forde

CISTERCIAN FATHERS SERIES: NUMBER SIXTY-NINE

Sky-blue is the Sapphire, Crimson the Rose

Stillpoint of Desire in John of Forde

Hilary Costello OCSO

CISTERCIAN PUBLICATIONS
Kalamazoo, Michigan

Translations are based on that of Wendy Mary Beckett, *John of Ford: Sermons on the Final Verses of the Song of Songs*, 7 volumes. Kalamazoo: Cistercian Publications, 1977-1984. That translation and this have been made from the critical latin edition prepared by Edmund Mikkers and Hilary Costello, *Ioannis de Forda, Super extremam partem Cantici canticorum sermones cxx,* Corpus Christianorum, Continuatio Mediævalis, volumes 17-18. Turnhout: Brepols, 1970.

Library of Congress Cataloging-in-Publication Data

John, Abbot of Ford.
    [Super extremam partem Cantici canticorum sermones CXX. English. Selections]
    Sky-blue is the sapphire, crimson the rose : stillpoint of desire in John of Forde / [edited by] Hilary Costello.
       p.   cm. — (Cistercian Fathers series ; no. 69)
    Translated by Wendy Beckett.
    Includes bibliographical references (p.   ).
    ISBN-13: 978-0-87907-569-9 (pbk. : alk. paper)
    ISBN-10: 0-87907-569-4 (pbk. : alk. paper)
    1. Bible. O.T. Song of Solomon—Sermons. 2. Sermons, Latin—Translations into English. 3. Catholic Church—Sermons. I. Costello, Hilary. II. Beckett, Wendy. III. Title. IV. Series.

BS1485.54.J64213 2006
223'.906—dc22   2005028787

TABLE OF CONTENTS

INTRODUCTION

JOHN OF FORDE lived from about 1145 until 1214. His death was at a time when the universities were filled with students during the early scholastic period. Although he reacted at times rather strongly against the tendency to make theology into a mere exercise of the reasoning faculty, his spirituality was in fact one of the crowning glories of his age. A contemporary cistercian nun, Beverley Aitken, wrote of him a few years ago before her death: John of Forde

> has been described as a man of unfailing courtesy and charm, a master of the spiritual life, a wise and holy writer. I find him a lovably generous and passionate person, whose sermons are peppered with superlatives: 'fully', 'wholly', 'always', 'never'. Paul is healed, for example, not by a 'look from Jesus' but by a 'long look from Jesus'. Again, it is not just the 'silence' of the infant Christ, but "the thunder of his silence". John is sure of himself, sure of his teaching, profoundly prayerful and humble.*

The excerpts printed here are all taken from John's Commentary on the Song of Songs, written during the period when he was abbot of the monastery of Forde in Devon, from 1191 until his

---

* 'John of Forde: Twelfth Century Guide for Twentieth Century Monks', in Hilary Costello and Christopher Holdsworth, edd., *A Gathering of Friends: The Learning and Spirituality of John of Forde*, CS 161 (Kalamazoo: Cistercian Publications, 1996) pp. 189-198, here 189.

death. He had already been chosen or elected as abbot five years earlier when, in 1186, he became abbot of Bindon, a daughter-house of Forde. He was well known even then as an author of distinction. While he was prior of Forde during the abbacy of Baldwin, who later became Archbishop of Canterbury, he wrote the life of Wulfric of Haselbury, a local hermit and one of the most noted saints of his time (†1154). This work still exists in four manuscripts of the twelfth century, and at the time of writing is being prepared for publication in Latin and in an English translation. John was also author of a commentary on the prophecy of Jeremiah which has not survived.

In addition to being an exegete, John was also a well informed member of the Cistercian General Chapter which he was required to attend each year. There were occasions when he was absent—and because of this he was given a penance. Nevertheless he was appointed as the representative of the Order in undertaking some difficult assignments; in particular he was commissioned to sort out the problems at Margam Abbey in Wales, where the laybrothers had staged a revolt against the decrees of the General Chapter.

In his sermons on the *Song of Songs* John of Forde follows the time-approved method of interpretation used by the Church Fathers. On one level, namely, according to the literal meaning, it is simply a love-song between the spouse and his bride. It starts with the desire for a kiss, an embrace, and goes through every emotion of romantic and erotic endearment, every hidden yearning for nuptial and sexual experience, and describes in vivid and poetic language every feeling and motion of love. On that level, one might question its inclusion in the Bible, as has been done by many authors both recent and ancient. There seems no place in the Sacred Scriptures for a song that is so frankly erotic. Yet that is not the interpretation given to it by the Fathers of the Church from the time of Origen onwards, and indeed by their jewish forebears. For them the Song of Songs is fundamentally an allegory, an expression, that is to say, of the love God has for his people, and more particularly, in christian thought, the love between Jesus Christ, the Spouse, and his Bride, the Church. To read it in any other way would have been for them a complete betrayal of its true meaning. As far as they are concerned, it must not be read merely on the literal level; to do so would embroil the reader in sexual fantasies that are far removed from the true meaning of the Song. That is not to say that they despised or ignored the literal meaning. On the contrary, they looked to it for some basis on which to gain an insight into the allegorical or spiritual meaning.

In this tradition, which John of Forde never questions, the 'Spouse' of the Song is Jesus Christ and his 'Bride' is first of all the Church, and then, by participation in the membership of the Church, the Bride is anyone who 'loves the Lord Jesus'. He devotes many of these sermons to the 'Spouse', to the praise of the Lord Jesus Christ, either in his divinity or in some particular aspect of his human nature. At the same time he adheres faithfully to his principal focus, which is that he is writing for his monks. He desires above all to arouse in them 'that bold, wild eagerness of longing to desire the desire of Jesus' love, so desirable and lovable'. This is the over-riding theme of all John writes. He was, however, too much of a theologian and too well-versed in the great tradition to leave it at that. There are two phrases that sum up the essence of his thought: *sponsa Christi*, the Bride of Christ, and *sponsa Verbi*, the bride of the Word. The former, which often occurs at the end of a sermon, refers to the ancient patristic tradition that the church is united with Christ as a bride with her bridegroom. Saint Paul uses the expression 'Christ is the Head of the Body' to express the same thought, that the Church is the Mystical Body of Christ.

Saint Paul writes, *Now you are the body of Christ and individually members of it;* in the same vein John of Forde raises the insight:

> Consequently, there is a twofold sense in which it is
> said, 'Chosen in thousands'. It can be understood

correctly in either way, whether it refers to a totality
or to separate individuals, that is to say, whether you
take it as the beauty of the whole, or each one in
thousands. God is wonderful in his saints in both
these ways, wonderful in all, wonderful in each.[1]

We see here that, for John, the Church is not primarily an
institution, even though it must necessarily be embodied in the
framework of an institutional society. Christ as the Spouse or
Bridegroom of the Church must be considered as the most fundamental principle of John's ecclesiology. He tells us this quite
explicitly when he calls the Church 'the first and principal Bride
of Jesus'.[2] We find him saying almost the same thing in another
place, using the romantic words of the Song, 'It is easy to understand that the Church, which is the great and principal Bride of
Christ, should hear from her Spouse in a truly unique manner,
"One is my dove, one is my perfect one"'.[3] The reason for this is
that the Church has within itself the full power of Christ's resurrection; it is the sacrament or mystery of the Risen One who im-
parts life and resurrection to us through the Church. 'In its
deepest understanding the Church is nothing other than the
world in the course of transfiguration, the world that in Christ
reflects the light of paradise'.[4]

John of Forde often refers to the union between Christ and
the Church as a marriage. That symbolism brings to the fore the
love that unites them. Because the Church is so closely united
with Christ in love, theirs is a union that drives forward with a
dynamic surge towards the ultimate mystery that will only be
fully achieved in heaven.

The other well-established title, *sponsa Verbi*, the bride of the
Word, is at the heart of these sermons. In the language of the
Song of Songs, the person who enters on the way of the spiritual

---

[1] Sermon 5.2
[2] Sermon 56.3
[3] Sermon 54.7; Sg 6:8
[4] Olivier Clément, *The Roots of Christian Mysticism* (London: New City, 1998) 95.

life is as yet a 'young maiden', *adolescentula*, who stands in need of conversion. *Adolescentia* is the time for self-examination and self-knowledge. But as the beginner advances in virtue and strives by deep longing and humble repentance for union with Christ, he or she enters ever more deeply into the way of contemplative love and thus becomes 'a bride of the Word'. This growth demands the full discipline of the following of Jesus by means of compassion, prayer, silence, the reading of Scripture and the pursuit of 'wisdom'. True silence is not mere taciturnity but the following of Jesus who gave no answer to those who accused him: 'My Lord Jesus was silent before the scribes and pharisees, silent before his judges, silent before those who punished him with scourging and crucifixion'.[5] His silence is full of grace and truth. Who will give his heart, John challenges us, to being a loving imitator of this sacred silence? Who will enter the school of this hidden philosophy and sit at Jesus' feet?

John often talks about the need to read the Scriptures. The person who ponders the Scriptures day and night, who enters as far as possible into a spiritual understanding of the reality revealed therein gains that knowledge of the Word which is essentially a gift of the Holy Spirit. Although John himself was thoroughly imbued with the Scriptures—to such an extent that every page of his sermons is, as it were, a catena of quotations, he does not confine himself solely to Scripture reading. He invites his reader to discover the Lord in all the works of creation. In this he is at one with Saint Augustine, who calls the cosmos 'the first Bible'. You can search for God in everything, like the bee that buzzes from flower to flower in search of the nectar that it transforms into honey. This honey is the understanding of the infinite mystery of God's revelation of himself in Jesus Christ. Understanding and contemplation, two aspects of 'wisdom', are inextricably linked.

John of Forde uses the word 'contemplation' in several ways. Sometimes it means gazing on the earthly life of Jesus as

[5] Sermon 22.3

described in the Gospels. We can do this by forming pictures in the imagination when we dwell lovingly on some episode of his life. In some lovely passages John invites us to go with him and imagine ourselves, for example, with the Magi gazing on the face of the infant Jesus in the manger or at his mother Mary's breast.[6] This simple form of contemplation, which more modern writers would probably call meditation, John proposes as a preamble to that deeper form in which the bride gazes long and steadily on the face of the Eternal Word.

With candid humility John of Forde confesses his own lack of experience in high matters.[7] Yet in the same sermon he has recorded something of his own personal ardor:

> There are times when my Lord comes to me to tell me more joyful things than I, for my part, had expected or hoped for . . . . When I ponder this well, relishing it with an indescribable sensation of sweetness, I think to myself, 'He has called me to the marriage feast'. This thought makes everything a delight, everything a glory.[8]

In the following sermons he is able to go on to something deeper still. Yet even at the height of his rapture and joy in the Lord he retains the due balance of true christian discretion and a certain sedate restraint, so that 'when the bride is carried out of herself, she is not carried away from herself more than is right and proper'.[9] Not for John the excesses of certain modern cults who work themselves up into uncontrolled frenzies and undignified emotional outbursts. The experience of a bride is a lot deeper than that; at its deepest level it is a marriage with the Word.[10] By long exposure to a special bond of union with the Holy Spirit,

---

[6] Sermon 11.6
[7] Sermon 43.12
[8] Sermon 43.5
[9] Sermon 43.6
[10] Sermon 4.5

the heart and mind of this chosen soul is endowed with joyous wonder and conformed to the likeness of the Word with a peace that surpasses all understanding and invades the whole of her being.[11]

As with the other cistercian writers, John of Forde has a tender devotion to Christ's humanity. Every word in his commentary is redolent with a yearning for Christ's love. One gets the impression that his whole life has been given over to this love from the moment he entered the monastic life at Forde Abbey. There is no explicit indication of his age when he started this commentary, but by the year 1200 he must have been well into his fifties, possibly nearing sixty. He clearly states in his Prologue that he has lost something of his first fervor, and he therefore longs 'that my whole soul might catch fire from these words of burning eloquence that I am commenting on'.[12]

John takes up his Commentary at Chapter 5:8 of the Song. This is the point at which the commentary of Gilbert of Hoyland breaks off. Gilbert, abbot of Swineshead in Lincolnshire, had followed on from the commentary begun by Saint Bernard of Clairvaux. Bernard's commentary comprised eighty-seven sermons and reached Chapter 3:3. It is highly unlikely that Saint Bernard ever intended to complete his Commentary. The words of the Song had provided a spring-board for his insights into the ultimate purpose of life and they reveal his passionate love for the Lord Jesus. Has anyone ever surpassed the poetry of this yearning love? In his final sermons he gave expression to his most profound thoughts on the subject of 'love'. There is no indication at all that he intended to take his commentary much further before he died in 1153. Nevertheless, the Englishman, Gilbert of Swineshead, took up the challenge and got as far as Chapter 5:10 before death claimed him too, in 1172. John hoped to pursue his own Commentary to the end of the Song, and succeeded in one hundred-twenty sermons.

[11] Sermon 68.3
[12] Prologue 6

John of Forde does not attempt to copy the subtle brilliances of Saint Bernard. He has his own distinctive charm. He speaks from personal experience. His enthusiasm and his longing for full and undivided love of Jesus draws us to emulate his own ardor, an ardor that is often grounded on careful observation of nature and life. Yet, 'Among the Cistercian writers it is John's special gift to have pierced the secret of Christ's interiority: his self-emptying'.[13] Saint John, 'the beloved disciple' understood the full depth of Jesus' love, and he it is who reveals to us 'the grace and truth that have come through Jesus Christ'.[14]

John's reliance on the Fourth Gospel is brought home to us by an abundance of quotations. He loves to ponder the meaning of the Word's dwelling 'in the bosom of the Father' from the beginning, and he lifts our contemplation of this mystery to the ultimate vision of the Word's glory. This phrase and its equivalent occur more than twenty times in these sermons. It sums up succinctly the relationship between the Father and the Son and the Son with the Father within the unfathomable mystery of the Blessed Trinity. We can only stand in awe before this mystery, which is totally beyond our comprehension. Modern scientific discoveries, even when they take us, as it were, to the very threshold of the act of creation, allowing us to glimpse at wonders of energy and power that stop scarcely short of the Infinite, only leave us with a greater sense of wonder. John hesitantly places a toe within this sanctuary and invites us to imagine the Father looking out from this hidden splendor at the world of his creating, and deciding to choose Mary, the lowly handmaid whom 'all people' call blessed. She found grace most richly in his eyes, not for herself only, but for the whole of creation yet to come.[15]

The full power of John's teaching is revealed to us in his reflections on the resurrection. For him, the resurrection dawned when the Lord Jesus chose us to greet the new radiance. Christ

---

[13] Beverly Aitken (above, n. 1), p. 190.
[14] Jn 1:17
[15] Sermon 19.2

triumphed over death so that we may claim a huge share in the glory of the resurrection and dwell with him in the heavenly places. Like an eagle he bears us to glory—bearing us as eaglets to the heavens. The glory of the resurrection is perceived in the fact that the Word, while retaining the flesh he once assumed, is now totally steeped in the glory of the new immortality which will never, for all eternity, be shed. Taken up together with him we too may render indescribable and glorious praise to God the Father.

It is this glory of the resurrection that is perhaps the theme that shines through all John's thought, because he sees that glory as ours, something we have a right to as true friends of Jesus. 'Whatever is lacking,' he says, 'in the share I have of his glory, is most richly made up to me in the rich fullness of his glory, to my unbounded joy and delight.'[16] For us, then, it is faith in the resurrection, granted to us by the Father, that joins us to all the holy men and women who have arrived at the goal of their longing. In this sense death is a grace because it takes us into the garden, that scented garden where the saints are alive, incorruptible, and immortal. It is a garden that the Saviour has transformed from glory to glory; rather the Saviour himself is the garden in which he has transformed us by the glorious joy of his unceasing resurrection.

John of Forde called death 'a good messenger'. Death is good because it ultimately brings the good news, the news that Jesus is there waiting, willing to transform us into his own glory. This good messenger came to John on 14 April 1214.

For seven hundred years his inspiring thought and remarkable teaching remained largely unknown, and certainly never attained the impressive interest that its publication thirty years ago has generated. Suddenly he has become one of the few outstanding writers in the cistercian pantheon. His charm for his readers today lies in the genial simplicity of his style, which speaks

---

[16] Sermon 27.8

directly to the heart. His style is simple and direct. Yet at the same time what he says is profound and often distinctly original. Here is a theologian with a flair for language that appeals to ordinary folk. Feminism was not prominent on the agenda of theologians in the thirteenth century. It is only in the past hundred years that it has become an important, even aggressive, perspective. Yet here we meet a theologian with an expansive heart who is not afraid of deep emotional feelings when dealing with fundamental questions. He enters, for example, the compassionate heart of Jesus with all the tenderness of a mother, broken with grief. There must be few spiritual writers who can achieve such poignancy without trailing some note of misjudged sentimentality. Drawing on his personal experience of the courts of law, both civil and ecclesiastical, in Sermon 10 he sets a scene of passionate conflict between good and evil, between innocence and wickedness, personalized in the huge burden of human sin placed on the shoulders of the savior, a dramatic scene both imaginative and emotional.

Not everyone today may be prepared to tackle the seven volumes of the english translation, especially as John of Forde was intentionally rather prolix in his commentary. I have therefore tried to condense the essential themes of his thought into one volume so that his teaching may become more accessible to the average reader. For myself I have found in him a source of constant inspiration and an awakening to new life.

Hilary Costello OCSO

Mount Saint Bernard Abbey
Coalville, Leicestershire

EDITORIAL NOTE

John of Forde's sermon-commentaries on the Song of Songs reveal a man of prayer and profound insight, a man who knew Scripture intimately and who strove to live according to its teaching and to lead others to experience the presence of God.. By presenting the marrow of his thought in a thematically structed anthology, we hope that those who may find the prospect of sifting through one hundred twenty sermons somewhat daunting will be introduced to this spiritual master.

In choosing passages from the sermons of John of Forde to provide this flowing narrative which accurately conveys John's thought and style, the editor has omitted some of the meanderings of medieval monastic exegesis which modern readers sometimes find distracting. Omissions have not been indicated by ellipses. Those wishing to read the full texts should consult the translation of Wendy Mary Becket, *John of Ford: Sermons on the Final Verses of the Song of Songs,* Cistercian Fathers Series 29, 39, 43-47. While the translation of John's sermons is based on Sister Wendy's translation, the editor has worked from the latin text and at various places altered the translation.

Direct quotations from Scripture have been italicized. Allusions and paraphrases have been set in roman type and identified in the notes without an intrusive *Cf.* or *Cp.* Scriptural citations have been made according to the hebrew enumeration.

I

SEEKING THE LOVE OF THE WORD

AN OVERVIEW

J OHN OF FORDE does not attempt to give an ordered theological framework to his thought. Rather, he takes each verse of the Song as it comes and draws out its spiritual meaning for his reader. For this reason I have not tried to put his thought into a precise or tidy structure, but simply to weld together certain themes that seem to represent, in his own words, the aspirations of his heart. If this inspires you to a greater devotion to and love of Our Lord Jesus Christ, then John of Forde would be well pleased and I will have been a tool in this beautiful work.

We begin this first section with the soul's yearning for Jesus. This implies that a person has already been looking for a meaning to life and has found that meaning in his or her search for God by reading, prayer, and other forms of human endeavor. There is no point in reading a book like this unless you are sufficiently convinced that the journey towards God is worthwhile. John of Forde's enthusiasm is catching, and I have tried here to choose those passages that bring out this captivating passion as a solid entry into his deeper thought. He is, of course, writing for monks. But there is no need to confine his words to them. Many people these days are just as keen as he and his monks were to devote their lives to the quest.

This journey is like setting out to discover the source of the river that runs at the bottom of your garden. The journey is sometimes pleasant and takes you through green fields and sun-drenched shades; sometimes it is difficult as you plod

3

through freezing rain and muddy footpaths. Yet when you arrive at the source you find the water has already invaded your soul; your spirit is filled from the rush of living water. The quest was not your own, but poured out on you from the Spirit of God. You move on, drenched in secret streams of grace. In Sermon Seventeen these streams flow from fortitude to withstand the devil's wiles, prudence to discern the working of the Spirit, the understanding that reveals the deep meanings of Scripture, the wisdom that delights in nothing except God alone. The apostles too were drenched with the Spirit, but also set on fire with burning tongues of fiery eloquence to unite all people to Christ.

Any person thus immersed in these waters of grace is well-pleasing to the Father and, to change the metaphor, has become adorned with the rich gold ornaments that befit her state. Each is clothed in the gold of love according to the degree of her preparedness: one person may offer to the Lord Jesus the gold of her original innocence, another may present to him the gold of sorrow and repentance, a third may bring him the purest gold from Arabia, a mysterious gift that Jesus accepts from those who are not yet with him but waiting with their treasures at hand. All look up with eager longing to their king, the Lord Jesus in his risen glory resplendent as a sapphire, sky blue like the heavens, one with the Father in the embrace of the Holy Spirit.

In the second part of this section I have concentrated on the theme of the Church as the principal Bride of Christ. From Sermon Three through to Sermon Ten John of Forde focuses upon Song 5:10, 'My beloved is all radiant and ruddy, chosen in thousands'. These eight sermons may be the result of a conscious desire on John's part to match Saint Bernard's first eight sermons on the Song, where he develops the theme of the Word 'kissing' Jesus' human nature so that two natures are united in one Person. John of Forde takes the opportunity of portraying Jesus in all his divine and human beauty. Radiantly white in his resurrection, he

is nonetheless covered in the red blood and shame of his crucifixion. At the same time he is fully united with the many thousands of those who follow him; the greater the intimacy the
more he is one with them in the Church. On the one hand he is
totally apart because of his unique relationship with his Father;
on the other hand he is totally within his Church and in all who
are his. Totally within the Church as a whole, he is totally within
each of its members by grace. In each of them he is within by indwelling power. Although he is the fairest of men, his beauty is
totally for all. 'The Lord Jesus is himself your beauty, your
flower.'[1] This beauty can refer to the totality of the Church or to
each separate individual within the Church. God is wonderful in
his saints in both ways: wonderful in all, wonderful in each. John
has a vision of the Church which is impossible to convey in
words, but if you remain with him in your search for the Lord,
before long you will enter into his vision and be filled with his
incomparable joy. True, this vision is no other than that of Saint
Paul when he dwells on the mystery of the Church, yet John was
able to bring out in all its meaning its deep significance by the
persuasive force of his eloquent language that flows from a rich
interior conviction.

John is not yet well known, but day by day his stature grows
as the vital content of his thought is more and more appreciated
by discerning readers and theologians.

[1] See Sermon 5.1

Burning with Love
for One Who is So Lovable

YOU KNOW, MOST LOVING JESUS, that it was because of desire for your love that I over-reached myself. Support me with your hand in case I fall, and speak out on my behalf. Most tranquil, most gentle, most wise of Lords, set in motion and direct in your servant's hand this pen, the obedient servant of your love. At your good pleasure, steep it in the ink of your spirit. For to you, most beautiful among the sons of men, into your power has the Father given the ink of writers, so that from your ink into our little vessels you may pour according to the measure of your giving.[†] *It is love that I have undertaken to serve in this work to the praise of your holy name. Burning with the desire for your love, I said to myself in thought:* 'Who will give me of the fountain of the living waters of my Lord,†* so that I may drink and be inebriated and forget my wretchedness? Who will intimate something of the art of loving?' *All of a sudden while I was thrashing this out with my soul, the thought came to me of the song of your love, your holy nuptial canticle in all its sweetness.*

At the beginning of this song I find your bride—that soul, whoever it is, whom you deign to call by this glorious title—I find her yearning and sighing most ardently that she may deserve to enjoy the kiss of your most sacred mouth. I hear your

^{Eph 4:7}

^{Jer 17:13}

consoling words to her, in which you gladly bestow on this bride of yours the kindest looks and the sweetest speech. There was enkindled within me a bold wild eagerness of longing, Lord, to desire the desire of your love, so desirable and lovable.

Moreover, it is my ardent intention and my duty, under your inspiration, to draw my brothers towards the aroma of your ointments.† *It is my duty to serve them outwardly, but yours to work within, you who teach men wisdom, touching the heart with spiritual unction. My task will be to display in speech or writing the significance of your words, but it is yours by the Holy Spirit to write deep in the soul what these words mean.*

Sg 1:3

I searched deep within my heart for the purpose of my writing. First and foremost, that I might offer the Lord God my Saviour the service of my lips as a sacrifice of praise. Secondly, to serve fraternal charity and to discharge to some degree the debt that I owe to my brothers. Thirdly, that my own soul might catch fire from these words of burning eloquence that I am commenting on. Nothing could be more effective to drive away coldness of spirit than the fire of this nuptial song at which the Bride of the Lord does not restrain her soul from fainting and melting away.

To you, Lord Jesus, I entrust this work of mine. Grant that from this little sowing I may reap some fruit of edification for my brothers. May you, O God, who are the seed in the hand of the sower, be also a sheaf in the hand of the reaper! For you are the end and beginning of every good work, the aim and the reward, the glory and blessing of your faithful people, Spouse of the Church, praise of the angels and

Wisdom of God the Father, who with the Holy Spirit lives and reigns, God, for ever and ever.

From the Prologue

THE DESIRE FOR LOVE: JESUS MY FRIEND

THE SPIRIT OF FREEDOM is the cause of the bride's love, and it is also what makes her able to love and to be loved. The bride casts away any veil of modesty, and seems to forget the heavenly majesty of Jesus, her Spouse, to forget that his least command makes the pillars of heaven tremble.† She simply glories that Jesus is her friend, while the maidens look on. She says, Such is my Beloved and he himself is my friend, daughters of Jerusalem.†

Job 26:11

Sg 5:16

To your praise of him, he replies with equal praise of you, and we find the testimony he bears very sure.† His testimony, then, is that you have spoken in a spirit of humility, no less than in a spirit of love.

Ps 93:6

She says to her daughters, 'You have heard me speak many things in praise of my Beloved. Yet this is more wonderful than all I have said that, although my Beloved is such as he is, he has nevertheless stooped to become my friend'. The Only-Son of the Father himself has stooped

in friendship to a sinful woman. The son of the
virgin has not been ashamed of the embraces of
this ethiopian maid of his.† He, whom the angels desire, is not abashed to be called 'friend' by
his least and lowliest handmaid. That face in
which the heart of the eternal Father takes delight has now bent down to his waiting woman,
longing to kiss her lips with love. He pays her
this honor so frequently, that from now on I can
confidently dare to call him not only 'beloved'
but 'friend'.

Sg 1:5

Let none of you accuse me of pride, for in
glorying before you I have been moved by love,
not by vanity. If *I have become foolish, you forced
me to it.*† For if I am beside myself, it is for my
beloved; or, if I am in my right mind, *it is for your
sakes.*† Both my self-possession and also my loss
of it are serving for your benefit. My beloved has
led me into his wine cellar, and there I have
drunk as much as I desire.† I have come out of it
and, as yet, that is a place where I cannot bring
you. What I can do is let you feel the wine upon
my breath, making you aware, by its scent, of the
sweetness I have imbibed. The sweetness you
then taste will draw you too to a fuller and more
ardent longing for that sweetness in its fullness.

2 Cor 12:11

2 Cor 5:13

Sg 2:4

To be full of charity does not imply being free
from compulsion. In fact, is there a need more
compelling than love?† It is a twofold love: the
love I love my Beloved with, and the love I have
for you. Both impel me. Because I love Jesus, I
long for him to be loved by everybody. Just as I am
ill-fitted to his love, so I am wholly inadequate
by myself. His beauty is so lovable, his loveliness
so desirable, that it is far beyond any expectation

2 Cor 5:14

of the wishes of lovers, and so it is only fitting that it be desired by everyone in his inmost heart.

My daughters, my passionate love for you—for in a special way you are my responsibility—has laid upon me the need to speak of those things which should rather be wrapped in secret silence, and so I appear before you as a fool. You must forgive me. I shall gladly endure being thought of as a fool, on your account, as long as I feel that this is helping you towards wisdom. In your progress I find joyful compensation for the damage done to my personal sense of modesty. Moreover, I recall that in the beginning I warned you about making judgments of this kind, in case, seeing me arguing with you so boldly, you should look askance at my swarthy skin, and think me less beautiful on that account.[†] God knows what spurs me onwards, and if I speak too freely to you of what has been stirred up within me by his Spirit, then it is he himself who forces me to it. Yes, and you force me, too![†] So if what I have done has spoiled anything of my beauty, then the love that took the beauty away has the power to make it anew.

O then, do not be careless! Since *he is my Beloved and he is my Friend,*[†] you too, if you are not careless, will be able in a little while to make just the same boast. O then take pains, strive your hardest! Let his gracious condescension towards me, mighty though it is, give you hope. Let the desire to love as I do strengthen you to the same bold confidence. I beg you, I adjure you,[†] that you too should hasten along the path that I have followed.

Sg 1:5

2 Cor 5:14

Sg 5:16

Sg 2:1

What at the moment seems to you impossible, God's grace will make easy, if only you are resolute, not only fixing your whole desire on him alone, but also believing that he will strengthen and perfect your desire. For he never fails those who seek him, he never disappoints those who trust in him,[†] he who is the Spouse of the Church, the Only-Son of the Father.

Jdt 13:17

Sermon 39.3–7

Seeking and Yearning for the Love of the Word

DAUGHTERS OF JERUSALEM, IF YOU FIND MY BELOVED, TELL HIM I LANGUISH WITH LOVE.[†]

Sg 5:8

THE BRIDE ENDURES JESUS' ABSENCE because love endures all things. She strains with sighs and ardent longing to draw him from the bosom of the Father. While the Spouse delays, the bride makes progress in love. Jesus delays the joys of his chosen one, but this delay, as the bride recognizes, is for her good. He uses his very absence to test the fidelity of her love, according to the words, *The Lord is testing you to know if you love him or not.*[†] What heavier trial for the soul seeking God, than to be kept from finding him?

Dt 13:3

The bride shuts out everything that could offend the eyes of her Spouse. She bolts the door in case, according to his custom, the doors being shut Jesus may wish to enter.† The Spouse is wont to appear at midnight while all things are in silence in the middle of the night.† The secret and hidden lover of Jesus makes darkness her hiding place,† so that she may give herself more utterly to the embraces of her Beloved. She spreads wide her arms, she opens out her heart, she pours forth her soul, in spiritual longing she draws to herself the breath of his love.

Jesus is absent, he is not here. She goes *about the city*,† sharing the word of love with each person she meets: imparting wisdom to the mature,† feeding the weak with milk.† She calls on those who are walking the paths of life in the streets and lanes. Sometimes the Lord Jesus is accustomed to reveal his richness more readily to those who inquire about him than to those who dispute about him. To reward listening more copiously than speaking is his way, and often those are accounted more blessed who hear the word of God than those who proclaim it.†

She seeks him on the couch of secret and assiduous meditation, and she does not find him. She sets herself to find him in the exercise of holy preaching, and she is not rewarded by finding him. Finally, she betakes herself to a third kind of seeking, namely that of humble listening in silence. First she seeks him in the chamber of inner peace; then in the service of brotherly edification. Lastly, she comes down from the teacher's chair to the humble position of a pupil, so that Jesus may regard the lowliness

Jn 20:26

Ws 18:14

Ps 18:11

Sg 3:2

1 Cor 2:6

1 Cor 3:2

Lk 11:28

of his handmaid. Her desired appears: he steals into her arms, there to be clasped all the more closely, enjoyed all the more sweetly, held all the more strongly because the search was so long, the finding so long delayed.

The sharp arrows of love fly so thickly that not only does the Spouse confess that his heart has been wounded with love by his bride, but she herself adjures the 'daughters' to let the Bridegroom know her languor.[†] So the bride of the Word believes that when she is with her Almighty Spouse she has no need at all of busying herself with petitions. The Spouse keeps away so that such sweet and holy love may remain untouched by any kind of trivial remedy. Look at her humility. She feels certain that her Beloved who has gone from her will have been found by the 'daughters'; the joy denied her is being offered to her 'daughters'. The greatest comfort of souls all on fire and languishing with love is to be able to set others alight with the same fire and wound them with a like hurt.

Sg 5:8

The images you find in the Old Testament are but examples. The sacred reality you can behold more clearly in the bride of the Word of God. Seeing her 'daughters' hasten to enter the happiness of her own condition, she adjures them not to delay in imitating the ardor of her love. It is a love to be longed for and desired above everything else which makes her suffer and burn and languish. They too will run to the embrace of the Word of God; they too will sigh for the kiss of Christ Jesus.

Be attentive then, run forward. Do not delay, I beg you, but tell the Spouse that his chosen languishes for love.† You are bearers of good news to the Spouse, with those words you will come very close to the Word of God.

Sermon 1.1-7

THE SAPPHIRE

WHEN SHE GOES ON to speak of the heart of Jesus as *emblazoned with sapphires*, she is describing his love not only as like a bone but almost as if it were a stone. Love is indeed a gemstone, taking all emotions to itself, and making them insensible of any other attraction whatsoever. O, how precious are stones like this! Anyone who finds them immediately sheds his sensual way of responding to things and takes on instead what one might call the loveliness of a serene heaven. A fruitful field to find these stones, if we are to believe the bride, is none other than the ivory heart of Jesus, that is, the holy and unfeigned love of Christ. We know that they are indeed at hand there for the bride, because the heart of the Spouse lies open to her chaste hands in the freedom of the marriage bond. He offers his very heart, not only for her to come close to it, but for her to caress it.

The bride speaks of a heart 'emblazoned' with sapphires, suggesting that there are very many of them and all different. She wanted to symbolize the grace of the various consolations with which she is often most joyfully visited by her Spouse, and the joy takes various forms. Who could number them or say what they are like, except perhaps the blessed one who experiences them? In fact, it was her wish to tell us nothing about it, except only this: that the heart of her Spouse is emblazoned with these stones. But what form this takes, she judges should not be revealed to our ears, either from a sense of modesty or because of the limits of our understanding. If anyone thinks it a valuable thing to learn, let him give himself to it and experience it! Let him yearn and pray unceasingly, and exercise himself in this matter of love. Let him give no sleep to his eyes and no rest to his eyelids.† Let him give no rest by night or day to the God of peace and love until the love of Jesus comes forth to him from out of his bridal chamber and bursts into flame before him, like a burning lamp. Then the love of Christ will be with him very often, *coming to meet him like an honored mother.*† Love will multiply its consolations and come in an infinite variety of ways. When that day comes, blessed experience will make what is heard meaningful, and to every soul who is so disposed it will be clear what is meant by this encrusting of the Spouse's heart with gems as blue as the sky of heaven. There will be no need then for anyone to ask the Spouse any questions.

May it be granted us to know this experience and to understand what we hear, through the grace of the Spouse of the Church, Our Lord Jesus Christ.

Sermon 29.5-6

Ps 132:4

Sir 15:2

THE RADIANCE OF JESUS

Sg 5:10   MY BELOVED—JESUS—IS ALL RADIANT.†

PRAISE AWAKENS LOVE and preserves it.
So praise is the food of love. If deep within you
there is a little spark of sacred love, do all you
can to apply to this spark the oil of your praise,
so that your tiny fire may live and grow. With
this oil you anoint Jesus, enriching love. Love
waxes strong on praise, and in turn praise is
enkindled by love. Love is dumb without praise,
and praise, though it speak with the tongue of
1 Cor 13:1   angels,† is still mute without love.

Jesus' radiance is not just any kind of radiance, but a whiteness above all others. There is a
whiteness of milk, a radiant whiteness of a lily,
of snow, and of light. But far be it from me to
believe that any radiance of this sort is being
praised in Jesus, especially by her whose eyes are
Sg 4:1   as the eyes of doves,† and who has learned to
gaze on her beloved spiritually. If you have
known Christ, not according to the flesh but in
2 Cor 5:16   the spirit,† you will assuredly see in him the
whiteness of milk, of lilies, of snow, and of light.
There is an innocence of children and an innocence of adults, an innocence which penitence
restores, and one which the resurrection bestows
at the last day.

The first is like milk. Milk is fitting for little
ones who keep joyfully and easily the innocence
that came with them from their mother's womb
and was sanctified in them by the waters of life.
Blessed are they who are carried in the arms of

grace, and grace, like a mother, brings to perfection by so short a way, hiding her little ones from the sight of evil.

The Lamb of God is surrounded with companions, closely conformed to him in every way, so that even that period of Christ's life may have those who play and rejoice with him, who follow him wherever he goes. Praise the Lord, you children, you have rich matter for praise! Lovely is the perfect praise and graceful eulogy that sounds on your virgin lips which no stain has defiled.

O mother grace, you claim them totally for yourself as children free from the stain of sin through the blood of Christ, as sharers in so great a glory through no effort of their own. Out of their mouths you have perfected praise, to confound the enemies of grace who rely on their strength and merits, and so fall from grace. Jesus commanded the little ones to come to him, explained to them the kingdom of heaven, and then even tenderly embraced a little child himself. How wonderful was this for little ones, how great his motherly affection, how it pours itself forth and spreads itself wide. How he yearns over them as a mother bird over her young.

Sermon 3.1-2

ORNAMENTS OF GOLD FOR ADORNING

GOLD OF LOVE FROM THE INNOCENT, FROM SINNERS, AND FROM THE JEWISH PEOPLE

I HAVE HEARD that the bride betook herself to the goldsmith, Bezalel,† so that from the small amount of gold which she had, he might make golden earrings for her. She wanted to win the favor of her Beloved so that when he saw her so adorned, the King would desire her beauty.† She started to think about gold necklaces and bracelets and rings, about a dress of cloth of gold with golden fringes† and all the other finery of an elegant woman that could stir the heart of the beloved.†

Her hope is not disappointed. When the Lord Jesus sees her thus attired and carefully following him and seeking his face, he thinks her worthy of the kiss of his mouth for which she has longed, and she becomes united and made one with him. She has entered into the joy of her Lord, she has been made free of all the possessions of her Beloved and she overflows with delight. Blissfully she enjoys the company of Jesus her Spouse, judging herself to know but him alone, and clinging to him with whom she has become one spirit.†

I myself have gone to a good counselor: *My advice*, he says, *is to buy from me gold tried in the fire, that you may be rich.*† This counselor is a great King, the richest of all kings, who has such a store, such an infinite treasure, of gold that in his sight silver is accounted worthless.† In the

Ex 35:30-32

Ps 44:10

Ps 44:14

Sg 4:9

1 Cor 6:17

Rv 3:18

Ws 7:9

land where he lives there is gold, and the gold of
that country is very good.† When he came

Gn 2:11-12

down to our level and became a child in our
midst an edict came from the Father that all the
gold that was anywhere on the earth was to be
brought at once to the Son of the King and
placed in his treasury. To him alone all love is
rightly due. By him alone it was created and created for this sole purpose, and then only is it
blessed when totally poured out for him alone.
So they came from everywhere to lay their
treasures before the King: from the east† and

Cf. Mt 8:11

from the north, some from Arabia, others from
Saba, many from Tharsis.†

Ps 71:15; Is 60:6;
Ps 72:10

From the east: some from the beginning
have come running to offer him their love, still in
its first freshness; and from that in itself they derive an incentive to love, knowing that they could
not have loved him in this way had they not first
been loved by him and set apart. So those who
came from the east are the first of those who love
him. They hastened when Jesus was still a baby
to consecrate to him the dawn of their lives, and
they followed him wherever he goes.† This is the

Rv 14:4

gold which the wise men from the east offered to
the King of heaven in his manger.†

Mt 2:11

From the north: coming from a far off land
they cannot arrive so quickly. The later they
begin their journey, the more swiftly they travel,
the more fervently they run. They draw great
matter for loving, for they would not have been
summoned from such a great distance had they
not been intimately known and loved. Nor can
the thought of such love ever leave their memory. My elder brother does ill to be moved

against my Father, if of his bounty he bestows
on me also the grace which he has kept for him.
My Father offers me greater reason for love. But
my brother fears for himself, thinking that since
I come from distant lands with a richer supply
of gold, my greater love will make me more
loved; or because I am loved more, I will have a
greater love. To be true, I am bound to a greater

Lk 10:42

love. This is *the one thing necessary.*† I beg my
most merciful Father night and day, and shall
not cease to beg, that he who gave the motive
will also give the reality. My particular possession is his death and burial and resurrection with
the thief and with Mary Magdalene at the cross
of Christ. Here is where I shall find healing for
my wounds, forgiveness for my sins, and an end
to my old life, the hope of a new beginning.

Why does it say: *It will be given to him* from

Ps 72:15

the gold of Arabia?† Not just 'gold of Arabia'.
This gold is from that Jerusalem which is in

Gal 4:25

bondage with her children.† She has given our
King a little gold from her store, but that little is
the best and very pure. Isaiah said: There is *a*

Is 6:13

holy seed which remains in her,† a seed which *the*

Is 61:9

Lord has blessed,† and in which the Lord has
blessed all her kindred throughout the earth.

Opening up his great stores of gold, he revealed many things and discussed their depths,
and he found no end to his treasures. But that
huge crowd which stood with Jesus in the level

Lk 6:17

ground,† meaning Arabia, could not go up to
him on the mountain and understand the
heights of perfection. They were not strong
enough to give all their gold to our King, but
from their gold they gave him the trifling

amount they could manage. He, most generous
in giving, is likewise most gracious in accepting.
He rejects no offering, however small, as long as
it is from their gold.† Since they cannot worship   Ps 72:15
him on his holy mountain, they will in the mean-
time worship at his footstool for that is holy.

Sermon 11.5-7

FULL FLOWING STREAMS

HIS EYES ARE DOVES, AT REST NEAR FULL
FLOWING STREAMS.†   Sg 5:12

THE *FULL FLOWING STREAMS* are the four
rivers of grace: fortitude, counsel, understanding,
and wisdom. A mighty spring, arising from the
middle of paradise, a stream of living waters did
the Holy Spirit divide into these four rivers, especially at that time when, coming with a violent
surge, he gladdened the city of God† and filled   Ps 46:4
the whole house where they were seated.†   Acts 2:2

FORTITUDE. Then in a spirit of fortitude he
strengthens the bars of the gates of Jerusalem,
and builds a tower in the midst of her,† a tower   Is 5:2
of fortitude in the face of the foe. From that day
forth the Lord has set them like a horse coming
down to the field of glory, surefooted, sniffing
the battle from afar. He presses on quickly to

meet the warriors, and when he hears the trum-
Job 39:25
pet sound, he says: 'Aha!'† *The Lord of Hosts is*
Ps 46:7, 11
with us, and who is against us?†

COUNSEL. From the spirit of counsel they drink
counsel and prudence, so that their city is not
only furnished with horses and arms but also invincible in its battle-leaders and the wise counsel of its elders. Fortitude is indeed a horse, and
a strong one, ready for the day of battle, but it is
Ps 33:17
a vain hope for safety† if not controlled by the
restraining spirit of counsel. If fortitude is to remain unconquered, let it take as its rider the
spirit of counsel, and under its guiding rein let it
come down into the field, prepared for fighting.
    Zechariah is our witness that *What is upon*
Zec 14:20
the bridle of the horse will be holy to the Lord.† It is
the spirit of counsel he is referring to, for when
that is absent, the horse stumbles, and his rider
Gen 49:17
also tumbles behind him.† Just as they became
brave and strong through the spirit of fortitude,
so they became wise and prudent through the
spirit of counsel, choosing cautiously, for the
most part, to avoid danger to save themselves
for the greater good of the Church. Nor did
they think it right to hasten their own glory at
the cost of causing harm to the many, for they
had been instructed by the Holy Spirit in the
laws of charity to seek not their own good but
1 Cor 13:5
that of others.†

UNDERSTANDING. From the spirit of understanding they received a great book, every creature of God, and there, as he opened and
unfolded it, they read of the goodness and wis-

dom of God. Under his guidance they learned of
his power and greatness through the things he
had made.† The same spirit kept constantly before their eyes in the words and deeds of Jesus a
book of easier understanding. As it is written of
him: *The Holy Spirit whom the Father shall send in
my name,* he says, *he will teach you all things and
bring to your minds whatever I have said to you.*†
Strengthened by this spirit, they bore with equa-
nimity the loss of Christ in the flesh, doubtless
understanding the meaning of that saying: *It is
expedient for you that I go away.*† So this spirit
calmed and enlightened their whole understanding, so that the spirit of wisdom might
then enkindle and strengthen their will.

WISDOM. For by the spirit of wisdom charity
takes delight in everything which the understanding sets before it. It almost seems to taste,
in a heavenly and living way, what it understands, and hence to evaluate it rightly. And it
spreads through each individual part of the soul,
giving life to all the senses and powers. Through
this spirit they were clothed with the wisdom
which is from above, people of true wisdom to
the extent that they savor only God and the
things of God. So violent was this flood of the
spirit upon them that, being unable to contain it
wholly themselves, they chose to open themselves to every soul and to strive to make all
those who shared their nature become a sharer
in this savor. In this most loving attempt to save
all people, the same spirit of wisdom provided
not only good will, but a tongue as well. With
these burning tongues they were on fire with

Rom 1:20

Jn 14:26

Jn 16:7

fiery eloquence and could speak with the tongues of all, seeing that they desired to unite all people to Christ.

To sum up: As we were saying, therefore, it was beside these full flowing streams that the doves were resting. Through the ministry of these same doves, by the generous gift of the Holy Spirit, we have all received a share in their fullness according to the measure of the gift of Christ, and he uses these same doves as his dispensers. We also are at rest near the same streams, for they intercede for us with the giver of all good things, the Holy Spirit. Restfully then we pray to the Holy Spirit, who with God the Father and his only-begotten Son, our Lord Jesus Christ, lives and reigns, God for ever and ever. Amen.

Sermon 17.10-11

CHOSEN IN THOUSANDS: JESUS IN THE CHURCH AND IN SOULS

Sg 5:10

RADIANTLY WHITE AND DEEPLY REDDENED

JESUS THE SPOUSE has a glory *as of the only Son of the Father*,† and this he graciously pours into his bride. O truly a great mystery, as the apostle witnesses,† because of the great love, the great bond, the great union!

Jn 1:14

Eph 5:32

The bride has understood this and conveyed it to the daughters of Jerusalem by adding to her praise of Jesus' radiance and redness that he is *chosen in thousands*. She did not say: 'My beloved is all radiant and reddened, chosen *before* thousands' or 'chosen *in the midst of* thousands', but 'chosen *in* thousands'. Surely she is signifying that he is chosen in his chosen ones, he is radiantly white and brilliantly red in the thousands who are his own. He is indeed the *fairest of the children of men*,† but the form of his beauty is for the children of men. He himself says: *The beauty of the field is with me* † and *I am the flower of the field and the lily of the valley.*† Do not be confined in your personal poverty. The Lord your God is himself your beauty, your flower, your lily. He is glorious not only in that beauty by which he is equal to the Father, but

Ps 44:2

Ps 50:11
Sg 2:1

25

also in that apparel which he washed in the wine of his blood. It is written: *He is glorious in his apparel.*† I am speaking of the Church of Christ. Even if, before his passion, it was soiled with stains and creased with wrinkles, the robe of glory prepared for it was reddened by the blood of her Spouse, radiant and reddened, and made into a robe no less radiant and reddened, having *no stain or wrinkle or any such thing.*† He changed it like a garment, and it was changed,† in its turn changelessly and inseparably befitting such great splendor and majesty.

Consequently, there is a twofold sense in which it is said 'in thousands'. It can be understood correctly in either way, whether it refers to a totality or to separate individuals, that is to say, whether you take it as the beauty of the whole, or of one individual by himself. God is wonderful in his saints in both these ways, wonderful in all, wonderful in each.

Let me say something briefly about the first wonder: what is more wonderful than that he bound together the whole of creation in his body, and by a great law he differentiated the parts of this body, so that in a marvelous way what seems less honorable in it he surrounds, as the apostle says, with more glory?† Does not the beauty of the whole person, head as well as body, belong to every part, even the least? This is the glory with which he has united this same church of his to himself in the bond of marriage. He has redeemed her and washed her clean in his blood. He has endowed her with the Holy Spirit. He has finally even enriched her with his own kingdom. What glory is like this?

Is 63:1

Eph 5:27
Ps 102:27

1 Cor 12:24

Rightly, I repeat rightly, *shall my very bones say,*
`Lord, who is like you'.† To make one who was Ps 35:10
deformed and dissimilar not only beautiful, but
conformed and similar to yourself, you made
yourself similar to him. You became as one who
had no form or comeliness.† Among all the mar- Is 53:2
vels of God, what marvel is equal to this: that
the king of glory came as a servant to rescue his
bride from the yoke of servitude? Blessed are
the eyes of the bride who in the total emptying
of Jesus, her Solomon, crowned with a crown of
thorns, not only took no scandal, but all the
more eagerly, all the more lovingly, ran to his
embrace and to his kisses! How happy are you,
bride of God, you are the reward of such loving
servitude, the fruit of such a long and drawn out
pilgrimage, the prize of such a difficult undertaking, the price of his precious blood.

Sermon 5.1–3

THE INEFFABLE FULLNESS OF HER GLORY

CHOSEN IN THOUSANDS† Sg 5:10

THE CHARIOT OF GOD is attended by ten thou-
sand, many thousands of those who rejoice.† If, at his Ps 68:17
first ascension, the chariot of the Spouse is so
many thousands of those who rejoice that the

huge crowd of those triumphing with Christ overflows into many ten thousands, what, I ask, will be the chariot of his second ascension? If such is the harvest of the firstfruits, what will be the riches of the full harvest, when the reaper fills his hand?[†] And he fills not only his hand, but his barns too, right up to the very top. On that day how will Abraham complain that anything is missing from the promise God made to him and to his seed, that anything is missing from their shining to everlasting ages like the stars of the sky,[†] from their number exceeding all reckoning like the sand on the sea-shore.[†]

Finally, the bride does not pass over in silence the ineffable fullness of her glory. When she adds to her description of her beloved *chosen in thousands*, she wants us to understand by those thousands the whole assembly of the saints. She accepts them from the generosity of her Spouse as the gift of his great promise: *As I live, says the Lord, you will be clad with them as with adornment*—referring to the saints and to the Bride, the Church—*and you will take them to yourself as a bride.*[†] Who would be astonished if she herself is astonished, rather if she sees and is rich, and her astonished heart wonders and is enlarged?[†] She is enriched with two blessings: a weight of unimaginable glory, and a countless number of souls in glory. She has indeed found the Lord at her desire, as it is said, and has found God at her pleasure; she has found a Spouse after her own heart.[†]

Sermon 5.4–5

Ps 129:7

Gen 15:5
Gen 22:17

Is 49:18

Is 60:5

Acts 13:22

THE FULL TALLY OF THE CHURCH
IN GLORY

HE WHO BLESSES enumerates them as increasing in three ways: *I will increase them,* he
says, *like a flock of men, like the flock for sacrifice,
like the flock at Jerusalem during her appointed
feasts.*† I think the *flock of men* is that multitude   Ez 36:37
of the faithful who have turned away from the
likeness of animals and have either preserved
through grace or repaired through repentance
the image of God within them to which they
were created. Living *sober, upright and godly lives
in this world,*† they look forward confidently to   Ti 2:12
the blessed hope promised to the faithful. What
is it like, what is the size, this great crowd of so
many generations of people, tribes and tongues?
From so many ages past, even to this day, it has
been gathered together, and it must still be
gathered up to the very end of time. What delight will be yours, O Bride of God, when all
these have come to you in assembly, when that
flock of so many thousand persons, new and
marked, display before your eyes the image of
God, clearly marked on every countenance, and
in every face, as in the brightest of mirrors,
when in them you see and adore your Creator?
  Lift up your eyes higher still to the *flock for
the sacrifice* which the Lord your God is going to
bestow on you. In my opinion these are they
who in order to become holy and, once holy, to
become holier still, have entered upon the path
of consecrated life. They have said to one another, *Come, let us go up to the mountain of the*

Lord! † According to the angel's counsel, we shall more easily be saved on the mountain, or according to the great angel of great counsel, the Lord Jesus, the only road to perfection is for us to leave all things and follow Jesus.† At the sound of this word, which the rich man would scarcely listen to when Jesus spoke it†—it is even written of him that *he went away sorrowful*—an infinite multitude have opened their ears, have risen up with joy, have run eagerly forward. Abruptly snapping all the ties that could hold them back, they have suffered the loss of everything that is of this world, even the loss of their own will, so as to fill up the ranks of the kingdom of heaven. The advance guard of this multitude were those in the very beginning of the primitive Church of whom it is written: *They were of one heart and one soul.*†

Rise up higher still; stand on the heights and lift up your eyes. Turning you will see a flock with a glory more excellent still, the flock clearly pre-eminent, 'the flock at Jerusalem'. These are the great friends of God, exceedingly honored, overwhelmingly consoled. Here the patriarchs hold the first rank,† because God bequeathed to them his covenant and magnified his mercy. So from them all fatherhood on earth takes its name,† making them not only the fathers of all who believe, but also the ancestors of Christ according to the flesh.

Following them come the venerable company of the prophets, aware of the hidden things of God and explaining them to the children of men. Even in those days they preached to the world what we now, with our own eyes,

Margin notes:

Is 2:3

Lk 5:11

Mt 19:22

Acts 4:32

For ranks, see the hymn *Te Deum*

Eph 3:15

see fulfilled in us, and to which we look forward to contemplating in all its wholeness.

Next to them is the glorious company of the apostles, by whose preaching the world was saved, through whose government the world is ruled, at whose tribunal the world will be judged. Then the impenetrable and uncountable army of martyrs, marked with so many of the wounds of Christ, refined to purity by the fire of many tortures, carrying into heaven many banners of victory. After them the pastors and doctors, who by their teaching and example, by their signs and wonders, made the catholic faith and the christian religion shine forth more brightly than the light, indeed, like the splendor of the starry sky. Finally the virgins, whiter than snow, following their Spouse wherever he goes; and most of these, not content with a single glory, have also washed red with martyr's blood their robes of radiant virginity. Who begot in you these children of such great glory, O fruitful mother, O Bride of the King of glory? Truly that flock of yours is a joyful flock, a festive flock, establishing for you a festal procession with branches,† and that for ever. Ps 118:27

Sermon 6.2–4

Chosen in Thousands
in Each Little Member of the Flock

Sg 5:10

CHOSEN IN THOUSANDS†

WE TOOK THIS as referring to the universal
beauty of the Church, as if the bride were to say,
'My beloved is wonderful in his saints and beautiful in each individually, but he is far more
wonderful in his whole Body, that is, chosen in
the thousands that are his own'.

If it seems better to take the words *chosen in
thousands* as meaning chosen in each one sepa-
rately, then it can also bear this meaning. It is not
the same thing to be chosen 'with' the chosen as
to be chosen 'in' the chosen. In the one, God is
present by cooperating grace; in the other, God
is within by indwelling power. One we yearn
after, to receive; the other we breathe in, not to
lose. What flock, however little it may be, is not
blessed, and blessed too each little member of
the flock, who has such a great one as this to
choose it? God himself is chosen in each of
them. Blessed is he whom you chose, O Lord,
yet one chosen for distinction is more blessed
still when you give him your aid in doing good.
And most blessed of all when you repose in him
as in your own home, and say, *Here is my resting
place for ever, here I will dwell for I have chosen it.*†

Ps 132:14

Now, O Lord, Father and Ruler of my life,†
give me the wisdom that sits by your throne,† *the
Lord Jesus, that he may be with me and toil, and
that I may learn what is pleasing to you,*† *standing
before you at all times.*† *May he labor with me,*

Sir 23:1
Wis 9:4

Ws 9:10
2 Chr 9:4

helping on my weakness; may he shed his light upon my unknowing. Yet even though you walk with me like this, and take hold of my right hand, your indwelling grace is indispensable, that is, your mercy, that it may follow me all the days of my life.† Ps 23:6

And now, Lord, remember me. Look upon the face of your Christ, living and moving in us through your grace, and since it is through him that you save us, save your king, save your Christ who lives and makes his abode in us! To make certain that you will listen, he himself intercedes with you from within us on our behalf; from the ends of the earth, from all the deep places of our hearts, he cries out to you in supplication, Abba, *Father!*

Whoever you are who desire to be included under the name *daughters of Jerusalem,* do not take little account of the thousands of chosen ones, because he alone is chosen in them. Take great and watchful care not to despise one of these thousands, not to condemn, not to scandalize anyone at all of these little ones. The ones you think lowly are of a mighty stock, they have a mighty Father, a most renowned Brother, mighty friends, mighty servants. Act like a careful investigator, peep through the lattices, take a good look at how bright it is inside. Granted there are coarse clothes and earth-colored pelts, but have you eyes for nothing else? You should rather be looking for the ark of the Lord hiding beneath these coverings of fleshly weakness, and then you would not be disturbed. You would begin to feel reverence, you would look, and wonder! Look closer still. Take great care that it is not Jesus you are despising, clad in his dirty rags!

Sermon 6.6–9

II

JESUS CHRIST
THE MAN IN ALL HIS
RESPLENDENT BEAUTY

AN OVERVIEW:
ENCHANTING GRACE

I N THE SECOND SECTION we turn our gaze to the
Lord Jesus in his life on earth from the moment of his conception until his ministry among men and women.

John had often seen a wood-carver at his lathe, fashioning
useful things for the monastery. He uses this image to express in
symbolic language the fashioning of Jesus' human nature. The
Son co-operated with the Father working vigorously at this excellent craft. 'Marvelous craftsman, who fashioned his own self
so as to refashion us'.[1] From this springs the reverence Jesus had
for the Father, and on another plane the reverence for his
mother. John of Forde always has the Virgin Mary in mind when
he is talking about Jesus in his birth and in his death. This is
truth he loves to dwell on.

Here we find the elements of wisdom. Wisdom is the foundation for all the creative forces in the Universe. Even looking at
it from the perspective of the twenty-first century and the remarkable discoveries of the past eighty years or so, we see wisdom at work in the evolution and ordering of particles and
galaxies. The creation of the elements that became the building
blocks of life came into existence through the action of God the
Creator which we must call a quite extraordinary wisdom. The
men of the Middle Ages knew nothing of the discoveries of
modern physics, yet they perceived the essential Intelligence that
is inherent in its overarching plan (which modern cosmologists

---

[1] Sermon 25.5

seem to miss). From the beginning, the primordial act of Creation, God had ordained the Universe towards life. We are perhaps on the threshold of discovering life on other planets, though there will be little indication, if any, about the nature of that life, unless we discover intelligent beings that have reached a similar development to that we have reached on earth.

By faith we know that the apex of this creative craftsmanship is the Lord Jesus Christ, who united God and Man in his own person. Here we find the highest expression of wisdom, for in this case wisdom is identified with God. Jesus Christ is Wisdom. The quest for wisdom must be considered essential to the understanding of medieval monasticism and mysticism. It often claims the major part in medieval thinking. The word *sapientia* (wisdom) occurs on almost every page of John of Forde's sermons. It is particularly associated with Christ's passion and death which is seen as the highest expression of God's wisdom over against the wisdom of society, i.e. human wisdom. In the Fourth Gospel the Word is identical with God, the Word was God, yet Saint Paul insists that Jesus Christ is our Wisdom. Wisdom thus reveals a complex of meanings. There is the wisdom of God over against the wisdom of the world; God's Wisdom is one with the Word, and one with Jesus Christ. Every manifestation in the life of Jesus is a source of wisdom in itself, but it is also a source of wisdom for us. John therefore presents us with many aspects of Christ's life because each one of them is a marvelous manifestation of wisdom for us. Christ's speech is an outpouring of wisdom, but also his silence teaches us the wisdom of God. His healings come from his wisdom; his miracles are a revelation of Wisdom. Everything in the gospels is a revelation to us of Wisdom Incarnate.

This Wisdom is revealed to us primarily in the relationship between Jesus and his Father. Jesus himself said, I and the Father are one.[2] This leads John to consider the reverence Jesus had for

[2] Jn 10:30

his Father. John declares, 'No one knows more clearly than the soul of Jesus how the majesty of the Creator is to be revered, adored with awe, and held in the highest wonder'.[3] The glory of the Father is, as it were, reflected in the very being of the Son, because the Father images the totality of his own glory into the Son. This reverence for the Father is seen throughout his life. In his childhood, every decision Jesus made was controlled by the wisdom given him from the outset. 'The Wisdom of God wished to live like us, and he chose to savor to the full whatever was human, to contemplate heavenly things through his experience' of life.[4] He took upon himself the study and meditation that was well suited to his boyhood. The parables and teaching during his ministry were the direct product of his early years and youth. These years were filled with preparation, like the bee producing honey for future use.

It is in this area of the preparation in Jesus' human nature and the glory accorded to it that John loves to dwell. He has perceived that Mary, the Mother of Jesus, was accorded a vital role in the physical and mental inheritance and development of her Son. This would be taken for granted today, but in John's time it was held to be very advanced thinking. To avoid any charge of dabbling in innovative thinking, John is obliged to appeal to those who have preceded him in this insight. The wonder is that he stuck to his own opinion, realizing as he did that Mary's mothering role was not simply a passive one, but a fully active cooperation in the qualities and virtues of her Son, Jesus.

Chosen from the beginning, she was singled out by the Father to be the mother of his Son. From before time the Word looked on Mary. Here we have the essence of Mary's role in our redemption. The Word, in the bosom of the Father before time began, looked on Mary and chose her.

We do not know whether Mary ever possessed the type of sweet-smelling nard that Mary Magdalene poured out on Jesus'

---

[3] Sermon 9.6
[4] Sermon 37.4

feet. In any case it should be taken as symbolic of the spiritual aromas that come to us from Jesus' own person. Its symbolic value is found in the aroma we become aware of when we experience his gentle dignity, his cheerful quietness—like a bloom on his cheek. We are admonished to listen reverently to his incredible gentleness and kindness that reconciled sinners to the Father. 'That most delicate of perfumes breathed forth its scent for him alone because no one knows the Son except the Father'.

If wisdom is a sort of taste of virtue—*sapientia* is said to come from the verb *sapere,* to taste—it clearly transcends the natural senses and takes on a deep spiritual meaning. Spiritually we are to become, as it were, swallowed up into Christ, source of all sweetness, drawn down into the interiority of salvation and, using pauline terminology, become one spirit with him in mystic union.

Jesus, The Craftsman:
Fashioning the Man

GOD'S HANDS ABOUND in *riches and glory*,[†] when he opens wide to the person who loves him the riches of salvation, the treasuries of holiness, and makes her rejoice in them, like one who has found all riches. And what a flight of glory takes her upwards too, coming from the testimony of a good conscience and the hope of sharing the glory of the sons of God,[†] quite apart from the supreme privilege of being wedded to a Spouse so gloriously great!

Prv 3:16

Rom 5:2

So the left hand is glorious indeed, yet not as magnificently so as is the right. In the right hand is the fullness of justice, as Scripture tells us: *Your right hand is full of justice.*[†] In the time and place assigned to earning our reward, it is however the left hand that is specially active, while the right hand has for its sphere the task of apportioning glory, of gathering together the sons of God and distributing to them their inheritance.

Ps 48:11

Furthermore, those hands were shaped for the only Son of God as if they had been rounded off by a certain skillful use of the turner's lathe. From the workshop where this craft is practiced, the hands were to go out as craftsmen themselves, fashioning our salvation.

41

It is the Father of the Jesus who fashioned these hands, and yet Jesus himself, like the Son of a workman, worked vigorously with his Father at this most excellent of crafts. Marvelous craftsman, who fashioned his own self so as to refashion us!

Ps 52:9

I shall thank you for ever, Lord Jesus, for what you have made.† You have made yourself into my salvation, you have made me into a prized possession through your salvation. You have made hands for yourself in order to save me, made them with skilful artistry, with speed too, yet with toilsome labor. First of all, like a wise designer, you raised a workshop for this craft of yours: the soul of your virgin Mother and her holy womb. A sublime workshop, vast enough for so great a craft and able to contain so immense a craftsman! But it would be truer to say that she herself, like the valiant woman, put out her hand to mighty things,† wisely working along with the Wisdom of God in the work of our salvation.

Prv 31:19

Since, then, the bride of the Song decided, by the Spirit of God, to adopt the image of this craft when praising her Spouse, there will be more of devotion than idle curiosity in lingering a little over it.

The craftsman sits with a piece of wood suspended above him and another, connected to the first by a thong, under one foot. By a movement of his other foot he raises and lowers the beam. Equally, the wood which is to be rounded is girded by the same thong, connected from the crossbeam in the centre, and so is in precisely the right position to be kept continually turning round in a circular motion as the foot moves up and down. Moreover, the craftsman has a chisel in his hand, and with firmness and great accuracy he brings this to bear on what is to be shaped, all his movements controlled by a craftsmanship that has become instinctive to him. So the work proceeds with great swiftness, and revolution follows on revolution so quickly that it outstrips the keenness of the eye and baffles the mind.

If we look for the underlying significance of this image, we find two beams of wood, very far removed from each other. One is exceedingly high, towering over our heads, while the other lies horizontal below. In other words, here are two natures, the Word and the flesh, which the unimaginable love of God bound marvelously into a unity. So God's love is the thong, itself imperishable, and it binds with a knot that can never be untied, using for the purpose a certain natural quality, namely the rational soul. Thus it connects the higher nature and the lower by an ingenious alliance.

Moreover, from the time of this most holy union, each nature is so utterly faithful to this amazing bond, that the Word stoops down to the lowliness of the flesh, and lowliness is lifted up on high to the sublimity of his majesty. In the spirit of humility, a man may enter the holy temple of God with the desire of glorifying the Lord our God. But God is not pleased with him and does not look with favor on his offering, unless he worships his footstool, for that too is holy.[†] This is the law, that the humanity, united to the majesty of the Word, is so taken up into

Ps 99:5

the oneness of the Person, that it can even share uniquely in his glory. Yet however much one position succeeds another, whether humanity raises itself on high or the divine Wisdom comes down low, this same humanity is truly in charge of the whole as the craftsman, pursuing our salvation. The business of our salvation is all arranged by the hand of Wisdom.

Sermon 25.4-6

THE REVERENCE OF JESUS
FOR HIS FATHER

COME, let Jesus open to us that book of the New Testament, the book of life, the book of wisdom, so that we may read in it the heart of Jesus and be taught by God. I see in it, traced by God's hand, the living letters of threefold humility. These are the letters: to be submissive to the divine majesty through reverential awe, to the divine will through obedience, to the divine glory through thanksgiving.

REVERENTIAL AWE. Clearly, among all the creatures of God, whether on earth or in heaven, there is none that knows more clearly than the soul of Jesus how the Majesty of the Creator is to be revered, adored with awe, and held in the highest wonder. His reverence was in proportion to his understanding. This is the reverence of the King's Son, loved and renowned through all his Father's house. He is honored beyond all others in the royal palace because of the inestimable dignity of his bearing and the awe-inspiring majesty of his countenance. Therefore, Queen Charity takes him to her side as an inseparable companion and orders that she must go nowhere without him, whether to the King's wine-cellar or to his chamber† —that is, to her prayer or to the deep silence of her love for him.

Sg 1:3, 11

OBEDIENCE OF JESUS. Listen, then, to the obedience of Jesus, listen and marvel and imitate as far as you can. Hear how holy and righteous it was, how voluntary and dedicated, how prompt and eager, how joyful and sweet, how patient and constant, how strong and unyielding. 'I have come to do the will of him who sent me'.† We see its holiness and righteousness in that it has nothing of its own, but makes Jesus completely subject and surrendered to him who sent him. We see its freedom and dedication in that it knows nothing of sadness or complaint, but wholly surrenders itself into the freedom of love: *My heart is ready, O God, my heart is ready.*† We see promptness and eagerness when Jesus anticipates his Father's orders and hastens forward before he is summoned for whatever he must do or suffer. *My food is to do the will of my Father, that I may perfect his work.*† There is also the joy and sweetness of obedience, which considers itself fed when it yields, and replete when all has been fully accomplished. There is patience

Jn 6:38

Ps 57:7

Jn 4:34

and constancy, in that it always burns with the selfsame ardor. To conclude: *Christ was made obedient to his Father even unto death, the death of the cross.*† What is stronger than this obedience, which triumphs so wonderfully over the Lord of hosts?

GLORY OF JESUS. Hear now how he was given up to the glory of the Creator, how wholly poured out in thanksgiving. Rejoicing in the Holy Spirit, Jesus said: *I give thanks to you, Father Lord of heaven and earth, for you have hidden these things from the wise and prudent, and revealed them to little ones.*† This is the voice of the true David who raises his voice in the psalms with such rejoicing and melody. This is the voice that cries to the Father: *I will extol you, O God my King, and praise your name for ever and ever.*† This same voice cries out to all the peoples: *Praise the Lord, all you nations, praise him all you peoples.*† This same voice cries to his own soul and all that is within him: *Praise the Lord, O my soul, and let all that is within me praise his holy name.*† This same voice cries to his lute rousing it to glorify God: *Awake my glory, awake, lute and lyre.*† This same voice cries out to heaven and earth and every creature, so that everything that exists may join in praising the Creator with all its might.

Hear also and imitate how Jesus kept his hands and tongue completely free from any reward coming from human approval. *The word which I speak, I do not speak of myself. The Father who is within me does the work.*† He often said: *If I glorify myself, my glory is nothing.*† Without

Phil 2:8

Mt 11:25

Ps 145:1

Ps 117:1

Ps 103:1

Ps 147:12

Jn 14:10

Jn 8:54

doubt, blessed and to be blessed for ever is he who comes, not in his own name, but in the name of his Father. All the graces flowing in great rivers to their fountain-head, namely the wellspring of the Father's glory, come pouring back with the selfsame power on him whom we confess and shall for all eternity confess, through his mercy. Through the one Beloved Son, Jesus Christ our Lord.

Sermon 9.5–8

The Beauty of Jesus
in His Virginal Conception

IN THE PSALMS David placed Christ's beauty at the forefront of his praises: *You are the fairest of the children of men.*[†] That appearance is truly the loveliest of all appearances, for in it the virgin's Son had the privilege of being taken up by the Beauty of God, the only Son of the Father. In this, my Lord Jesus has shown himself ideal in his surpassing beauty for all who have the favor of being admitted to his sight. From then on, those who have once seen this beauty yearn with insatiable desire to see it again and they yearn for this alone. As Scripture says: *He is more radiant than the sun, wonderful above all the starry constellations.*[†] Wondering at

Ps 44:3

Ws 7:29

him, every sense fails; longing for him, all seeing fades away; in comparison to him, all beauty seems dim.

We can understand why *the angels longed to* 1 Pt 1:12 *look upon his appearance*,† why they marvel to see him advancing towards them in the robe of his incomparable beauty, and why they cry: *Who is* Ps 24:8; Is 62:1 *the King of glory, glorious in his garments?*† This cry of admiration from the hearts and lips of the angels has never ceased, from the hour when the King of glory was clad by his Father in a robe of glory, crowned with the crown of the kingdom within his mother's womb. From then on *the stars of morning*—i.e. the angels—began to praise him, and all the children of God to shout Job 38:7 for joy.† The stars of the morning were eagerly watching for the morning rising of the Eternal Sun. They began to keep night watches of longing, in zealous anticipation of the first signs of his coming. They began to honor him with angelic praises, as he came lifted up with the glory that is his due, hailing him as God, bowing low in adoration. From that day on, there has always Lk 2:14 been 'glory in the heights of heaven',† in honor of the rising King. Jubilation has never faded from the heart nor praise from the lips, nor contemplation from the eye; insatiable longing from the soul. Does not the Father of Lights himself take pleasure in gazing on this beauty of Jesus? From the hour when he rested from all Gen 2:3 the works that he had done,† he gave himself completely to contemplating his beauty, taking his delight in that alone, with infinite pleasure.

This is a blessed day for you, Lord God, which gladdened you with the glad announcement of your Son. He is your Son, *descended from David according to the flesh,*† your exceedingly beautiful Son, the perfect Image of yourself to the point that whoever sees him will also see you!† On this day, and from this day on, may the day of my birth, as well as the night of my conception,† pass into oblivion forevermore. For this is why your Son was born, and why he came into the world,† that the appearance of his beauty might wipe away the disfigurement from the whole of his race. For this purpose, O Loving Lord, in the wonderful working of your power, a Son was born to you and, through your mercy, also for us, so that the very sight of his appearance might bring us back to you in friendship and incline you to us in love.

O holy Father, how we thank you! From that day you have taken such delight in this appearance of your Son, that for his sake you have determined to show mercy to his entire race. You have forgotten your just anger,† *so that you do not only delight in him yourself, but in him and with him, we too begin to be a delight to you. In a word, it has been your good pleasure, that we also should become and be called your sons,*† *in your Son and with him. Still, as is only fitting, the Son who is born to you from the Virgin daughter of David,*† *is your Son in a much more splendid way and with a nobler dignity. He is Son by reason of the grace of that most holy union which unites him in oneness of person to your Only-begotten Son. But as for us, we are sons through grace of adoption, and it was through him that you adopted us and united us to him in faith and love. O Father, it was your love that made you send forth the splendor of your glory to become*

Rom 1:3

Jn 14:9

Job 3:3

Jn 3:19

Ps 85:3

1 Jn 3:1

Is 9:6

intimately united with this man, the Virgin's Son, and it was love that made you clothe him with the robe of beauty to the glory and honor of all his brothers and sisters, your children. Truly, Lord, it is this love of yours, this tender courtesy, this grace that makes your new creation radiantly white. This

Ps 78:55

is 'the mountain of your holiness',† the mountain on which you planted your great cedars, i.e. the angels,

Mt 18:10

who are always with you.†

This, then, is that wonderful and truly glorious appearance of the Lord Jesus, on which, Lord, your eyes are always resting. His appearance is like Lebanon, because in every respect it is like the appearance of your own beauty. This is why this appearance gives you such intense delight, being 'the radiant mirror of your power and the image of

Ws 7:26

your goodness',† showing you within itself a most faithful picture of what you are, a most perfect representation.

Sermon 35.1–4

Mary's Role in the Glory of Jesus' Assumed Humanity

YOU ARE DAUGHTERS of Jerusalem. The bride herself is your mother, who brought you forth and gave you birth. She is the cause of your joy, the goal of your journey. The voice of

Jesus your Spouse and his Bride, the Church,
sound on your tongue and ring in your ears. We
are trying to find out about the glory which he
had from the beginning—the glory of his
beauty as the Son of man, *fairest among the sons
of men.*†

Ps 44:3

He nourishes the soul that gazes on him
with love. The flesh of Jesus is food indeed, and
his blood is drink indeed,† for those who have
thoroughly ruminated on the inexpressible love
and humility of his incarnation and passion.
Happy are those eaglets who, on assuming their
wings, soar straight to the body of Christ and
with an insatiable hunger—let me not call it a
voracious maw—devour his flesh and lap his
blood! Yet why should I scruple to say voracious
maw, when the law lays it down as part of the
ceremony of this meal that the flesh of the lamb
be eaten hastily, that is, voraciously, and the
head be consumed together with the entrails?†
This is the mysterious longing to see and be
united to the Incarnate God. Let us clutch our
prey, Jesus, and cling to him tenaciously.

Jn 6:55

Ex 12:3-11

Let us look at the radiance of the glory of
the humanity he assumed. It has four qualities,
and all of them exceed the grasp of human or
angelic comprehension: first, the complete innocence and perfect sanctity of that most holy
flesh; second, the complete wisdom and perfect
justice of that most exalted soul; third, the glorious assumption of that man into God; fourth,
the wonderful restraint of his humility from the
soaring flight of such great glory. If we cannot
conceive these in our words let us at least bring
them to birth in our delight in them.

THE FLESH OF JESUS. How pure and radiant was that flesh, brought forth by the virgin, conceived by the Holy Spirit. The glory of his holiness was inherited from his mother as well as from the Holy Spirit, and so it was inviolable in itself, besides giving health to the whole race. The wisest of virgins poured straight into her Son the leaven of innocence and sanctity by the wisdom and power of the Holy Spirit. So he was virginal, free from all corruption.

The Blessed Mother of God fashioned a garment for the sole beloved fruit of her womb, and the Holy Spirit wove it with her.[†] It was a garment woven throughout from above,[†] a garment of incomparable whiteness, such as before or after has never been seen on earth, a garment which no spot can bespatter or hand impair. This is the kingly garment which alone the King of kings has worn from his very beginning. It is for the King of kings and Lord of Lords.[†] This is the privilege reserved solely for the mother who bore him, a privilege reserved solely for the flesh of him so born.

THE SOUL OF JESUS. His soul was the mediator and it made the bond in that ineffable union by which human flesh was united to the Word of God. In that soul are hidden all the treasures of wisdom and knowledge,[†] all the riches of God's judgements so fully and immeasurably that nothing can be added and nothing taken away. In this soul the liberty of the human will, in the full dignity of its freedom, was restored to the integrity of the ancient decree, completely and peacefully, forever after to be enjoyed in its per-

Lk 1:35

Jn 19:23

1 Tm 6:15

Col 2:3

petual state, flowing from the peace he had beneath him, the justice he had within him, the glory of God he had above him. What joy there was in the soul of this peaceful King of ours! Many things come to mind about the glory of that ineffable union, wonderful things, but I can say little that will be worthy.

ASSUMPTION INTO GOD. First, I admit not knowing whether to wonder more at the dignity of the assumed nature or the dignity of the Person who assumed. Let us bless the Lord our God, Father, Son, and Holy Spirit, for having done so for us by a loving and similar agreement. They have not only made man *to* their own image and likeness,† but they have made a man who is their own image and likeness, something no man has dared desire or hope for. Blessed be the Holy Trinity and undivided Unity. O with what great joy was this done. With what great jubilation it was welcomed throughout that country! O with what great exultation it has resounded in our land!

Gen 5:3

JESUS' HUMILITY. The sheer dignity of the person who assumed this flesh and his full wonder will shine out all the more brightly from a comparison with the pride and blasphemy of the Assyrian, the devil. All envy shrinks away from him, far from his thoughts, for the goodness and loving-kindness of our Savior has appeared.† God freely gives us his Son and all that is his together with him, and in turn he communicates to him all that is ours.

Ti 3:4

Very sure are the decrees† of the divine humility, the stooping down of Majesty, the taking

Ps 92:5

up of human nature, the emptying out of wisdom and strength. The Son of Man says: I will
descend even to the likeness of man and be reck-

Ps 87:4

oned as one of those who go down to the pit.†
Truly, Lord, your works are great, fashioned to

Ps 111:2

your every desire!†

We have now spoken of three kinds of radiance pertaining to the glory of Christ Jesus: the
flesh, the soul, and the blessed union with the
Word of God. There is a fourth: his marvelous
humility by which he sustained the flight of
such glory, but this must be dealt with later.

Sermon 8.1–10

THE NOBILITY FOUND IN JESUS

IF YOU DESIRE to know more about Jesus
whom you love, ask the bride about him: 'Tell

Sg 1:9

me about your Beloved'.† The person who has
been enriched with knowledge of Jesus will tell
you: 'Jesus has a nobility in his nature in two important ways, and in both he is as wonderfully
renowned as he is beautiful and loveable beyond
all conceiving'. The bride quickly answers these
desires of her friends that are so lovingly conceived by the spirit of love, so gently too giving
birth to love, though not without pain and grief.
Here are pains like those of child-birth until the

love of Christ is fully formed in her. Now, whoever is a bride of the Lord and a mother of Jesus
groans in sympathy with anyone yearning for
the love of Jesus; and she stands by her when
that love is in labor. When at last she has
brought this love to birth, the bride ardently rejoices with her because a child has been born
into the world.†   Jn 16:21

'You want to know', the bride asks, 'in what
way Jesus, my Beloved, is more beautiful than
any other'. This is a vast theme in many ways.
He is a fire that shines and burns, especially for
his beloved Father, since he too is a fire, and a
font of light and heat for his only Son, and he
loves him with a love as marvelous as it is beyond our comprehending. He has poured into
him all the fullness of his glory and power. So
great is the force of love pouring out on him
from that font of love, that the Father and his
Beloved Son are not only coeternal and coequal
with each other, but they also have one and the
same essence, in every way undifferentiated.
This font of love is the primary channel of living water, a font of life to all who drink from it.

All holy love draws its joy from this font;
and in order that it may perpetually flow towards eternal life, from which it must also
spring, it wells up forever with desire towards its
font, rushing tirelessly back to its origin. So
great is the power of this love which flows from
the very deepest and primary font of love that it
unites its lover to its source. There is however,
no question of unity of nature, for that is something unique and incomparable that is possible
only in the Source itself. What we have here is

an indissoluble bond of union. For the person who cleaves to the Lord becomes one spirit

1 Cor 6:17

with him.†

In the same way as the Father is lovely and desirable, just so is his Only-begotten Son. Radiant from pure light, red-hot from burning heat. Seeing that my Beloved is truly a fire, he shines and burns exceedingly. But he does this as one whom the Father loves and he is in turn loved totally with an equal charity, for the Father is the source of light and infinite heat to his loved and loving only Son. So together they are one light and one heat, since they are in essence wisdom, truth, holiness, goodness: Wisdom, the artificer of all things, having all knowledge; Truth, vanquishing with its brightness the shadows of error, the lurking places of deceit; Holiness, totally erasing all corruption and impurity; Goodness, freely communicating its very self, even to the unworthy. This light strips away all the darkness of blindness and ignorance in which night had enveloped mankind.

O most beautiful Light, O radiance of light eternal, you were that from the beginning, you were like that, O everlasting loveliness, in those everlasting days of yours, in the years of your eternity. You were like that, O Lord Jesus, wise, true, holy, good, but you were this for yourself and for your beloved Father who loves you. With you was the beginning on the day of your birth, and you were with him, and you were total joy to him, and so was he to you.

Sermon 7.1-3

Our Sharing in Christ's Anointing

THERE IS ONLY ONE SPIRIT OF ANOINTING, by which the Father anointed his Only-begotten, and also anointed the Church his Bride. But the Son possesses a triple privilege which sets him far above all those who share with him in this anointing. From the very first moment of his conception in the virgin's womb he was anointed. He was conceived through the Holy Spirit, and beyond all measure every last drop of unction was poured out upon him. So much so, that from him and by him the overflowing abundance of this anointing streamed down upon the hem of his garment,† which is the Church. First, then, he was anointed before all others, and second, above all others, and third, for the sake of all others, not just for himself alone.

Ps 133:2

Those who share in this anointing have grace poured into their hearts, for he distils it, but this does not mean they also have it on their lips. They are enabled to receive into themselves the grace that comes from heaven, and this in itself is without any doubt a sufficiently divine favor. With great truth John could assert: *No one can receive anything unless it is given to him from heaven.*† Yet really to produce it in others, in just the same extent as they have themselves received it, this is not within the scope of the grace or glory proper to men or to angels. This belongs only to him who is the only Son of the Father.

Jn 3:27

For as that same friend of the Bridegroom says, *he who is sent from God*, only he and not another, *he it is who speaks the words of God.*† For

Jn 3:34

the words of the Creator, unutterable by his creation, are the utterance of divine inspiration. Only words like these are words of strength, only they are living and life-giving. Only those who listen to them are alive, and whoever listens to them, although in the grave, rises immediately into life.† So whatever life-giving spirit these words breathe, those who hear them even if they stop listening for a moment will become deaf. If you, Lord, become silent even for a single second, I shall immediately die and *become like those who go down into the pit.*† Let my God speak without interruption to the heart of his servant, let him speak the words of God, and that means justice and peace.

I know well who it was who said, *I am he who speaks justice,*† it is he who is supremely the defender of our salvation. But only of the Son of the Father has it been written: *He will speak peace to the peoples.*† Oh, if only I too could hear *what my Lord God speaks within me.*†

With beautiful precision the Bride expresses the unique glory of her Spouse saying: *His lips distil the purest myrrh.*† It is as if she were to say, *No one has spoken like this man.*† For my Beloved speaks not only in human language, but as *the Only Son who is in the bosom of the Father*† from his divine lips he distils the mysteries of God into the ear of the heart. He speaks of ineffable things and in an ineffable manner. He speaks of what he has heard from his Father, and in the manner he has learnt from his Father.† What person is fit even to think of these things?

The lips of the Beloved seem to the Bride to signify the unique power and glory of his

Jn 5:28-29

Ps 28:1

Is 63:1

Zec 9:10
Ps 85:8

Sg 5:13
Jn 7:46

Jn 1:18

Jn 15:15

inner breathing within us, the distilling of his
gentleness and the wisdom of this breathing.
The finest myrrh of anointing is the excellence
and power of the gift he has breathed upon us.
For he alone is glorious and powerful who can
turn the mind of man, with the utmost speed
and ease, in whatever direction he chooses. He
alone is gentle and wise and knows how to do
this with calm unction and wise discretion. He
alone is good and humble who graciously shares
his own Spirit with his little ones. *To him be
honor, glory, power and majesty for ever and ever.*

Sermon 21:6–7

Enquiring about the Beauty of Jesus

WHAT IS YOUR BELOVED LIKE?[†]   Sg 5:9

THE YOUNG PEOPLE ASK THIS for they
have grown accustomed to seeing the glory of
Jesus, the Spouse, in the face of the Bride. They
have been wonderfully enlightened by her as
from some everlasting mountain.[†] Now the   Ps 76:4
time has come for them to contemplate with the
apostles the glory of the Lord with face un-
veiled, and in Light itself to see light.[†] A new   Ps 36:9
name is to be given them, one which the mouth
of the Lord has uttered. So it is that with cour-
teous kindness and humble charity, the Bride

shares all with these young people, all the good blessings that Jesus, her Spouse, has given her: the yearning for a holy kiss, the fragrance of choicest perfumes, the very secrets of the marriage bed, the most glorious of honors.

In this spirit John the Baptist sent his disciples to Jesus. He sent them away from himself, and handed them over to stronger nourishment and a more powerful master, proving himself a faithful friend to the Bridegroom. The bride, by the deepest law of friendship, hands over to them the most blessed part which shall not be taken away from her.† She pours it out on them, even desiring to be surpassed by them in this holy warfare of love. If the bride demands from Jesus anything just for herself, and looks for personal glory because she has been specially favored, she is sure to lose something of that glory of the bride whom the apostle describes as *splendid, without spot or wrinkle or any such thing.*† The bride desires, with an intense and universal love, that the name she has been given, a name splendid and distinguished above all others, should become their common property.

The young people say to her: 'You have seen his beauty; to you alone among mortals has that desirable face been shown. It is impressed upon your senses, stamped upon your inmost being. You are like a mother; instruct your daughters. Tell us young and ignorant girls what your beloved Jesus is like! We do not ask who he is, for we know that he is no other than Jesus Christ, the Word of God, the Son of the virgin. We want to hear about his loveliness and graciousness, the outward signs of beauty. Humbly

Lk 10:42

Eph 5:27

refraining from grandeurs and marvels beyond
us, we are content in this life to be taught from
your own lips. For your voice is sweet[†] (we have   Sg 2:15
Jesus' word for it), and your lips distil nectar.[†]   Sg 4:11
The sweeter the love, the sweeter too the
speech. Yes, your tongue is on fire and your
speech is enkindled,[†] and we long for you to   Ps 118:140
make our hearts glow again for your Jesus, for
he is totally desirable. Who is the wise person if
not the one who has an intimate relish for Jesus,
and whom Jesus relishes too?'

In your mouth, O Beautiful one, praise is beau-
tiful; honor befits you, O Worthy of honor.[†] You are   Sir 15:9
an overflowing cup, exceedingly lovely.[†] You are   Ps 23:5
a chosen arrow of the Lord,[†] and you strike   Is 49:2
straight to the heart, for it is from the bow of
the Lord you are aimed. May the Word of the
Lord be in your hand! May your Spouse Jesus
come to us from his bridal chamber, your heart,
for if we are to find him for you, it is first necessary that you manifest him to us'.

It is the bride's lips that guard wisdom; to
her it is given to speak as she pleases. She is the
one for whom the golden ring is fitting, also the
golden necklace, the golden ear-rings, inlaid
with silver, for she serves the cause of love in all
she does, thinks, hears. Everything in her is directed towards love. O fairest of women, these
emblems are yours.

Sermon 2.1–3

CHARITY IS MORE PRECIOUS
THAN THE PUREST GOLD

Sg 5:11   HIS HEAD IS LIKE FINEST GOLD.†

COME THEN, MY BROTHERS, let us too be on fire with holy love. Let us follow the Spirit of understanding in conformity to the principles of faith. If we can find the gold of which the bride speaks, our King will be most gracious in his recompense. In this case *gold* signifies love. Love just like gold is precious, is full of light, is weighty, is solid, and once purged by fire has learned to resist it. Love and charity are one thing.

Charity is precious. If we consider the value of gold, it is more precious than all the wealth there is. No one knows the price of it;† no one, that is who can only speak of earthly things.† When Jesus sat down at his Father's right hand it was love he diffused into the hearts of his elect. This is the pearl of great price, which is obtained by selling everything.† The repute of its value has drawn after him an infinite crowd of merchants who, having sold all, bear in their hand the price of the pearl, namely contempt of the world. The buyer says, 'It is worthless, it is expensive, it is a hard bargain'. But when he has taken the pearl from the merchant's hand he changes his tune, 'It is fine, it is inexpensive, it is a wonderful bargain'.

Charity then is full of light. It effortlessly shows up the darkness of sin, reveals the paths of holiness in the beams of its brightness, and

Job 28:13

Jn 3:31

Mt 13:46

makes the loving soul vividly aware of eternal life by an inner vision of it. Charity, like gold, has within itself an everlasting source and a power of shining with a glorious natural splendor. Although that which shines externally is bright, much brighter still is that which lies within, retaining a great deal of light for its own illumination.

Charity has its own impetus, with an impulse that bears it up to things of eternity. There is an upward surge just as there is a downward fall. Fire and water are both moved by their own impetus: One straining to things above, one whirling swiftly down to things below. For a rational being love is its impetus. Blessed is charity which draws us up to Christ, and pulls with more effective power the more it calls upon the hand by which it is drawn. Charity frees itself from things of earth for those of heaven. It hastens to him who sits at the Father's right hand through the tireless momentum of its pull. It can say: 'Beneath this nothing pleases, and outside this nothing delights, beyond this nothing is agreeable, within this is whatever most deeply and richly satisfies'.

Charity is solid. Like gold, if you hammer it, you make it spread; if you pound it, you do not shatter it, you extend its width; if you persist in hammering it, it also persists in increasing. It turns its losses into profit, whether beaten with hammers or thrust into fire. When charity is beaten, its substance expands just as gold does, and the brightness lying hidden within bursts forth into view. So through suffering and endurance, charity grows in a double fashion: it grows in charity and it grows in clarity. After various hammer-blows of trouble, if the fire of tribulation seizes it, it knows that this is to test it, not to consume it. Fire can only consume what is weak and base, but here it has no power at all, since it is here to serve, to purify, to burnish. When all impurities have been refined away by heat, fire is of no use to it and of no harm either.

Fire is of no further service save that which tends to glory, to the completeness of victory, to a marvelous triumph. Whoever draws near will be able to see, with Moses, a great and awesome sight: how charity, like gold, burns and is not consumed. And so the gold that the Bride speaks of is love which is charity.

Sermon 11.1-4

The Gold that is Jesus

Sg 5:11   HIS HEAD IS OF FINEST GOLD[†]

I HAVE NO HESITATION in calling this gold love. It is a loved woman who speaks, she speaks about her Beloved, she speaks to those who live for love. What is more lovable than love, what is dearer than charity, what is sweeter, stronger, more life-giving? But I promised to tell you about the 'golden-love' from Saba.

*All shall come from Saba, bearing gold and in-
cense.*† This is the land where gold and incense   Is 60:6
originate. What is this land of incense if not devotion in praying, purity of prayer and earnestness in prayer? In this land it is not just a handful
of incense that is laid in the thurible, but with
both hands a full amount of incense is thrown
into the furnace, so that prayer may be directed
like incense before God. Love abounds in someone to whom it has already been granted to desire it more than anything else that pleases. She
seeks from the Lord who is rich in love, begs it
from him who has himself commanded it.

Before pure prayer can be uttered, it must
be preceded by the spirit of love, for this sets the
incense of prayer burning, and directs its smoke.
Also, before love can be a living flame, sweet
scented and worthy of the heavenly altars, there
must be the incense of prayer. By the urgency of
your prayer you are laying up a rich treasure of
love for yourself; and the more abundant your
love, the more frequent your prayer, the more
powerful its effect, the more perfect its purity,
the more delightful its sweetness.

From this land came the Queen of Sheba to
hear the words of Solomon. She lived in the
land of Saba and was queen in it. She came to
Solomon laden with spices, more precious than
had ever been in Jerusalem,† and she carried   1 K 10:10
home with her far richer gifts from him. Here
we can see the quality of prayer, its greatness
and power. How sweet a fragrance this incense
[prayer] has. Prayer makes us long to see our
King in Jerusalem, and then it grants us what
we long for. As we come to him prayer loads us

with precious perfumes; as we go from our prayer he loads us with joys more precious still. I am ashamed, brothers, of our poverty in this matter. We appear to be holding in our hands instruments of sacred song and lyres of prayer, but we have hung up our lyres on the willow trees of vain thoughts and affections.† We should remember the holy angels who hear and join us in our praise. We seem to be keeping vigils, there is plainsong on our lips; but our hearts are asleep. *Awake, my glory, awake, lyre and harp.*†

Ps 137:2

Ps 108:2

What are we to think of the gold from Tarshish? Solomon brought huge amounts of gold from there in his ships.† These ships are our earnest, frequent meditations, directed towards increasing our treasures of love. In fact, Tarshish is the country of 'joy'. We seek for joy throughout this land. Truly joy is this country. It is a place of rejoicing, and her people are full of joy.† So the ships of Jesus, our Solomon, were sent to this country to buy gold there. Jesus is in charge of the voyage both ways; otherwise these ships would have been in great danger. As they came and went across the vast sea of this world, endless in its infinity of thoughts and desires, salty with deep anxiety, swollen with excitement, choppy with uncertainties, tempestuous with disorders, they would be fearful lest a strong wind should overturn the ships of Tarshish.† Jesus, the man of discernment, controls the helm.† The spirit of Jesus is a spirit all gentle and humble. He will command the wind and the sea, and there will be a great calm, everything will be safe.† But if you have wisdom,

1 K 10:22

Is 65:18

Ps 48:7

Prv 1:5

Mt 8:24-26

Jesus will go before you in the ship and taking his seat as an oarsman, will hold the rudder.

We must apply ourselves in every possible way to love. This must be carried out with zeal and discretion. As long as I hear eternal happiness offered to me on a condition, I do not rely on my own efforts. Even if the Lord freely pours down on me as much rain, i.e. grace, as I could desire, increasing it and blessing my soul,† I am convinced that the more he blesses me the more I should be fearful. Since his gift comes from heaven, I will open myself as wide as I can, in order to draw the Spirit of love in the desire of my soul. So even if the ships of meditation come to grief, let us not on that account drop the whole undertaking or engage in it with less enthusiasm. Yes, the harbor to which these meditations happily steer is nothing else than the investigation of joy.

The goal of this blissful meditation is nothing else than the fruit of holy contemplation, which is love, and you know the fruits of love. Their names are: joy, peace, patience tolerance, kindness, integrity and many like them, which the apostle Paul enumerates.†

Mal 3:10

Gal 5:22

Sermon 12.1–4

THE SIGHT OF JESUS

Sg 5:12

HIS EYES ARE DOVES BESIDE SPRINGS OF WATER.†

Mt 26:10

WHY DO YOU TROUBLE ME,† you crowd of my cares, you tormenting worries, you unruly mob of thoughts, all wasting and racking my heart?† I will go, then, and with all the strength I can muster, I will try to tear myself free from the crowd that presses and oppresses me. I am small in stature, so I will climb into some tree, where I may at least catch sight of the face of Jesus as he passes by.† I will at least catch sight of the face he wears now as he comes to visit his wandering exiles.

Job 17:11

Lk 19:3-5

ZACCHAEUS: I recall, in fact, a man who was blessed with a longing for this kind of vision, and he grew suddenly to such a stature that he enjoyed the sight of Jesus at will. He was able to receive him with joy as he came nearer and nearer, to act as his host, to possess him as an intimate companion.† I remember others too, burning with the same desire, though as yet gentiles and sinners, I remember them saying to Philip: *Master, we desire to see Jesus.*† Surely these were men of low stature, and by the measure of the age which is in Christ Jesus, they were perhaps the least of all. Deliberately, then, they climbed a tree to see Jesus. Thereupon Philip went to Andrew, and Andrew together with Philip were found to be faithful messengers of this holy desire for Jesus. It was a loving desire,

Lk 19:2-10

Jn 12:21

and Jesus responded lovingly: *The hour has come*, he said, *for the son of man to be glorified.*† For it is true that if a man ardently seeks the face of Jesus, he has already come in this hour to glorify the son of man, he has already gone to the feast, the day of festivity has already dawned on him.†

Jn 12:23

Jn 7:10

Scripture says of those gentiles that they went up to Jerusalem to worship at the feast.† So this is a sign to you that you have seen Jesus: if you have glorified him, praising and blessing him with all your heart, if the sight has filled you with wonder, confusion, emotion; if all the arrogance of your heart has melted away like wax before his glory; if finally you have feasted and exulted at the sight of him and are jubilant with joy,† your whole heart rejoicing in him, because your eyes have seen the salvation of God.†

Jn 12:20

Ps 68:4

Lk 2:30

O face more desirable than anything else,
never holding yourself back from those who
    seek you,
and glorifying with your own light those who
    see you!

Yet as is said here by Jesus himself, this festivity and glory takes place for an hour, and that hour is very brief and exceptionally rare. *The hour has come*, he says, *for the son of man to be glorified.*† But happy the hour and weighty the business of this hour, in which he in turn gives glory to those who glorify him. Lord God of hosts, convert us, show us your face and we shall be saved.† The sight of the face of Jesus truly saves us, truly gives life to us. No one will see his face without immediately dying to himself and taking new life in him. Blessed are those eyes

Jn 12:23

Ps 80:19

Mt 13:16

alone, and blessed are all those who have seen his face.†

Sermon 18,1–2

THE EYES OF JESUS

I FIND IT DIFFICULT, my brothers, to let myself be wrenched away from the sight of those eyes of Jesus, so infinitely to be desired. I appeal to that knowledge you share among yourselves, which has deserved even once to enjoy this sight, to bear witness to how good it is to be attached to it, how wholesome it is to lose oneself in it, how full of gladness it is utterly to lose oneself in it. To rest your strength on it is to stand firm; to lose yourself in it is to be more and more enlightened; to cleave to it will be finally to be made like to it, to be made one with it.

To look at those eyes is to have received a promise of grace; to be looked at by them in turn is to have received grace itself, here and now. In a word, nobody is holy, nobody is or can be just or good if he has not found grace in those eyes. Those eyes are full of grace, or to put it better, they are themselves the fullness of grace, because a look from them suffices for every outpouring or confirming of grace in the

children of grace. But those eyes have many different ways of looking and they apportion the
work of salvation according to the various reasons that make it necessary. To sum up, Jesus
from the shore beheld Peter and Andrew, as
well as James and John, and he drew them from
the restless waves of this present life to the shore
of the sea,† that is, to contempt of the world.   Jn 21:2-14

On the mountain, accordingly, he lifted up
his eyes to them and their fellow disciples and
called them, by his words in their ears and his
grace in their hearts, to greater heights of virtue.†   Lk 6:20
At the beginning of his passion, when he was already taking his place in the courtroom, he
looked at Peter†—the sacrament of our redemp-   Lk 22:61
tion was already under way, and he was preparing Peter in advance for the penance and pardon
that would flow from it. From the cross he
looked at his crucifiers and at all who were guilty
of shedding his most sacred blood—I shrink to
say and I dread not to admit that at some time
we too have been among them. From the cross
then he looked at all us sinners, fastening our
sins to his cross and pleading with his Father for
transgressors, that they might not perish.† From   Lk 23:34; Is 53:12
heaven he looked at his disciples, gathered to-
gether into one, when he poured out upon them
the abundance of his Spirit and created from
them new heavens for his delight. From them,
also, as if from his holy throne, he looked down
on all who dwell on the earth,† and he poured   Ps 33:14
out his Spirit upon all flesh through their hands,
drenching them with sacred unction.

Indeed, even before these glances of his,
when he was still in his most holy and hidden

resting place, the bosom of the Father, he looked on the lowliness of Mary, his handmaid, whom rightly they call blessed and all genera-

Lk 1:48

tions shall call her so.† For she found grace most richly in his eyes, and not for herself only, but

Est 7:3

for all generations which are to come.† From the bosom of the Father, Jesus saw the one to whom, by a unique and irrevocable privilege, he gave the name of mother, so that he who was

Lk 1:32

the son of the Most High† was also the son of

Lk 1:46-48

his most lowly handmaid.† The Lord is high,

Ps 138:6

and from his height he looks on the lowly,† all the more because by his unchangeable decree

Lk 18:14

everyone who humbles himself will be exalted.†

Now, if I am not mistaken, it is clear to you why the eyes of the Spouse are said to be like

Sg 5:12

doves beside rivulets of water.† You can see that it is only on the small and lowly that Jesus looks or the Spirit rests.

Sermon 19.1–2

The Cheeks of Jesus

I KNOW YOU ARE WAITING eagerly to hear what these cheeks of the Spouse really are. Unless you have some better opinion, it seems to me that his cheeks are his gaiety and gravity. The whole of a person's face becomes very pleasing in appearance if gravity gives it dignity and gaiety gives it an appealing charm. Ripeness of years brings a solid stability that protects the mind against inexperience and heedlessness. On the other hand, cheerfulness dissolves the clouds of sadness, smoothes away the wrinkles of irritation, stops gnawing envy inflicting its spiteful wounds, or cures the bites it has already inflicted. . . .

MY CHEEKS. I lift up my eyes to the venerable gravity of those ancient patriarchs whose faces were full of gladness, yet *the light of their face did not fall to the earth.*† They shame me. I hear any one of them thundering forth in tones of terror when his brother gives way to frivolity. 'In the presence of heaven and earth,' he says, 'we are about to render our account to God, and do you cackle?'

Job 29:24

Then there is this, too, to consider, that in our own household we have a gardener to take care of these things. I am referring to Saint Benedict. For many years now he has been toiling in the little garden-patch of my soul, and as well as he can he has surrounded it with a wall, divided it into plots and sown it with scented herbs. To this very day he is waiting patiently, but I am sadly afraid waiting in vain to gather small bundles of fragrance from my cheeks. In their place, I fear, the time of harvest will discover thorns and nettles, the things that usually grow in the field of a lazy man.

Alas, how often this beautician of mine, trying to renew the surface of my cheeks rises threateningly against me. He accuses me and

instructs me, speaks to me and makes announce-
ments, condemns in every place throughout the
monastery all buffoonery and outbursts of laugh-

RB 6:8

ter, does not permit me to open my lips to them.[†]
What answer shall I make to this perfumer as he
extends his pruning knife, as he opens out his
hand and spreads wide the fold of his cloak?
What am I to say, especially when he begins to
call as witness against me the very frequent warning he has given me and the very profession of
my vows? It was my own mouth that once pronounced these vows, and I called God and his
saints to be my witness.

THE CHEEKS OF THE BRIDE. As soon as the
Word of God has kissed her, the bride seems to
make progress in the beauty of her cheeks, while
charity is just beginning to take root in her.
Among the first words honoring her with
praise, she hears with deep happiness from the
lips of her Spouse: *Your cheeks are as lovely as*

Sg 1:9

those of a turtle-dove.[†] Surely, through the power
of his Spouse, the bride has made her cheeks
like those of the dove, in that the absence of her
Spouse leaves her wretched beyond all solacing,
sick beyond all healing, poor beyond all wealth,
insensible to every joy there is? But when her
Spouse is at her side, she learns to let nothing
trouble her and to stand firm against all injus-
tice, with a quiet heart and a cheerful gravity.
She sees to it that her beloved is always in her

Ps 16:8

sight,[†] she ponders constantly upon his face, she
esteems everything else as nothing in comparison with her longing-love for him. So she is
very like the turtle-dove in its purity. She main-

tains inviolable her loyalty to her Spouse and to him alone. She clings faithfully to him when he is with her, and she sighs after him with still greater faithfulness when he is away. While he is alive she is determined to live at least for him, but when he is dead, she offers the rest of her life in daily funeral, in ceaseless mourning.

SCENT ON HIS CHEEKS: JESUS' MEEKNESS AND POWER OF HEALING. *Therefore, O Jesus my Lord, O honey-sweetness, O scented delight, O font of all that is sweet, draw me in the odor of your cheeks! With their rich beauty and perfume cleanse from our cheeks what is unclean, blow away what is fetid. Teach us at every hour to fix our whole thought on your cheeks and borrow from them some fair semblance for our own cheeks.*

According to what we have received from your perfumers—I mean the prophets and evangelists—we hear reverently that in your unspeakable kindness and gentleness, for the sake of reconciling sinners to God, your Father, you gave them to others to be plucked.[†] That was a very great day, the day of your Father's harvest, when he gathered to himself bundles of spices from the beds of spices which are your cheeks. With those bundles he filled his lap, there to remain stored with him for all eternity. That most delicate of perfumes breathed forth its scent as if to him alone, because *no one knows the Son except the Father.*[†]

On that day, too, the Bride of Christ, the Church of God, gathered her harvest of firstfruits from the beds of your cheeks, and from that day until the end of time she never ceases

Is 50:6

Mt 11:27

to reap an ever-fresh harvest from that scented seed.

Those who harvested these beds were not Jn 4:37 those who sowed them.† They were sown by prophets, who spoke at length of the holiness and meekness of the Lord Jesus, as if in the fullest and most brilliant light of the Gospel. In the Gospel the Church has, for the most part, gathered nothing more than their hand sowed in their prophecies. Let me pluck a little and hold it to your nostrils to smell its scent.

Nothing could be clearer than the words of Isaiah: *I gave my body to the strikers and my cheeks to those who plucked them; I did not turn my face* Is 50:6 *away from those who mocked and spat upon me.*† Other beds of the holy seed have been sown by other prophets, all in the same spirit, all thickly planted. It is into their labors that the Church Jn 4:18 has entered,† brought there by the loving gardener. So that we may smell more distinctly something of the gentleness of Jesus in his suffering and innocence of heart, absolute in its submission, he went on to say: *He will not* Is 42:4 *mourn or be disturbed,*† he will not cry out or contend, but he was *silent as a lamb before his* Is 53:7 *shearers and he did not open his mouth.*†

Let anyone with nostrils to smell with, come near! Let him gather for himself and carefully press between his fingers that bundle of spices! Let him breathe in from them the odor of every kind of gravity and serenity. Then, like the careful Bride of the Lord, let him store his Sg 1:12 bundle between his breasts,† so always to have close at hand a reminder of his sweetness, especially when a time of temptation assails, when his gravity and cheerfulness in good times as well as bad is destined to be put to the test.

    Lord Jesus, 'be our strong arm in the morning, and our protection in time of trial,† perfuming us on every side and breathing sweetness by day and night. From the scent of your cheeks may there flow to us at all times the certainty of salvation and a continual source of healing.*   Is 33:2

Sermon 20.4–7

JESUS' THROAT:
THE LIFE-GIVING VITALITY
WE RECEIVE FROM HIM

HIS THROAT IS MOST SWEET, AND HE IS WHOLLY DESIRABLE.†   Sg 5:16

THAT THROAT is most truly an overflowing fountain of all sweetness, to which nothing can be compared, and he is so wholly desirable that he is greater than any yearning and more powerful than any desire. In him there is food for all our sustenance, all the support we need for vitality, all the life of our spirit. Through his throat all the nourishment of our spiritual life is drawn down into his interior—which is where we are. Through his throat the wholesome breath of God, his Holy Spirit, spreads out to make us living and full of vitality. Through his throat we breathe, drawing in his Holy Breath (Spirit) through our continual desire.

You, Lord Jesus, understand our needs, you heal our weakness, you give us all that will help us. Through your manifold wisdom, which is the secret sweetness of your throat, you distribute to each separate one of your members what will bring them fully to life, make them responsive and strong, as far as each of us has need of it.

Lord Jesus, you are uniquely sweet and infinitely desirable. For so many ages already, your holy angels have taken delight in you, and yet it is as if they were only now seeing you for the first time, so deep is their longing still to gaze upon you. O sweetness ever ancient and ever new, to enjoy you to eternity is to be constantly aroused to desire, to possess you completely is to be constantly stirred to new longings. O morning splendor of eternal brightness, how joyfully you irradiate those who enjoy you! You are always with them, and yet you are always breaking upon their eyes like the 'morning splendor' of the rising sun. Truly, one day within your courts is better than thousands elsewhere,[†] *because of its lovely freshness. What an amazing miracle of happiness this is: complete satisfaction that is never endangered, because desire is always stretching ahead of it! Yet there is no room at all for desire to feel unhappy, because of the completeness with which satisfaction abounds. Repletion cannot enter into it, as the longing is always intense, and yet the yearning can know no pain, for its hunger is full of joy.*

Surely, Lord, this is what is meant by that blissful and eternal 'circle' of which the psalmist sings. You are mighty, O Lord, and your truth is

Ps 84:10

a circle round about you[†] —*the circle of those who* Ps 89:9
seek the face of the God of Jacob,[†] *of seeking and* Ps 24:6
finding, blissfully finding and nonetheless ardently
seeking! For round that most true and brilliant
light which is yourself, there circles that blessed so-
ciety of whom you said in the beginning, Let there
be light, and there was light.[†] *They cleave to the* Gen 1:3
Truth, and so they become the 'truth'. They most
truly circle around you, always seeking your face,[†] Ps 105:4
and rejoicing in having found you, they run to you
without exertion, they reach you without hin-
drance, they lay hold of you without pride, they feast
on you without repletion, they possess you without
possessiveness, they keep you without anxiety.

O Light most desirable, running so joyfully to
meet all who long for you! You present yourself so
sweetly. And above all that those who desire you
could hope for, you grant the complete, overflowing
enjoyment of yourself. Yet by those who enjoy you,
you are enjoyed with desire that is always new, and
every minute renewed, and they press eagerly for-
ward. You are sought and you are encircled, and it is
as though only for the first time, or better not even
yet, they have fully seized upon you. Who cannot
wonder at it? Since your throat is 'most sweet' its
indescribable sweetness has devoured them, but at
the same time, you are wholly desirable[†] *and they* Sg 5:16
enjoy you blissfully. They desire then to enjoy you
unceasingly, so that in one kiss of peace they may ex-
perience simultaneously that bliss of desire and the
desire of bliss.

This is the same happy kiss which justice and
peace for ever give each other in the glory of
heaven.[†] For justice could truly be described as Ps 85:10
the passion of holy desire with which God is

loved, and peace could be spoken of as abundance, referring to that peace *which surpasses all under-*

Phil 4:7

standing,[†] even the understanding of those who have been worthy to enjoy it most abundantly. This abundance is not on earth but up above,

Lk 2:14

where there is *glory to God in highest heaven,*[†] and

Ps 122:7

abundance within the towers of Jerusalem.[†]

Sermon 38.1-6

THE HUMILITY OF JESUS

THE BRIDE is not well versed in the wisdom of this world, or rather, because she is bride to the Word, her foolishness is wiser than men. She has woven a cloak of praise for her Beloved and wants it finished off with golden fringes. So, after all his other praises, she adds finally the praise of his humility.

The bride has made a wise decision. All the virtues, not only of virtuous people, but even of the very Lord of virtues, find their completion in humility. That is why her Spouse is wonderful both in heaven and on earth. He is the First,

Ps 113:4

and *his glory is above the heavens,*[†] and yet at the same time, he is the Last, and his humility is lower than the very lowest of the lowly. So the bride, well aware of this mystery, adds to her loving description of his beauty by praising his humility, which is the highest praise his beauty can have.

Although the marvelous power of his beauty makes him incomparably more glorious than all God's chosen ones, nevertheless, in his humility he makes himself like the others, counting himself among the cedars of God.† He forgets the honor that is his due, and devotes himself wholly to loveliness. It costs him nothing to break up, as it were, the glory of his appearance and bequeath it to his little ones to be their glory. He lays aside his primacy, and hands himself over even to the least of his members in a state of complete sharing and equality. *God, above all things and blessed for ever*† makes it his glory to become like a cedar, stretching out to them his branches.

So in the eyes of those who love the appearance of Jesus and gaze on it directly, his beauty is all the more wonderful for his placing himself at the feet of all in humility, as though he no longer remembered that he was wonderful or lovely in appearance.

In the bride's hands, we find praise of Christ's genuine humility; there is nothing feigned. Her aim is to please him whose approval she covets, and for the King to desire her beauty.† So with ease and joy she often watches herself reflected in the mirror of Christ's humility, as if she heard her Spouse saying to her, *Go and do likewise.*†

[A long section on the pride of the devil follows]

The glorious beauty, rashly sought by the devil, has been vindicated and reclaimed for the Only-begotten of the Father.

Sg 5:15

Rom 9:5

Ps 44:12

Lk 10:37

Is 52:10

When *all the ends of the earth see the salvation of our God,*[†] and see, on the one hand, Christ in all the glory of his ineffable loveliness, and on the other, the evil one in the foul stench of his hideousness, the face of Christ Jesus will testify to his humility and that of all who share his wisdom. Then, in comparison with the terrible repulsiveness of the evil one, the appearance of Jesus will be even more beautiful than before, and it will be said to him: 'Truly, Lord our God, you are beautiful and gracious, and in either of your natures, the classic grace of your loveliness is very wonderful. Although in your divine essence you are truly coequal with your Father, you have come down to the depths of human nature in order to restore what the rival of your glory violated. He set his heart on the highest place, you submitted to the lowest. His ambition was to lord it over the heavens, yours to be a servant on the earth, rather to be servant of sinners. He was the beginning of ruin; you, the first beginning of all that is, are the beginning and cause of restoration. He fouled his beauty and tainted the glory of his fellows; you were clothed in flesh, born of a woman, living among sinners, and you kept yourself free from

Ws 4:19

stain and bore the sin of the world.[†]

Yet your humanity too has infinite beauty. Although in that humanity you were taken up by the very form of God, you did not relish your greatness, but conformed yourself to our nature and made yourself like the humble. Now you have the glorious position that Lucifer desired;

Is 14:14

you are made like the Most High,[†] indeed you

Lk 1:32

are the Son of the Most High;[†] yet this high

dignity did not raise your heart to pride. From the moment of your conception, when you were adopted by the Son of God, you never cease giving thanks to the Lord God your protector. Your heart is full of prayer and thanksgiving to the God of your life, and you cry out to God, *You are my Protector.*[†]   Ps 42:11

You are most humbly obedient to the election by which God chose to take you up, and you abase yourself before the Majesty through and in which you were exalted, giving incomparable thanks for the grace by which grace and glory were lavished upon you. In short, although, O Lord our God, you are great beyond measure,[†] you came to live among your little ones as one of them.[†] You did more. Taking up the burden of every kind of service, you emptied yourself completely and put yourself at their feet, not their fellow-servant, but their drudge.[*] Even on your throne at the right hand of your Father, you have not laid aside for one moment the measure of your earlier humility, so that to all ages you are both the highest of all and, equally, the lowest. May you hold in everything the Primacy.

Ps 104:1
Sir 32:1

* Guerric, Sermon
1 for Palm Sunday;
CS 32:55-56.

Sermon 36.1–6

THE SWEETNESS OF HOLY MEDITATION

Sg 5:16 HIS THROAT IS MOST SWEET.[†]

THE BRIDE wants the *throat* of the Spouse to signify the pleasant sweetness of 'interior tasting'. Not everything tastes alike. Butter has one flavor, honey another; pure honey differs from honey in the comb; bread differs from fish, milk from wine, fresh fruit from dried. Christ, after the resurrection, was offered Lk 24:42 a comb of honey[†] and he also ate bread both be- Mt 26:26 fore[†] and after resurrection, and he also partook Lk 24:32 of fish after he had risen.[†]

What hope is there of conveying the true figurative meaning of these flavors? But we must try. One might call butter a rich smooth disposition of charity, sharing through love in all our brothers' concerns, good and bad.

Let me call honey the sweetness of glory which true Christian hearts, eager for the glory that comes from God, gather for themselves from various flowers. Not only from perfect flowers, but even from the flowers of the field that bloom today and are cast into the oven Mt 6:30 tomorrow.[†] It is possible, by holy meditation to extract an imperishable glory from these flowers of the field, if only you are rich in those keen desires which made holy by the Holy Spirit have learnt the way of making this honey. Any flower at all, however insignificant, is still a unique mirror of God's eternal glory. It has this tremendous importance, that in it the heavenly beauty seems to have left some traces of its

beauty in this *beauty of the meadow*,† which is Ps 50:11
here among us, i.e. the glory of the world. Anyone who makes wise use of it can gather the
sweetest honey from its flowers. With that
honey of meditation in his mouth he will acquire the experience that makes the glory of the
world appear like a nauseating bitterness, and
that makes his throat eager for the glory which
is in the heavens, the pure honey of glory.

In his boyhood our Emmanuel knew how
to reject evil and choose good. This sweet and
gentle training is well suited to his boyhood.
Not that he needs these flowers in order to contemplate the unseen glory of God, being himself nothing less than the flower of the meadow† Sg 2:1
from whom the whole swarm of heavenly bees
gather the finest and rarest honey. But the Wisdom of God, taking flesh, wished to live like us,
and in this way he chose to savor to the full
whatever was human and to change into the
contemplation of heavenly things whatever he
experienced in his fleshly senses.† Rom 8:5

Fed every hour on the sweetness of the
sacred honey that was within him, he was himself that honey. It was stored up for him in that
honeycomb which the Wisdom of God so wonderfully fashioned when he took his spotless
body from the Virgin.† His great glory is that Jn 1:14
honey, placed in the comb and there concealed,
growing ever sweeter within the virginal body
and marvelously containing itself within those
virginal limits.

Whenever he chooses, our Emmanuel eats,
now his pure honey, now the honeycomb with
his honey. The Virgin's Son has equal freedom

to glory at his good pleasure in the greatness of the Word who lifts him up, and to render indescribable and most glorious thanks to God the Father and to his Word, because in lifting up his flesh, the Word has given it such joy. But after the triumph of the resurrection he alone has the right to glory and to say to his Bride: *I eat my*

Sg 5:1

honeycomb with my honey.[†] That is: through the glory of his resurrection the honey has been returned to the wax from which it came. Not that the Word deserted even for a moment the honeycomb of the flesh he once assumed—rather with the total extinction of mortality, he has now totally steeped and clothed his flesh with the glory of a new immortality never henceforth

1 Cor 15:54

to be shed for all eternity.[†]

Do you too long to feed Jesus with food like that? Then, in the secrecy of your heart, like the ingenious bee, first hang up the clinging wax of holy thoughts, breathing out the love of Christ. Then drench them with loving dispositions, as if sprinkling them with honeyed dew. The Holy Spirit will help you to arrange your comb by the skilful dexterity of your hands and feet, so that one meditation harmoniously follows another. Each one helping the other with identical support and mutual aid, they can together raise a marvelous structure for the angels to gaze upon. Then you will be able to gather for yourself

Ps 49:11

honey from *the beauty of the meadow,*[†] which is not of this earth, from the roses and lilies of the valley, i.e. the martyrs and saints, among which

Sg 2:16

the Beloved makes his pasture,[†] that is, from the holy joy of the celestial spirits. Above all, you will be able to gather honey from that flower on

which rests the sevenfold Spirit,† because in
him dwells all the fullness of what is sweet.†
The oftener you come to taste his honey, the
more blossom you will find in him, and the
more overflowing. Eagerly then, buzz round
that flower and lose yourself within its holy
depths. He himself must first feed you on himself, and then in time to come, you in turn will
be able to feed him.

By meditation and love carry the gift of
heavenly bounty away into the secret chambers
of your heart, digest it and conceal it. Imitate
the wisdom of the most prudent of bees, of
whom it is written: *Mary kept all these words,
storing them in her heart.*† Believe me, the Lord
Jesus will be more delightfully fed by a honeycomb of this kind of honey, than by honey that
flows from your hand. Solomon says: *It is the
glory of God to conceal his word.*† To a great extent, the very concealment of glory confers a
certain degree of taste in the glory itself, and for
this reason the throat knows very much more
sweetness.

Sermon 37.2–5

Is 11:2
Col 1:19

Lk 2:19

Prv 25:2

III

THE FATHER'S LOVE FOR THOSE WHO SHARE IN HIS SON'S PASSION

AN OVERVIEW

THE BOOK OF JOB begins with a scene in the courts of heaven where Satan confronts God and issues a challenge concerning the just man, Job. God takes up the challenge. The afflictions of Job and his vindication by God are the thrust of the whole demanding dialogue that anticipates our redemption.

This epic poem provides a setting for one of John of Forde's most moving creations. A scene in heaven predicts the drama of men's redemption in the heavenly court before the judge, God the Father, and the defendant, condemned mankind, whose huge sackful of sin is vicariously accepted by the Son, Jesus Christ. The angels stand amazed in the court as sentence is pronounced on the Son. He, steeped in his free willingness to obey his Father's verdict, manifests his love of humankind by his acceptance of the infinitely dramatic reparation demanded of him.

Here John puts to God a rhetorical but very pertinent question: Why punish the just man who has done no wrong? If God is just, then surely he cannot punish the innocent? A good question. Using human logic and justice it is unanswerable, it is unreasonable. But John searches the infinite wisdom of God's wisdom and finds an answer which is found in the latter part of sermon 10, not without a considerable display of emotion and powerful insight characteristic of his style.

Again, in Sermon 28, we find the flood of John's emotion and compassion as he touches the sorrowing heart of Jesus who is grieving over his imminent and necessary departure from the disciples.

The agony was caused not by fear, John insists, but by loving mercy.

No word could be more eloquent than a word from the Word. No wisdom more wise than the Wisdom of God, except perhaps his silence. He, who with a word of power could have called on all the angelic might, remained silent before the judgement seat of Pilate. This silence is the incomprehensible silence of God in the face of the Holocaust. It is the silence of God who watches with infinite compassion on the tragedy of evil and diabolical sin, our sin. Only this silence, when supported by faith, can bring a meaningful peace to the soul. 'Which of you, my dearest brethren, will give his heart to becoming a loving imitator of this sacred silence?' He who truly seeks wisdom will enter this school of philosophy where he will sit with Mary at Jesus' feet, or stand with her at the foot of the cross.

No one can comprehend the power and meaning of the cross. We know that Jesus chose this way. We know that his love for his Father, for the Church, and for you and me drove him to embrace it. Infinite in its meaning, each person and each generation will find unlimited scope for contemplation in a suffering that subsumes all suffering into one pure agony. John of Forde speaks of the cross in many places in his sermons. In Sermon 30 he follows the allegorical meaning of the Song where praise is given to the legs of the Bridegroom. The commentary makes it abundantly clear that he is not talking so much of the physical legs of Jesus, but raises his sight to the everlasting and changeless strength on which Jesus rests. His soul is firmly established on the will of God; therefore his patience and long-suffering are marks of the divine strength on which he stands, rather than the innate weakness of physical bones—though in this unique case God preserved those legs intact through the unbreakable law of prophecy. Not a bone of his body shall be broken.[1]

[1] Jn 19:36

Let us stand by the cross. 'Let us return quickly to the cross of Jesus with the blessed mother of the Lord and her companions'.[2] If we would gain some insight into the love of Jesus, we must return again and again to the cross in our meditation. 'Let us stand there together. Let us draw one another by our mutual love to the contemplation of that immense love.' *'Vivat'* cries John of Forde,

> May it live. May that death live, may it live and may it breathe eternal life into our understanding. This death is alive eternally with the Father, it is alive in the heavens, it lives in its cause, it lives in its fruit. I will be your death, O death, says he who on the cross died for me.[3]

In saying that John was constantly meditating on the death of Jesus, I do not mean that his spiritual teaching was negative. On the contrary, he comes back again and again to the triumph of the cross, its power to conquer. 'O victorious death, what is there still to be conquered? Everywhere is bright with your triumphs, everywhere the banner of your victory flies in splendor'.[4] It is possible that this sermon was written before the wrath of King John and his conflict with Pope Innocent III plunged England into the dark chasm of the Interdict, and before the king's depredations brought the abbey of Forde to the brink of ruin. But I think that John was able to transcend all the evil around him with the spiritual vision of faith, a faith that glowed white-hot with hope. His faith ultimately transfigured his soul with the purest spirituality.

That faith was a dark shadow over the disciples when Jesus died. His death and his absence were and still are for all of us the darkest of nights. His presence among them had been so desirable because he was so totally desirable: 'The Lord Jesus is desirable

---

[2] Sermon 26.8
[3] Sermon 26.8
[4] Sermon 26.8

when he is present, desirable when he is absent, desirable as the light he is, desirable also is his shadow. Everything about him is desirable to those who love and live for him."[5] His absence from them was a dark night taking away all meaning to their lives, total abandonment by God—the very darkest of nights. But faith is still alive in the soul. She says: 'I have confidence that morning will follow night. You have let me watch for you in the night' and by your gift 'I shall watch for you even at the break of day'.[6] The night and the shadow are therefore gracious, full of saving power, and when grace seems lost, it brings back the desirable presence, symbolizing protection.

For John this is the 'royal road'. It is by no means an easy road. It is for those who are eager for perfection, who strive to run along the straight and narrow road. John knew what it was like to be in the presence of the king and queen of England. He knew that theirs was not true royalty. It violated the meaning of the word. Only those who have entered on the royal road are truly 'royal queens'. They have the joy of the kingdom within them; even here below they reign with Christ.

We too can prove ourselves truly children of our Father in heaven,[7] if so great a light glows within us that we are eager to show ourselves heirs of our Father's love. Then we are truly kings and queens because we are children of the Most High, because the Father loves those who share in his Son's passion.

---

[5] Sermon 38.7
[6] Ps 118:117
[7] Cf. Mt 4:8

The Patience in Suffering of Those Who Love God Deeply

THERE ARE SIXTY QUEENS, AND EIGHTY CON-
CUBINES, AND MAIDENS WITHOUT NUMBER.[†] Sg 6:7-8

ROYAL QUEENS. The first are those who, eager
for perfection, strive to hasten to perfection by
the straight and narrow way.[†] The second, who   Mt 7:14
have experience of Christ's love,[†] follow him in   RB 58:8
sweet and gentle ways. The third, who have no
interior experience of the sweetness of Christ,
have all the same an ardent longing to obey and
practice this holy warfare.

Obviously the first kind are *royal queens* because, having entered on the royal road, they
think it intolerable to have to wait upon the future. They have the joy of understanding something of what the kingdom of Christ means and
they hasten, even here below, to reign with him.[†]   2 Tm 2:12
They say: His kingdom is certainly not of this
world,[†] yet all the same it is *in* this world. For   Jn 18:17
the Kingdom of God and his Christ is right-
eousness and peace and joy in the Holy Spirit,[†]   Rom 14:7
and anyone who shares in these things already
reigns with God.[†]   Rv 20:4

When the Lord Jesus preached the Good
News of the kingdom of God, he said that
the blessed ones were the poor[†] and those who   Mt 5:3

95

Mt 5:10

suffered persecution for justice' sake,† and he did not simply 'promise' the kingdom, but he placed it right in their midst. They are now in possession of the kingdom. They are kings of the kingdom of which the Lord our God is also King.

For the love of the glory of heaven they hold in disdain everything which savors of vanity. Rejoice greatly, exult, and sing for joy!† *Do*

Ps 31:11

not fear, little flock, for your Father has been pleased to give you a kingdom.† I tell you, the Lord has

Lk 12:32

Ps 126:2

done great things for you.† Sing praise to God, for what he has done for you. To what other kings than to you and kings like you can it be said: 'they have heard every word from your

Ps 138:4

mouth?'† Blessed be God! Over the whole world we see that many nations are this kind of kingdom. We see it, we hear it: *For see, the kings*

Ps 102:22

of the earth assembled, they assembled all together.†

Mt 5:10

When they *suffer persecution for justice' sake*† they look for the crown of the same kingdom, but now reproduced with twofold merit, though they do not so much look for this crown as receive it. They glory in the confidence of God's children, but they also learned from Christ how

Rm 5:3

to rejoice in afflictions.† Paul thought this so precious that he says: *Far be it from me to glory in*

Gal 6:14

anything except the cross of our Lord Jesus Christ.†

HOLY REPOSE. We too, dearest brothers, have not been defrauded by God of a share in this glory. All who wish to live godly lives in Christ Jesus will suffer persecution. I pray that when persecution does threaten, we may not be weary of remembering our crown, and that we may be ready to defend bravely the honor of our kingdom.

There is a third kind of perfection, having no less than either of the other kinds, which the Lord referred to when he said: *Love your enemies, do good to those who hate you, so that you may be the children of your Father who is in heaven.*† A little later: *You are to be perfect as your heavenly Father is perfect.*† This is a high and arduous path, but it leads to the heights. It is the more excellent way of charity, one that is not only long-suffering, but also warm and generous.† This is the most precious of all the gifts. Our sun is our charity, warm with benevolence and radiant with practical kindness. We shall prove ourselves truly children of our Father in heaven,† if so great a light glows within us that we are eager to show ourselves heirs of our Father's charity. We too are kings, because we are children of the Most High.

Tragically, it is evident in us how far we are from the glory of those *queens* who were bound to Solomon by holy wedlock, because they learned from Solomon, that with those who hate peace, they must make peace.†

It is of these that Scripture speaks: *holding swords and expert on war.*† The number sixty makes it clear that in both places the same people are being referred to. Every soul that longs for interior peace finds here the very great eagerness, the courageous and tireless warfare that is needed to encompass the couch of Solomon. For the true Solomon these queens bear noble children, destined very soon to be a mighty nation, the inheritors of renowned inheritance. They proceed from poverty into a deeper poverty, from endurance to a deeper

Mt 5:44

Mt 5:48

1 Cor 12:32

Mt 4:8

Ps 120:7

Sg 3:7

Rom 5:4
1 Jn 3:16

endurance,† from love to a deeper love,† but always they approach the couch and bear away from it some fruitful blessing.

Sermon 55.1–7

THE SOLEMN TRIBUNAL IN HEAVEN

Sg 5:10

'MY BELOVED IS REDDENED' WITH CONFUSION.†

AS FAR AS JESUS' feeling of shame is concerned, it is not without a loving movement of compassion that we hear the cry of distress: *Let

Ps 69:6

not those who seek you be ashamed because of me.†* Jesus indeed bears our shame.

Something more humiliating lies hidden within this shame. By the will of the Father, providing for us something better than our utmost hope could have envisaged, all the sins of all of us were bound tightly together, and he bowed his neck beneath them. God the Father has sat down upon the judgment seat on his high and exalted throne. He has summoned Jesus, who stands in readiness before his Father. Around him presses the whole heavenly army, eager to hear what new thing that day is to be achieved or decreed. The Father speaks to the

Ex 3:9

Son: *The cry of the children of Israel,†* O my Son, has thundered in my ears; it has moved my heart with its bitter misery. This is the time well-pleasing to me in which I send you, my only Son, into the world. For the sake of those who will have to descend into the pit, it is necessary this day for you to become like those who go down into the pit.† The iniquity of my people† is so great in my sight that there is no way in which it can be expiated except in your self abasement, in your blood. I am sending you, my one spotless lamb, that in you I may reconcile to myself whomever I have destined for salvation.'

Ps 30:3
Lm 4:22

Then he who sat upon the throne† gave orders that the huge sack containing all the sins of Adam and his children, which had been sealed and hidden† in the royal treasury, should be brought out into their midst. He ordered that planks should be brought and the sword. Then the king said to his Son: 'You see before you the sack of your race, sealed. Unseal it, take out all that is in it, examine it, count it, weigh it. As I live I shall require all these things from you, and you will bear all this iniquity. Pierce your hand and wound your foot;† groan, blush for shame, and do penance for all of this. You are my firstborn, my Only Son, and I have given all things into your hands. Behold, accept these planks for your cross, inasmuch as your father transgressed through a tree, and under a tree your mother was corrupted.† *What I have written, I have written.*'†

Rv 5:1

Rv 20:12

Lk 23:33; Jn 19:37

Sg 8:5; Gen 3:6
Jn 19:22

At this pronouncement of the King, so dread and inflexible against his only Son, the whole court of heaven stood aghast and trembled. But he, standing with deep attention by the judgment seat, immediately prostrated himself on the ground in adoration, bending his knees before his Father, and stretching out his hands: 'Everything concerning me, everything in me, be done according to your will, O my Father. For as you know, Lord, *my meat is to do* Jn 4:34 *your will.*† For this I have come, for this I live. First of all, this sack of sin, which you have placed upon me, although huge and heavy, I take up with glad devotion. I will do penance for these sins in your sight, enduring most patiently, that everything be laid at my door as much as at the door of my father and brothers.

'There is only one favour I crave of your goodness: grant that your wrath may pass over to me, and be diverted from your people. In my blood may all your creatures be reconciled to you in peace, so that my blood be the sign and everlasting cause of the eternal covenant between us.'†

He finished speaking, and all who heard were lost in wonder at the willing obedience of such great majesty. The angels in the judgment hall reeled in their seats, and began to say to one another: '*Truly this is the Son of God,* for his very speech betrays him'.† The Father, recollecting in his heart all the words and feelings and compliances of his Son, was stirred in the depths of his being. 'Because you have done this,† and have not spared your soul, in your deed all the earth will be blessed. Because of you I forgive men all my anger, and I will no longer hold in memory the old complaint. But it is not enough for me that you bring back to life the tribes of Jacob, but rather that in you and your obedience, the whole family of the earth should be blessed.† Even this is not enough in my eyes, because it is

Heb 9:14

Mt 26:73

Gen 22:16

Gen 22:15-18

my good pleasure to restore all things in heaven by your blood and to bring peace to things in heaven and things on earth.† From this day forth, I will give you a name so glorious as to be above every name, which every tongue will confess, before which every knee will bow'.†

Eph 1:20

Phil 2:9-11

After these words there was great exultation, joy and rejoicing in heaven, such as has not been from the beginning of creation, rejoicing first over the ineffable goodness of the Father, then over the wonderful obedience of the Son, thirdly over the reconciliation of human nature, fourthly over the restoration of the celestial city. So the sound of the wings of the cherubim was heard from afar, and the whole city was stirred with the cries of exultation,† with the shouts of praise and thanksgiving.

Ps 132:16

Sermon 10.2-5

A SINCERE ENQUIRY

MY SPIRIT meanwhile burnt within me to seek out and discover, if this was at all possible, what was the reason for this overwhelming and mysterious sentence that the Father passed on his Son. For what was the logic of a law or the quality of a sentence by which, though I am the one guilty of death, another is given up to death on my behalf? With full knowledge and deliberation I have committed murder: how is it that I am released, and the blood that I have shed is demanded of another? I have stolen from my Lord a very large sum of money, ten thousand talents.[†] I am caught with the evidence of my theft and dragged to the court. I am patently guilty, everyone pronounces sentence on me. The cross is prepared, I am immediately hauled to it with my hands bound. I am pale at the nearness of death and no idea but that of death present to my eyes. Behold, suddenly a voice rings out from the throne, ordering me to be brought back and released, while someone else, who has done nothing wrong, is dragged to the gibbet and fastened to the cross. Where is the appearance of justice here, what manner of judgment is this?

Here the order of justice is reversed, with the justice of the just falling upon the wicked and wickedness of the wicked upon the just.[†] All of us have eaten sour grapes, and it is innocent teeth, teeth whiter than milk, that are set on edge.[†]

I am speaking to you, O Lord my God, although I am but dust and ashes.[†] If justice and right are the foundation of your throne,[†] and you absolve the guilty and condemn the innocent, then show me, O Most Holy, with what justice you have done it. I see indeed that in all this I have been treated very mercifully, but as you show mercy, show its justice. I believe that in heaven, in your own domain, you have some new kind of justice, not revealed before that time but to be revealed on the day of salvation with salvation itself.

Mt 18:24

Ezk 18:4, 20

cf. Ezk 18:2

Gen 18:27
Ps 89:14

At this I seem to hear the Lord saying to me in my inner ear: 'O man, my charity, this is my justice. From the beginning I so loved the world as to give my only Son,† first to mortality, then to death, even death on the cross.† Him alone I have found: a man after my own heart,† a just man to all generations, chosen in thousands† whether of men or angels, one both able and willing to fulfil my will and become my salvation in heaven and on earth. Or is it not lawful to me to do what I please?† Who could set a limit to my kindness and love, to lay down a law?'

I give you thanks, Lord God, for this most gracious reply, and for the incomprehensible depths of your mercy. I clearly see that your charity is your justice; since indeed you are all charity, our God, you are all justice. With you to abound with the riches of mercy is absolutely just, because proper, natural and instinctive. It was in the truest sense your justice to hand over your only Son as a ransom for us all, and it was the justice of that only Son of yours to obey his Father's will so lovingly and effectively. At your command he pursued even unto death the iniquity of mankind, so hateful to your holiness; he fixed it with him to the cross, and utterly removed it from your sight by his blood. Therefore, as was just, you have given him the first fruits of universal joy, immediately transforming his flesh with the oil of your anointing, establishing him as the first-born from the dead,† the cause and beginning of all who will share with him in rising from the dead to incorruption. He is thus your Beloved, and the Beloved of your holy Church, and the Beloved of every holy soul, radiant from his immaculate conception (candidus ex conceptione immaculata), *red from his*

Jn 3:16

Phil 2:8

Acts 13:22

Sg 5:10

Mt 20:15

Col 1:18

voluntary passion, glowing and flaming with the love of your justice, namely, the obedience of his will. Passionate in his hatred of sin—that is, in expiating it—, ardently burning in the joy of the resurrection, Gal 1:14 *he is above all his fellows.† May we become partakers with him, we beg you, most Holy Father, beseeching it through the love of your only Son.*

Sermon 10.6-7

THE NIGHT OF JESUS' ABSENCE: THE SHADOW OF HIS POWER

Sg 5:16   HE IS WHOLLY DESIRABLE.†

THE BRIDE CALLS HER BELOVED *Desirable* and *Wholly Desirable*. Now, he is desirable to his bride in the pleasure of his presence, and in the pain of his absence. Especially when he is absent, she longs for him to be present and never stops turning over in her mind how pleasant is his desirable presence and what it has meant to her. Obviously, the more painful his absence the more desirable his presence; yes, and the more lasting his memory the more self-abasement in the recollection of it, the more passionate the expectation of his coming. Hence the words: *My soul longs for you in the night, and* Is 26:9 *my spirit in the depths of my heart.†*

'*In the night*,' she says, '*my soul will desire you*'. By *night* she means the absence of her Beloved, when his glorious countenance does not irradiate her with its usual serenity; and it is for her Spouse to decree whether this night lasts for a shorter or for a longer period. The bride says, 'The more he protracts his delays, the more shall I protract and draw out my desire! Surely this night is given me to keep vigil, to stay awake all its course, especially since it is my duty to watch carefully for the hour of his coming?† He has chosen to keep this hour a secret from me, to help me keep drowsiness at bay'. She says '*my soul*'—that is, all my loving desire—'it was with this that I love you, O Lord my God, and it is this soul that will *yearn for you in the night*.† It will be watchful in its love, impatient in its longings, carefully keeping vigil until you come'.

 Reason will come to assist emotion, suggesting to my soul thoughtful meditation, so that 'from the depths of my heart' the memory of your goodness may come lovingly to help me. 'My soul will desire' the desirable face of Jesus, because when he shows it to me, my love increases and my will becomes fertile with fruits of virtues; because he has only to appear, and the spirit of wisdom and understanding which is within me, small though it is, is more fully illuminated with his light and can think right thoughts about him.

 'It is good to wait quietly for the salvation of God'.† The soul is confident that in a little while she will have the perfect fulfilment of her wishes, and she sings: *I will watch for you at break of day*.† I have complete confidence that

Mt 25:13

Is 26:9

Lam 3:26

Is 26:9

morning will follow the night. You will not dis-
appoint my hope, Lord. You have let me 'watch
for you in the night', and by your gift 'I shall
watch for you' even at break of day.†

We see, then, that when a soul is languishing
with love, the Lord Jesus is desirable to it for two
reasons: when his grace is present, it rouses the
heart with the desire to hold him, and when he is
absent, he stirs up the desire to seek him. How is
he 'wholly desirable'?† The intention of the bride
is to signify that even his very shadow will be 'desirable'. She said, 'I have sat down under his
shadow'.† Small wonder if, sick with desire, she
should believe that the shadow of him she desires,
the shadow of the 'tree of life' should bring her
healing. Even the shadow of Peter was a symbol
of the wonderful power of healing and refreshing
in every way which made him come to help the
sick with no less power than compassion.† While
that shadow brought health to sick bodies, it was
proclaiming with great clarity the strong light
that illuminated Peter and so made him cast a
shadow. In its very self, it was proclaiming to
those whose strength was returning the strength
of the light, as if the shadow itself was telling
those who fled to it for refuge, 'Why do you fix
your eyes on me or on Peter? It is not we who do
these things, it is the Light, which has shone
upon Peter, and so produced me, Peter's shadow'.

If there is such great power in Peter's shadow,
what ought the Bride to expect from the shadow
of her Spouse? That shadow is the protection, the
cool, the concealment, with which he graciously
over-shadows the soul that loves him, hiding her
within the secret of his face.† There it is his cus-

Ps 118:117

Sg 5:16

Sg 2:3

Acts 5:14-15

Ps 31:22

tom to shield her, at one time from the glare of fleshly temptation, and at another, from the far more dangerous heat of spiritual sin. It is a gracious shadow, full of saving power, and sometimes, when grace itself seems lost, it comes to our help in the sickness of various temptations, providing refreshment. It is a specially gracious shadow in that it brings back the desirable presence of the Spouse for the moment, symbolising protection. For a shadow represents what it is a shadow of, by imitating its outline.

So then, there is nothing that is not desirable in him who is 'wholly desirable'. His absence brings healing, his lingering brings salvation, his keeping us waiting brings us closer to virtue. Under this desirable shadow, the shadow of him she desires, the Bride finds rest and comfort. She sits there under his shadow, patiently waiting until some ripe fruit from the 'tree of life' should fall into her lap as she waits. It is impossible that the Lord's Bride should be disappointed, because *the Lord hears the sighs of the poor*.† It has all turned out as she hoped, her destiny has fulfilled all her expectations, and so she says, *And his fruit is sweet to my throat*.† In this case, then, the Lord Jesus is seen as 'wholly desirable', desirable when present, desirable even when absent. His light is desirable, and his shadow too; in short, everything in him is desirable, everything that has the taste and the fragrance of Jesus, Only-Son of the Father, Spouse of the Church who together with the Father and Holy Spirit lives and reigns, God for ever and ever. Amen.

Ps 10:19

Sg 2:3

Sermon 38.6–7

THE LORD'S MATERNAL LOVE

WE CANNOT BUT KNOW the heart of our God in all its tender mercy. It is something we must never forget. It is how the *Daystar from on high*,[†] Jesus, came to us and comes to us still. How great the heart, how wide, how incomprehensible! In the nature of things what can be imagined as more loving than the heart of a mother or the heart of a father? Such are the riches of God's heart that he has bound us to himself by a double cord of love: both as a father, shaping us into his own image and likeness;[†] and as a mother carrying us within the womb and bringing us to birth, even at the cost of suffering.

The Lord, my God, holds within himself the love of both parents and he brought me forth in holiness and immortality. Listen to him, as a mother yearning over her children: *Can a mother forget her child, and not take pity on the child of her womb? And even if she should forget, yet I shall not forget you.*[†] And again: *As a mother cherishes her children, so shall I cherish you.*[†] And once again: *I was like a nurse to Ephraim, and they did not know that it was I who looked after them.*[†]

But now let us come to the very words of Incarnate Wisdom, words sweeter even than honey. His passion was close at hand and he was on the point of going down into that vast ocean of suffering. Yet he comforted his little ones with words so tender, he gave them such gentle teaching about love, he encouraged them with

Lk 1:78

Gen 1:26

Is 49:15

Is 66:13

Hos 11:3

such gracious promises of soon sending the Holy Spirit, that he might well be considered as having opened the floodgates of his heart. When he had finished speaking, he turned to pray to his Father for them with greater privacy and earnestness.† At that time he was completely overcome with maternal love, enduring in his breast indescribable pangs of an utterly overwhelming affection at having to abandon them like orphans and be turned away from those for whose sake he did not hesitate to die. So he offered his heart to his Father and being in agony, as the evangelist says, his sweat became as drops of blood, trickling down upon the earth.† Perhaps someone thinks it was dread of his approaching passion that aroused anguish in the heart of Jesus and wrung a bloody sweat from his body. But both were caused, not by fear, but by loving mercy.

Lk 22:41

Lk 22:43-44

As the hour of his passion drew near, the gospels tell us that Jesus began to be weary, distressed and troubled,† but that was no more than the beginning. Suffering of that kind he underwent of his own free will, he controlled it by his own power, and he threw it off when he pleased. It was through love he accepted it, not through necessity, through tender compassion, not slavish fate. If you would understand the deeper reasons for this agony and sweat, there is one who lay on the breast of Jesus, John, and entered into a knowledge of this mystery: ask him.† He had the privilege both to witness and relate all that Jesus said in that lengthy prayer which breathed out solely love and tender mercy.† All who would understand that most sacred mercy

Mt 14:33

Jn 13:23

Jn 14 seq

will be able to see in those words what a struggle there was in the depths of the tender heart of Jesus, what tortures of compassion, what a battle of merciful tenderness, what agonies of love. The heart of Jesus is his love, but his 'belly' is his mercy. Now he could control his heart no longer. His heart became 'within his belly like melting wax',[†] because love turned all to gentleness from the intimate depths of tender mercy.

Ps 21:14

O loving Jesus! how merciful, how concerned, how rich in compassion was the desire of that heart as it prayed that the Father might keep them in his name, sanctify them in truth, unite them in love, join them to their head and make them happy in the vision of that glory which the Father had given him.[†]

Jn 17:11

So we too, who now appear on the scene after so many centuries, we too are held within the womb of infinite tenderness, and indeed, through his mercy, were held within it even then. Within his breast, Jesus held out to his Father not only every child of Israel, but all those also who through their word would come to believe in him.[†] If Paul's love was so great that it forced him to cry out,[†] how much more is the breast of Christ, hardly able to contain a heart so great; it stretches out into an immense infinity from the overflowing richness of tender mercy. For if the streams of living water pour with such abundance from the belly of Paul, or of any other of those who love him,[†] how much more must the belly of Christ be an abyss of tender mercy, wholly deep and unfathomable!

Jn 17:20
2 Cor 11:29
Jn 7:38

Sermon 28.2–4

THE SILENCE OF JESUS

MY LORD JESUS was silent before the scribes and Pharisees when they accused him, silent before his judges when they questioned him, silent before those who punished him with torture and crucifixion. Even today he is silent before the wicked and shameless people who challenge him every day and every hour. If this is so, then plainly that silence of his is full of grace and truth.†

The true tree of life is the fruitful silence of Jesus. It drew its patience from the true fount of wisdom, unknown to the wise of this world, and it said to the Father, *For you, O Lord, are my patience.*† And again: *Lord God, you are my helper, and so I am not put to shame, so I have set my face like a flint.*† The patience of Jesus is a flint, flint-hard, and yet anointed with the oil of gladness, and so very gentle.

Which of you, dearest brothers, will give his heart to being a loving imitator of this sacred silence? Who will enter that school of hidden philosophy, and sit at Jesus' feet? Who will fix his whole attention on Jesus' mouth and catch the drops of myrrh distilling from it to water the earth?† At the sight of Jesus keeping his peace in such tranquillity, who among you is willing to put his finger to his own mouth, to rank himself with those kings whose admiration at his virtue and with generous desire to imitate it, induced them to close their own mouths because of him?†

That silence of his is a living and effectual word,† and it is those *who have ears to hear*† who

Jn 1:14

Ps 71:5

Is 50:7

Ps 72:6

Is 52:15

Heb 4:12
Mt 11:15

hear it . . . . *The mouth of the just man*, says
Prv 10:31 Solomon, *has brought forth wisdom.*[†] Would you
like to know what the mouth of this just man
brought forth by keeping silent, and what the fruit
was of that bringing forth? The hands which men
had stretched out on the Cross, he stretched out to
his Father, and from the infinite riches of his patience he cried out this word of love: *Father*, he
said, *forgive them for they know not what they do.*[†]

Lk 23:34

Sermon 22.

THE WISDOM OF JESUS

IN THE PREVIOUS SERMON there was
shown the great power in the silence of Jesus.
What then will it be when he opens his mouth
and the grace of his lips no longer holds itself in
restraint? We have our witness from the mouth
of Truth himself: *The good man out of his good
treasure brings forth good, and from the abundance
of the heart the mouth speaks.*[†]

Therefore that *good man*, the only one truly
Mt 12:34-35 good among the sons of men, the only one truly
rich with boundless treasure, speaks as befits the
royal grandeur of his heart and resources. He
opens his mouth to words of grace, virtue and
wisdom, words beyond the reach of any utterance of man or even angel.[†] Only he whom God
1 Cor 13:1 sent and who is the true Son of the true God,

can speak the words of God, as John tells us in his gospel.† No words but those of God can be addressed to what is not, and give it being, to what is created, and make it continue in being, to what is living, and make it increase and multiply.† God is the only one who at his pleasure calls into life, and then sends to death, saying to this man, 'Come', and he comes, and to another, or rather the same man, 'Go', and he goes.†

Truly that man is the all powerful Son of the all powerful God who utters words not dissimilar to those of God, saying to the dead man, *Rise*, and he comes;† to the blind, *See*, and immediately he sees;† to the deaf ear, *Open up*, and at once it is opened;† to the man with a withered arm, *Stretch out your arm*, and he stretches it;† to the leper, *Be clean*, and straight away he is clean;† to the cripple, *Take up your bed*, and he takes up his bed.† He orders the sea to be still, and it is still, the winds to be quiet, and there comes a great silence, an immense peace.† When he curses the fig, it dries up.† When he rebukes the demons, they fall silent. When he commands, they come out, when he gives permission, they rush into a herd of swine.†

As the centurion had the faith to realize, this man is in all truth the Lord of armies.† Everything is a soldier in his ranks, and obeys him instantly. When the Lord draws near, there is no slightest trace of reluctance, but an eager haste to fulfil his least command. In his armies are health and sickness, life and death, holy angels and evil devils, and he says to one, 'Go,' and he goes, and to another, 'Come,' and he comes.†

Sermon 23.1–2

Jn 3:34

Gen 1:22

Mt 8:9

Jn 11:43

Lk 18:42

Mt 7:43

Mk 3:5

Mt 8:3

Mt 9:6

Mt 8:26

Mt 21:19

Mk 5:13

Mt 8:9

Mt 8:9

JESUS ON THE CROSS

THE BRIDE PRAISES CHRIST'S PATIENCE
AND LONG-SUFFERING

Sg 5:15   HIS LEGS ARE ALABASTER COLUMNS.[†]

HAD THE BRIDE paid heed to human modesty she would at this point have put her finger to her lips and offered greater praise by silence than public proclamation.

Yet I hear the Spirit of the Spouse, Jesus, making answer for his bride and within her. Let the bride then take courage in the Holy Spirit, let her take courage and give an answer: If I seem foolish, it is the love of Christ that drives

2 Cor 5:14   me forward.[†] Where there is the Spirit of my
2 Cor 3:17   beloved, there is freedom.[†] It was he who put the words of this holy song upon my lips, words that can be entrusted only to the chaste ears of those who also know Jesus by experience. These are sacred and burning phrases, which the fire of divine love has refined from all impurity, which only the zeal of lovers has real right to hear and savor.

They are wholly removed from flesh and blood, wholly removed from all that is uncircumcised and unclean. Let beasts keep far away, lest any of them should come too close, and touch this burning of love like an animal, i.e. with sensual understanding and feelings. For those who love the name of Jesus know only peace, there is no scandal for them in these

words, but only joy and an enkindling of holy
love. Come then, under the guidance of the
Holy Spirit, let us go nearer to the marriage
chamber of the Spouse and the bride. From
there the meaning of these words may become
audible to us.

With regard to 'the legs of the Spouse' I
cannot recall any place in Scripture where I have
heard anything that could be set under this
heading. The only exception is when they come
to Jesus on the cross to break his legs. When
they say he was already dead, *they did not break
his legs,*† because the law about the ceremonial   Jn 19:30
observance of the Passover bound them strictly
that not a bone of the lamb was to be broken.†   Jn 19:36
But the Gospel goes on to say that instead of
breaking his bones, an opening was made in
Jesus' side, and immediately blood and water
flowed out.† So the bride has every right to take   Jn 19:34
into her song of praise these legs of her Spouse,
which even the wickedness of his crucifiers
feared to harm and which the sacred witness of
Moses the lawgiver preserved from harm.

Perhaps even then Moses saw beforehand
the glory of the Father's Only Son. Under the
influence of the same Spirit through whom he
told how heaven and earth and all things visible
and invisible were created,† he reverently   Gen 1:1f
wrapped round the invincible patience of the
Son the holy veil of these words: *Not a bone of
his is to be broken.*†   Ex 12:46

The glorious fidelity of the martyrs, which
they borrowed from the divine strength of this
'bone', is celebrated joyously in the psalm: *The
Lord keeps all their bones, not one of them shall be*

Ps 34:20

Ps 42:12

Ps 138:14

Mt 7:24

broken.† On the other hand, the weak declare with feeble groans, *While my bones are broken, my enemies taunt me.*† Yet to the Only Son of God belong the words quietly whispered in his Father's ear, *My body held no secret from you when I was being fashioned in secret.*†

I shall now hold my peace, but I am sure that anyone who listens will observe how beautifully and becomingly and without wounding her modesty, the bride of Jesus has succeeded in exalting with praise the legs of her Beloved. But I think it is now also clear why she has spoken of them as 'columns'. For the legs of Jesus are his patience and long-suffering, resting on everlasting and changeless strength. They are 'alabaster' because they are strong, stable, beautiful, and of great worth. They are the columns on which the whole round world and all that is in it is supported. Not only the world, but without doubt heaven too leans upon these same columns, for it trembles and quakes at the good pleasure of Jesus. Any house not founded on these columns must necessarily fall.†

Sermon 30.1–4

THE COLUMN OF DIVINE PATIENCE THAT JESUS STOOD ON WHEN ON THE CROSS

THE COLUMN of the divine patience also stands on a golden socket. Set in this socket it bore with great endurance the blindness of all nations, right up to the last days. Now in the fullness of time, when his plan was ready, God has turned the blindness of Israel into the light of the nations. So the ruin of both Israel and the light of the nations may become the salvation of them both. For the first cause that lies behind all other causes, and their supreme fulfilment, is love.

It follows that the Bride of Christ has copious matter for joy and praise in this twofold patience and love of her Spouse. By Bride I mean her, who has been raised up from the nations to the dignity of being married to the Only-begotten of the Father *in genuine faith and sincere charity.*† 2 Cor 6:6 So much so that her swelling heart breaks forth into a cry of praise: Truly the legs of my beloved are the strong bones of his patience and long endurance, limbs concealed by the Father of Lights, limbs which the Father has set up to be the columns of heaven and earth. Upon these changeless celestial supports, he has erected the whole fabric of all that he has made.

Now the Spirit of charity, which my beloved bestowed on me, makes me feel compassion for the daughter of Zion. I pity her, . . . but I rejoice with her to the full now that we see the day coming when the bill of divorce will be torn up. A new bond will be made *which will stand firm for ever.*† When that day Ex 16:60

comes, I too shall go to meet her with exulting heart. I shall be there as a go-between to bring about a holy kiss, and in everything connected with her marriage bond I shall offer my help and mediation and testimony. It will be my delight to be present at that marriage, where I trust that I too shall be inebriated to the last degree of joy. For at that marriage will be present my Lord Jesus, and for the nuptial day his cellars will be filled with wine.† Meanwhile I am full of joy on my own account also, body and soul, because in divorcing his first bride, the Lord my God remembered me.

Jn 2:11

How can this new title be mine, and such great grace and mercy come down suddenly from heaven into my bosom, beyond all expectation? In addition, as a crowning grace, the former wife's divorce has meant that I, all unworthy and of lowly birth, have been raised to the dignity of her title and position.

So she has been left widowed, and I have entered without warning into her inheritance and marriage bed, to reap what I have not sown, and to gather what she, not I, has scattered.† What can I do to make some response, not wholly disproportionate to his greatness, in face of this stupendous honour? For my Lord has given up his own home, in order to be united with me, a woman of unclean race. What could be imagined more impressive, more noble, more passionate than this love, where solely for love of me, every other love is abandoned and outlawed? Why do not I concentrate on him all the affections of my heart, no matter what they are, no matter how great they are? He gave up everything that was his for me.

Mt 25:26

Not only has my Spouse freely handed over to my authority all the graces of his previous bride, but all that she did wrong has become for me a means of salvation. It was she who shed the blood of my Lord, and it is I who bathe in it and am cleansed. She provided the cross, in which I have been given the privilege of finding my glory.† It was she who brought about the cruel death through which I now live, and yet *it is not I who live.*† It was she who opened the side of my Lord, when he was dead,† but it is I who have entered therein. She has made for me a way of life into that inner, secret hiding place of the heart of Jesus.

There, from the side of my sleeping Lord, I have been fashioned,† for it was only to bring me into being that he chose to fall asleep. For it was not his former bride who cast him into slumber. It was rather my Lord's own Father who closed his Son's eyelids in sleep,† and of his own free will he slept and took his rest.† So in that sleep it was his good pleasure that I should come forth, bone of his bone, and flesh of his flesh.† He breathed his own Spirit into me, so that there should remain within me nothing that came only from myself.

In the end, fashioned wholly out of him and by him, I was brought up to him by the Father of mercies, so that he who had bestowed all these other gifts upon me, might not fail to add the glory of his name. Therefore he gave me a new name, a title which his own mouth pronounced.† As for me, I have not yet been granted the grace of understanding the dignity of this title. No one knows that until he has

Gal 6:14

Gal 2:20

Jn 19:34

Gen 2:21

Ps 132:4

Gen 2:23

Gen 2:23;
Eph 5:30

Is 61:2

Rv 2:17

received it.† However, by his grace I shall grasp the full significance of this name when the day of my marriage arrives, and the Bridegroom re-

Is 62:5

joices over the Bride,† and the Bride likewise enters into the eternal enjoyment of her Spouse, for this is his good pleasure.

May we too be made partakers of this nuptial joy by the Spouse of the Church, our Lord Jesus Christ, who reigns with the Father and the Holy Spirit for ever and ever.

Sermon 30.6–7

AT THE FOOT OF THE CROSS

LET US RETURN QUICKLY to the cross of Jesus with the blessed mother of the Lord and her companions, eager to measure the love of the crucified, as far as is right in view of our littleness. To stand there with greater strength and courage, let us, as the prophet says, *stand*

Is 50:8

there together.† Let us draw one another by our mutual love to the contemplation of this immense love. Let us stand together, and with hearts at one, let us marvel reverently at our prize and cleave to it wholly. Let our mouths be open wide to catch the liquid flowing gently from those wounds, more precious than fragrant balm, sweeter than honey. Let us swallow it with thirsting throat so that it may pour down into our hearts and there search out every one of our ills, and in the searching, cure them.

May that death live for us, may it be alive and breathe eternal life into our minds. His death lives eternally with his Father, it lives in the heavens, it lives in its purpose, it lives in its result. *O death, I shall be your death*† were the words of him who died on the cross for me. But this curse was for that death which devoured all our race.

Hos 13:14

But you, O death, which my Lord tasted through free choice, not by force of circumstances, and drained through love and not necessity, you are blessed for all eternity. You commanded the great whale to spew forth,† or rather, you yourself gulped down our death to annihilate it utterly, and wonderfully lodge us within yourself. The insatiable maw of that beast was ripped apart by your hook, which it carelessly took and arrogantly swallowed,† and now all the prey, greedily crammed into it for so many years past, is spilled forth. So you are alive from now into eternity, you are alive, you are triumphant, you are king.† You live in the putting to death of sin, in the destruction of faults, you live in the tears of the contrite, the comfort of the sorrowful, the remitting of punishment. You live in the virtue of faith, in the devotion of the sacraments, above all in the minds and prayers of those who love you. You live in the fidelity of the martyrs, you live in the life of the holy, and lastly and most blessedly, you live in their death.

Jon 2:11

Job 40:24

Jn 19:19

O death of my Lord, who could assess your priceless worth, by which you make the death of your saints also something precious?[†] You have made it possible for us not to flee from death, as from the sight of a snake,[†] but instead to flee towards it, running eagerly as to a mother's womb from which we shall soon be born anew as sons of life. Through your gracious mercy, we pass through death out of death into life, home to the fatherland. Let me say it again, you have made it possible for the death of the holy to be called rather an escape from death than a death, as the psalm says: *And to the Lord, to the Lord belongs the escape from death.*[†] For now that you have blessed it, the death of the saints is a coming safe to land from the vast sea of this long-lasting death, a restful anchorage, a harbour of peace, an entrance into joy.

O victorious death, what is there still unconquered? Everywhere is bright with your triumphs, everywhere the banner of your victory flies in splendor.

And then, you took flight to the heavens, where you ceaselessly present yourself to the Father of mercies on behalf of the sin of the world, and you make reparation for it.[†] You alone can repay the debt of Adam and his sons to that eternal creditor. Therefore you are imperial on earth, irresistible in the underworld, glorious in the heavens.

Sermon 26.8-9

Ps 115:15

Num 21:6-7

Ps 68:20

Heb 7:15

IV

OUR LADY, MOTHER OF JESUS

AN OVERVIEW:
MARY, OUR MOTHER

M ARY'S SPECIAL TITLE is 'Mother of Jesus'. The overwhelming contrast between Mary and Eve stems from the fact that Eve, who was the original *mother of all the living*,[1] forfeited her title at the 'fall' because her action brought the consequence of death to all her children. The title and the fact was transferred to Our Lady by God because she was to become the 'mother of Jesus' and consequently the mother of all those who are *in Christ Jesus*,[2] that is to say, the mother of all the living. The Son of God, when he was still

> in his most holy and hidden resting place, the bosom of the Father, looked on the lowliness of his handmaid whom they rightly call blessed. . . . He saw the one who, by a unique and irrevocable privilege which she has from the Holy Spirit, was to find grace most richly in his eyes not only for herself but also for all generations yet to come.[3]

Mary thus became the 'Mother of God'. This title was given to her in the eternity of God's predestination and is essential for our understanding of Mary's role. John of Forde draws a fascinating picture, comparing the divine designer to a joiner working with wood.

[1] Gen 3:20
[2] Rom 8:1
[3] Sermon 73.5-15

God's choice of this Virgin to be his mother fitted her for the unique work she was to perform. The oxymoron-like structure used by John, 'virginal fruitfulness and fruitful virginity', should make it clear to us that we are within a divine mystery that transcends human experience.

John loves to speak of Mary's humility. She was always aware of her utter dependence on God. Like a canopy over the ark, covering her and protecting her from evil, this humility also protected her from the overwhelming sun of the Divinity. John calls this 'the power of the virgin, high above all others, because the greatness of her humility more than anything else makes her sublime. It draws the Most High down from the heights to the depths of her being.'[4] At the annunciation an unprecedented cataclysm took place in the universe, but because it was totally spiritual, it was unobserved and unnoticed, perceived only by faith.

No doubt Jesus was fashioned and developed in the womb just like any other normal child. But even at that stage a potential for extraordinary wisdom was coming into being. Wisdom is to the spirit as honey in the mouth:

We may ask ourselves: Who can speak worthily of this conception or the solemn festival of his birth? For two thousand years now this feast has been celebrated everywhere throughout the world. *A child is born to us, a son is given to us.*[5]

> How pure and radiant was that flesh, conceived by the
> Holy Spirit, brought forth by the Virgin. The glory of
> his holiness was inherited from his mother as well as
> from the Holy Spirit, and so the wisest of virgins
> poured straight into her son, as his natural inheritance,
> the leaven of innocence and sanctity, by the wisdom
> and power of the Holy Spirit.[6]

---

[4] Sermon 4.5
[5] Is 9:6
[6] Sermon 8.4

John is embarrassed by his own boldness here and carefully gives his sources, though there is nothing that would disturb us today. We would take it for granted that Jesus inherited much of his own character and personality traits from his mother. We can however join John in his cry of admiration as he echoes the praise of the angels who also see the infant Jesus in the manger.

It was Mary's greatest sorrow and pain as well as her greatest privilege to stand at the foot of the cross. It was her privilege because it allowed her to enter fully into the redemption of the world. Did she know that the dire suffering she experienced was going to effect redemption? Pure faith in all its stark simplicity, faith in the unfathomable mystery of God, rooted her there. Her role was to bear the will of the Father in whatever way it showed itself, even this. Yet John goes further by placing us all in the shadow of the cross with Mary our mother, drawn by our own willingness to enter the mystery.

Here the mystery of suffering is revealed at its most poignant moment. Not only the suffering of the one Man on the cross and a mother watching her Son die in agony, but also the whole suffering of humankind taken up in a moment of sacrifice in which the totality of human suffering is subsumed. That was our mother Mary's role. To stand by the cross is to enter into the mystery of redemption. If we are willing to do this we will win a place for ourselves near the cross of Jesus, a very close place, one next to the Lord's mother who was both mother and bride to the only Son of God. Let us lay hold of the Lord who has laid hold of us; let us hasten back to the cross with the blessed mother of the Lord and her companions, eager to measure the love of the Crucified, as far as it is possible in view of our littleness.[7]

For John this is the most intense school of love and it is found in the heart of Mary. We have as our exemplar the Blessed Virgin herself, into whom the whole stream of love flowed freely, and who holds the teacher's chair par excellence in the school of

[7] Sermon 26.5-8

those who love Jesus. When she bore in her arms the Word of
the Father made flesh through her motherhood, John tells us,
she rejoiced with a joy that was more than human, more than the
angels' joy, something utterly divine.[8]

Then in Sermon Seventy, which is devoted entirely to Mary,
he has this wonderful paean of praise:

> Amidst all the ranks of the saints, the first place for
> humility, purity and tender love is held by the Blessed
> Virgin, Mother of Jesus, and in the same way she
> shines out gloriously above all who love God for the
> greatness of her love. That is why the title of unique
> glory, which the Spirit of Love in his gracious good-
> ness, makes common to all souls that love Jesus, has
> been bestowed by him with special reason on the one
> that loves him very much more, the title 'Bride of
> God', so that she is called God's Bride and is his
> Bride.[9]

[8] Sermon 24.4
[9] Sermon 70.1

PRAISE OF MARY, THE BLESSED VIRGIN, AND HER VIRGINITY

I WENT DOWN TO THE ORCHARD OF ALMONDS,
TO LOOK AT THE FRUITS OF THE VALLEY . . .†   Sg 6:10

PRAISE must be deliberately directed to Christ as its object, although he, who alone deserves to be praised, generously shares with his Bride, the church, what is said in his honor. He puts the praises of the Church in the mouths of those who praise him, and he who stirs them on to praise, is himself the rewarder and the reward.

The Spouse says: 'You do well to admire and honor your mother, but first and foremost you must look to the reason for it all. It was my coming down from heaven that poured out all this light, dawnlight and moonlight and sunlight. It was my human weakness that brought about all this endurance, that gave so terrible an appearance to an army of martyrs. I came forth like a bud from the shoot of Jesse's stump,† so   Is 11:1
that I might pass on to my native stock the lovely and sinless dawning of my birth'.

There is something very beautiful and fitting in Christ's describing the stainless purity of his mother, the Blessed Virgin, as an *orchard of almonds*, because it was from her that all this

129

precious family of herbs arose. From this one shoot thousands of shoots have grown, and this one virgin is the Mother of many, many virgins. She has brought them into the world through her chastity. Yes, it was fitting that the angel should bring to this virgin the good news that she had *found grace with God.*† She found what lay hid, concealed from mortal eyes; the finding of it was reserved for her alone. She found the beauty of this grace, its fruit, its fertility, its glory. There was beauty in the dignity of its holiness, fruit in its restoration of our nature, fertility in giving rise to so many virgins, glory in its being Mother to the Word.

But this going down did not happen first when *the Word was made flesh*† so as to dwell among us. He went down also at the time when, to sanctify the Virgin in the womb and consecrate her dawning and establish her formally in the state of holy virginity, he sanctified her, soul and body.

So the Blessed Virgin is the only virgin who is also a mother. Yes, it is she who is *the orchard of almonds*. She gives birth to virgins, she who is the model, the guardian and the glory of the chaste. She gives them birth, since she is the first and pre-eminent woman to pursue this state of life, and she has brought into the world the whole family of those who pursue this same grace. She is their model because, as if she were *a shoot from the stump of Jesse,*† who is Jesus, she strengthens them to the full strength of what they have undertaken to live, and with her example, she forms them to the right shape. She is their guardian, enclosing them round like *a gar-*

Lk 1:30

Jn 1:14

Is 11:1

den enclosed.† She defends them from the as- Sg 4:12
saults of the foe and overshadows them to protect them from the violent heat of their own
passions, just as the Holy Spirit overshadowed
her. She is their glory because, in the regenera-
tion of the saints, she will be the pride of those
whom for God she brought to birth, formed
and preserved in this grace of virginity.

Just as the maidens speak of Mary's charity
as the sun and her courage and steadfastness as
an army, so the Spouse graciously takes up these
praises, pouring them forth from the spring of
his most disinterested love, as much for their
profit as for the sake of his Bride.

He lays down the form of praise, he who is
himself the source of all their good qualities,
and the reason why, amid all these admiring ex-
clamations of theirs, they may well seem, in the
light of their very great excess of admiration, to
have rather under-expressed it. He lays down
the manner, too, as he clearly reduces their
praises to a more modest measure. The Spouse
speaks with the greater sobriety we would expect from him. Of course, there is more wisdom
in an admiration that takes its rise from God.
His words are: *I went down to the orchard of almonds.*† That is: My Bride, the Church, comes 6:10
forth rising like the dawn, because I have anticipated her, by my free gift, going down to my
Mother, Mary. Since I was about to take flesh
from her, I consecrated her to myself. I prepared
her for the universal church, to become the salvation of her people, the mediatrix with God,
the model of holiness, the patroness of virtue.

Sermon 59.1-5

In Praise of Mary,
the Mother of Jesus

AMID THE RANKS of the saints, the first place for humility, purity, and tender love is held by the Blessed Virgin, the mother of Jesus, and in the same way she shines out gloriously, above all God's lovers, for the greatness of her love. This is why that title of unique glory which the Spirit of charity, in his gracious goodness, makes common to all souls that love Jesus, has been bestowed by him with special reason on the one who loves him very much more, the title of Bride of God, and she is called God's bride and is uniquely his bride.[†] It is she who is truly *the mother of fair love*,[†] as the Church sings of her. She is the teacher of knowledge[†] of it, the craftsman who trains us in it,[†] its lawgiver, and go-between who brings about love's covenant with us.

Obviously, *happy is the person who watches daily at her gates and waits at her doorposts.*[†] After long waiting, such persons will be finally admitted to the heart of her holy marriage chamber, where they may be privileged to understand something of the perfume of the love of Christ, overflowing there in its scented abundance.

Everything in this marriage song is directed principally to Mary, the principal bride of Jesus. This is true whatever form the words take, whether from the lips of the Spouse to the Bride, or of the Bride to the Spouse. In her own self, Mary, the Bride, is the highest and most distinguished model of love, and from her over-

Sg 4:8
Sir 24:24
Ws 8:4
Ws 8:6

Prv 8:24

flowing fullness, every person receives as much
as their capacity allows.† Since she is *full of* Eph 4:7
grace,† it perpetually abounds in her, a source of Lk 1:28
marvelous pleasure as well as total richness to
every spirit, angelic and human. Believe me—or
rather believe the Holy Spirit—to gain the love
of Jesus, there is no shorter way than to contemplate the beauty of this unique, incomparable
and immense love that Mary has.

Mary's womb is a marriage chamber of
great tenderness, rich in the most noble seed,
and it contains a great and holy secret. It has
knowledge of great mystery and it bears very
great dignity. But clearly that womb was blessed
even before it carried the Lord. Day and night,
with a most pure desire and the longing of a
holy and consecrated love, it prepared itself to
bear its holy burden. In the silence of her heart,
Mary said to herself, *Let him kiss me with the kiss*
of his mouth.† There has never been another Sg 1:1
soul, or rather, there has never been one of the
blessed spirits, not even among that most blissful of the nine choirs that takes its name from
the fire of love and refreshes by the heat of its
immense love by the continual contemplation of
eternity and ceaseless praise of the Holy Trinity:
no, not even among the cherubim has any one
made progress like hers in desiring and receiving this kiss.

So then, to make her ready for such great
grace, she was fashioned from her mother's
womb† by him who *establishes the heavens*,† and Ps 138:13
every single moment, during the successive Job 28:27
stages by which God established her, the fullness of grace was built up. One day she would

Lk 1:28

become God's Mother, and then the angel would call her *full of grace*.† So her womb is blessed in the very manner of its establishment in blessedness, yet it is far more blessed when it finally, in a divine and indescribable way, received its most blessed burden. Blessed, indeed most blessed, is that womb when it bore him, when it formed him, when it was in labor with him, when it brought him to birth.

When Jesus left his mother's womb, in which he had been cherished and nourished, he left behind him a blessing. He sanctified her womb when he entered it, he filled it when he dwelt within it, and when he bade it farewell, he consecrated it and strengthened it with his full blessing. Jesus came forth from his mother so as to bless her virginal eyes also, by showing her his face. He came forth to sanctify her mouth by the beautiful kiss of his own mouth,† to make blessed her breasts by pressing his lips to them, to consecrate her hands, her lap, her knees, every part of her by the infinite sweetness of his sacred body as she held him to her.

Sg 1:1

Sermon 70.1–5

THE HUMILITY OF MARY, THE LORD'S MOTHER

YOUR NECK IS AN IVORY TOWER.[†]   Sg 7:4

THIS PHRASE has a very special relevance to the Lord's Mother. There may have been many who have been privileged to enjoy, here on earth, the embraces of Jesus, our Solomon;[†] but   Sir 47:12-17
there is one who is the chosen of her mother, of the woman who bore her.[†] Mary stands at the right   Sg 6:8
hand of the King of glory,[†] and sits down beside   1 K 22:19
him too, cleaving to him without intermediary. She is the holiest of virgins, the most fruitful of mothers, the happiest of women. Throughout this whole song, all the praise has her in view, first and foremost, because of the unique privilege which she has from the Holy Spirit, and this is specially so when it is the Bride who is being addressed or referred to. In this verse it is particularly clear that the praise of the Lord's mother has been thrust into our hands, so that it would be both imprudent and impermissible for us to be secretly anxious to turn aside from it. What could be more obvious than that the outstanding humility of the Lord's mother is being praised, when the bride's neck is compared to an ivory tower? This means that admiration of her most noble virginity is added to the wonder of her most exceptional humility. Who could not immediately see the reference to the glory of this woman, most radiantly white in virtues?

While nature stood in awe, this virgin Mother brought forth God and man, and her

Sg 7:3

breasts are the devotion and tenderness of this submissive mother.† It seems to me that a woman's two breasts indicate here two kinds of tenderness, so that she ministered to the Lord Jesus as to her own child, the virgin's son, the fruit of her womb, and also provided for the same Jesus as for the Lord of the Angels, the Son of the most High, acting now as the Lord's hand-

Lk 2:38

maid.† If the tenderness of the virgin Mother was twofold in this way, there were also two ways in which she regarded the twofold nature of the Word made flesh from her: in that personal and hypostatic union, she both lovingly adored and reverently embraced him. This wis-

Sg 7:3

est of virgins was given the name of *gazelle*.† Above all other saints, she had the privilege of contemplating most keenly the glory of the only Son of the Father, and she outran them all in the incomparable earnestness of her love. So she is the symbol of serenity because of the deep gaze of her contemplation, yet a symbol of allegiance because of her swiftly moving love.

It is a wonderful thing that, with God, a soul enriched with so many virtues so as to surpass all the saints, should in the end transcend her own self by her over-surpassing humility. So before all else, this beautiful description refers to the blessed Mother of the Lord, but while respecting her special dignity, it will also be in order to extend this praise to the Lord's Bride, the Church, under the same heading.

Sermon 73.1–2

The Compassion and Mercy of the Mother of God

YOUR EYES ARE LIKE POOLS IN HESHBON.[†]   Sg 7:4

IF I WERE TO TREAT of this wedding song and deprive the Lord's Mother of her praise—especially since that praise shines out more or less clearly from the mirror which we are looking at now—I am afraid that my own mouth would condemn me. If the whole song is about her in a particular way, it would be a sacrilege not to speak of her. However, it ill-becomes the tongue of a sinner to utter what is unutterable to the mouth of angels and give expression to knowledge which belongs to the saints; still, may she approve the stammering efforts of a mouth that sings her praise. We may think of the most tender Mother of Jesus in the same way as we think about her Son. He made perfect praise for himself *from the mouths of infants and suckling babes,*[†] so that their attempts became in his mind *perfect praise.*[†]

Mt 21:6
Ps 8:3

This verse, in which the bride's eyes are commended by her Spouse, is concerned with the eyes of God's Mother, her own eyes of mercy. In a previous verse her eyes were said to be *eyes of doves,*[†] and there the Spouse's intention was to praise the dove-like glance of her eyes and was meant to honor the sharpness of her spiritual penetration, which keeps her ever gazing with pure and loving insight into the face of her Spouse and the glory of her Son. But here, in comparison to the pools of Heshbon, what is

Sg 1:14

praised is the abundance of her tenderness and
the gentleness of her regard when she looks at
us. These most blessed and tranquil eyes preserve the happiness of their contemplation
utterly without intrusive effort. This contemplation is free of anything that would disturb it;
it is undistracted by any interruption. With a
sublimity completely above that of any other
creature, she contemplates 'the Word in the

Jn 1:1   beginning'† and God in man. Perhaps it was
intended that the penetration of that contemplation should be clearly seen as excelling all the
other saints who contemplate God's grandeur.

Or perhaps it was because the Holy Spirit

Mt 3:16   deigned to appear in the form of a Dove,† and
he is usually spoken of as 'the sevenfold Spirit'
on account of the seven spirits which have been

Rv 5:6   sent upon the earth.† It follows that Mary's eyes
were described as the eyes of 'doves' since the

Is 11:2-3   sevenfold Spirit makes his special abode in her.†
In a spiritual sense, this grace is assigned to her
eyes, because from the beginning of her very in-
fancy, she consecrated her eyes to the blessed vision of the majesty of God, and disdaining all
things of the flesh, she fixed her gaze and fo-
cused her attention on the one who absorbed all
her affection.

How very greatly the privilege of motherhood added to her virginal purity, and then the

2 Cor 4:17   great weight of infinite glory,† that came from
the Son of God's taking flesh within her, in-
creased this twofold glory beyond all measure.
No human has any inkling of the grace that suf-
fused her loving gaze. It was the gaze of one
who contemplated, eye to eye, that great mys-

tery of tender love, a gaze that beheld, face to
face, that great brilliancy of light.

Even if the human weakness of the child
she bore, and her constant knowledge of his
baby needs, should have sometimes cast a cloud
over her contemplation of his glorious face, the
Holy Spirit overshadowed her from that cloud,† Lk 1:35
and it was from the cloud that the Father of the
Lord Jesus thundered the words: *This is my
beloved Son,*† and he is your beloved Son, too. Mt 3:17
Who can tell the story of how, while she contemplated with her constant dovelike look the
Sun of justice, enveloped in her flesh, the sevenfold Spirit irradiated her with his overshadowing, and overshadowed her with his radiance?

Sermon 75.1–4

Jesus at Twelve Years Old

WHEN HE WAS TWELVE YEARS OLD† we Lk 2:42
find Jesus staying away for three whole days, to
the very great distress of his mother, Mary, and
father—we find Joseph honored with this name
by the Holy Spirit.† We hear of them searching Lk 2:48
through the streets and squares of Jerusalem to
find him *whom their soul loved.*† Their search for Sg 3:2
him was not in vain, for he soon gave himself to
them most fully, rewarding the loss of a small

stretch of time by making his abode with them for many years and most humbly submitting himself to their authority.[†]

Lk 2:51

There is something here which no soul who loves Jesus should merely listen to in passing, and that is the reply he makes, almost in rebuke, when they declare the reason for their anxiety. '*Why did you seek me?*' he asks, '*Did you not know that I must be about my Father's business?*'[†] If I am

Lk 2:49

not mistaken, by *his Father's business*, he meant to imply meditating on God's law, being peacefully attentive to his word, a most active and zealous devotion to understanding his truth, not boldly relying on one's own wisdom but humbly seeking the opinion of others. These things are the first sweet blossom of a good heart, the promise that in ripe old age, there will be rich fruit. The wise man tells us, *Speak, young man, only if there is necessity. Wait till you are asked twice, and then make a brief reply.*[†]

Sir 32:10

So Jesus in his youth is eager to show the traits proper to his own age, those that reveal him as a boy like any other. He goes to where the teachers are seated, and there, in their midst he sets up his chair of humility, quite obviously sitting at their feet.[†] He hides his wisdom by humbly asking them questions, showing them every mark of respect and shunning the least trace of presumption. But by the wisdom of his replies, as though compelled by power other than himself, he involuntarily revealed the hidden treasure of his wisdom. All are filled with wonder,[†] and he eagerly opened the door to their reverent knocking, running lovingly to meet their zealous search.[†] And so, very rightly,

Lk 2:46

Lk 2:47

Lk 11:9

occupations like these Jesus calls *his Father's business*, because wisdom, which *dwells with prudence*[†] and is found in the scholar's reflections, as scripture describes, is occupied, works and plays amidst these things in his Father's presence.[†]

Prv 8:12

Prv 8:30

Though, my brothers, at this point, this should be brought to your attention so that 'when you all come together'[†] you may be concerned 'to be about your Father's business'. We must set ourselves always to have something on our lips that concerns his Father's will or the glory of his kingdom, something that will help us to serve him better, that arouses love, that has the savor of Jesus about it. Let us ask questions, duly, about the things of God, and let us give gentle answers. Let both question and answer be pleasantly seasoned with salt, *the salt of grace*[†] as the apostle calls it. Finally let all your conversation be made perfect with words of great gentleness and peace, so that it never happens that anger and bad feeling find tinder from what should be matter for love.

1 Cor 11:20

Col 4:6

Sermon 42.3

Love as Strong as Death:
Its Meaning for Me

Death was always an important and constant reality in the lives of medieval monks. Not a morbid thing, not something to be avoided at all costs, but simply the ultimate reality which gives positive meaning to their whole monastic life. Death was seen, not as the end, but as only the beginning—the entry into eternal life and love without end.

ON THE TESTIMONY of the Spouse, who alone knows the strength of love since he himself is love's overflowing source, *love is as strong as death,*[†] no less, and in fact wrestled with death and triumphed over it. However, if it is true that death and God's life, with their strengths arrayed on either side, joined in combat, and that, death having been defeated, love left the field victorious and rejoined her lover, why then is due praise denied her? After this, why is it not described as stronger than death, and not merely as 'strong as death'? Perhaps the answer is that the fight with death is still on, and that love's praise must be deferred in this life until the trumpet sounds and the battle is absolutely over. Then the whole Church can shout together with equal joy: *Death is swallowed in victory. Death, where is your sting?*[†]

But as long as life lasts, we have to await the end of the combat with a certain dread. We must wait until the end before we can praise the

Sg 8:6

1 Cor 15:55

love which is in Christ Jesus, how it fought strongly against death and won a glorious victory over it. The reason why we must wait is that he undergoes this same combat all over again in each one of his beloved, strength once more matching itself with strength. But at the end, all his praise will be chanted aloud, for the time will have come when God *gives his beloved sleep.*† That will be a deeply tranquil sleep, but it will also be deeply alive and watchful,† and in it, there will be the death of sin. It was because of sin that there first came the wall of division,† making the union of body and soul a thing that would disintegrate under the necessity of death. Now it will be wholly swallowed up by life, the old complaint utterly removed from sight: *Unhappy man that I am, who will free me from the body of this death?*†

Moreover, the death which unties the knot between soul and body, or rather, sets the soul free from the body, should be described not as death but as sleep. This is what our Lord indicated when he said: *The girl is not dead but sleeping.*† He said too: *Lazarus our friend is sleeping.*† So we find the apostle does not want us to mourn for the sleeping as if they were dead, giving us the incontrovertible reminder that just as *Christ died and rose again,*† so will it be for them. Through the power of his resurrection, they too will rise up from their sleep, when they have fulfilled the time that must be spent sleeping.

Then there is the death which comes when souls have left the prison of the body and suffer a dire penalty in purgatory. But the *love* of Christ still *as strong as death*, assails and destroys

Ps 127:2

Sg 5:2

Eph 1:14

Rom 7:24

Mt 9:24
Jn 11:11

Rom 14:9

this death, eating it away little by little and consuming it, until joy comes in its fullness and completely absorbs it.

There is also the death which will come at the end, when we resume again our bodies, the death that thrusts the unwilling spirit into its bodily prison, there to suffer in confinement for ever. The same *love* of Christ is here too, *as strong as death*, and by the price of his own death and the prize of his resurrection, he has changed this death into the joy of a blessed immortality for his beloved ones. It is then that the strength of Christ's love will receive its full praise, for the full number of his beloved ones will have won the full victory over even this death.

Finally, there is that death which we mentioned above as being the most bitter of all, namely, the communion of all the lost in their wretched unhappiness, where each one destroys the other in their common ruin and they mutually devour one another in partnership. The love of Christ is fully strong enough to avert this death from his beloved, immersing them in the ocean of eternal happiness in a blissful communion where there are as many blessings as there are those to be blessed.

Love is as strong as death, then, and is openly zealous for its loved ones until it can *make* all their *enemies a footstool* at their feet.[†] Death, which Paul called *the last enemy*[†] has many forms, and love must either destroy it by direct attack or supplant it by prevention. Utterly good and precious is the advice from heaven that tells you to set Jesus and him crucified as a seal upon your heart.[†] Ponder and pon-

Ps 110:1

1 Cor 15:26

1 Cor 2:2

der again, print and imprint what Christ once did by dying for you, and do it very often in commemoration of him.† Think deeply over the strength of that love that emptied out all the ointment of so great a love.†

Recognize clearly the strength of Christ's love, which dissolved itself so generously in the winepress of death,† and then poured itself forth so wonderfully and pressed itself out so purely. Go to the winepress, O Bride of Christ, if you long to be rich in these joys; press out for yourself the love of Christ from the death of Christ, since *love is as strong as death.*†

Sermon 105.5-9

Lk 22:19

Mt 14:4

Is 63:3

Sg 8:6

V

CHRIST'S PASSOVER
AND GLORIFICATION

AN OVERVIEW:
THE TRUE PASSOVER

'IT IS THE LORD'S PASSOVER'.[1]

JOY is an intangible quality that breaks into our lives, often at unexpected moments. It can touch us briefly when we walk barefoot soon after dawn, through dew-sprung grass as the sun glistens on clear hedgerows. It leaves the echoes of a memory hanging in our heart, and if we are lucky it carries us away to a God-filled place. More lucky still was Moses, who was lifted up out of himself and by prophetic foresight glimpsed the face of God in the beginning of creation. This vision embraced the King in his splendor, reflected or imaged on the transfiguration mountain. A brilliant new light shone in his eyes, and even his ears knew joy in his excess of rapture.

What did Moses see? The meaning of the true Passover. When he came down from the mountain, his face shone with the glory and splendor that streams from the face of Jesus. He saw the future. This is the christian interpretation of that mysterious passage in Exodus 34:28-35, when the skin on Moses' face was radiant with glory as he spoke with Yahweh face to face. 'Tomorrow,' Moses said, 'is the true Passover, when Christ our Passover, our Lamb, will be sacrificed, and we ourselves shall celebrate it with him'.[2]

[1] Ex 12:12
[2] 1 Cor 5:7; Sermon 31.1-3

Historically the Passover was the celebration of the escape from Egypt, and indeed of the Chosen People's entry into the Promised Land. In christian terms it is transferred allegorically to 'the great and solemn celebration of the true Passover when the Lord passed over from Israel to the Gentiles'.[3] For this reason the apostles set out to proclaim the grace and glory of the Word-made-flesh to the gentiles. From then on the glory of Jesus shines on us who have been adopted by the Father as his heirs.

In the Song the Bride sings, *His hands are rounded and as of gold.*[4] John of Forde makes this an occasion for delving into the golden rays that blaze for God's right hand. Five rays of glory may be perceived. Chief among them and the basis of them all is the moment when the Word united himself to man in the Incarnation. This union of God and man in Jesus Christ, our Lord, was effected with the utmost graciousness and irresistible strength, though inevitably beyond the power of the human mind to understand. This glory was the glory that the Son had with the Father before the beginning of the world but manifested in a hidden way within the person of Jesus, shining forth briefly at the Transfiguration, because *the Father and I are one.*[5]

It may seem strange that John of Forde calls the greatest christian feast, Easter, only the 'second glory' of Jesus. Nevertheless it is the moment when Christ burst forth from the sepulcher and brought the glory of the resurrection to all who believe in him. We need to remember that Easter and Ascension, Christ's third glory, are a unity: the former marking the glorious moment of triumph and victory, the latter proclaiming his ultimate return to the Father's final embrace. In this respect the second and third glory are the counterpointed harmony of a single refrain, while at Pentecost, the fourth glory, Jesus pours out his Holy Spirit on the whole earth without restraint and causes the living water of grace to flow into our hearts in a way that John will explain at

[3] Sermon 32.6-7
[4] Sg 5:14
[5] Jn 10:29

greater length in Sermons Seventeen, Eighteen, and Nineteen. The infinite and final ocean of Jesus' glory is achieved only when he is on his glorious throne of majesty, when time has come to an end.

It will be seen at once that, in order to highlight the principal points of Christ's glory, John of Forde is making only a brief summary of a huge area of theology. Each subject will receive further treatment in other parts of the commentary. In Sermon Thirty-Four it is the final glory that is the main theme. John looks beyond. He turns his gaze away from the 'here and now' to the 'there' of the Parousia. This he does, not in order to avoid present realities, but to direct our lives towards their ultimate goal. 'There love burns bright and understanding is vigorous. There good-will is ever eager and memory wide-awake.' The sight of the Word in glory fulfils every desire of the human heart, transforming the lover into the Beloved so that every face is lit up, in the Father's eyes, with the Image of his own Son. It is this glory that transfuses our life on earth with purpose, because 'if something of his appearance shines in our hearts now, it comes from the fullness of this city which is above', that is to say, from the appearance of the Son and the Father.

The Song, in another place, sings the praises of the Beloved's hair. John suggests that we should find here a reference to the Gospel saying, *Not a hair of your head will perish,*[6] and he interprets this as 'the thoughts and desires of those who are firmly rooted in the love of Christ'. These are signatures of the martyrs, men and women whose imperturbable courage has made them beautiful in the eyes of God and grounded their hearts in him alone. 'When the blast of persecution threatens, these thoughts increase in depth and number'. The incontrovertible sign of discipleship is the grace of martyrdom. It is the glory that Christ gives to his chosen few. He it is who creates the poignant thoughts that express the willingness to die for him.

---

[6] Lk 21:18

'He creates them through the promptings of his Holy Spirit'. The thoughts of those awaiting martyrdom, like our own Atlas martyrs, are first washed clean by the Holy Spirit with the grace of compunction, then they are arranged in order by the grace of prudence, and made pleasing to Jesus through the spirit of humility. United in this way to Jesus on the Cross, the martyrs go forward with steadfast courage.

There are a few, not many, who can even rejoice in their sufferings. Few and far between, they have advanced to the very height of discipleship. They have become like lofty trees in the garden of the Lord's planting.

Although martyrdom is reckoned as the greatest proof of a person's love for Jesus— 'greater love than this no-one has than that he lay down his life for his friends'— nonetheless the majority of Christians will never have to face this choice; their discipleship will be found in patiently accepting the more minor trials of life. Here a strong faith is required, a faith that compares with the faith of the martyrs even though these people are not called to that glory. People with this faith believe that everything comes from God, that 'nothing is done by Jesus that is not in accord with his name'. Their confidence has deep roots in Christ who is their whole aim and the intention of their lives. In this faith they already have a foretaste of eternal joy. John of Forde himself had tasted the bitterness of this patience during the painful time of the Interdict that halted religious life in England during the last years of his life, but he also knew the sweet peace of Christ that accompanied the full acceptance of it as God's will for him.

If joy is intangible and patience a daily necessity, it is hope that binds them into unity with other demanding virtues. One of the driving themes that dominate John's thought is this pervasive hope. 'To share one day in the eternal blessedness of Christ's glory' dictates much of his encouragement for his monks. He draws them on to fix their sights on heaven, because it is 'in highest heaven Christ's glory resides, supremely radiant and sublime'. The whole thrust of his concern for their spiritual welfare, the basis for his teaching on contemplation, the urgency of his demand for patience rests ultimately on his belief that the purpose of monastic life is to ensure them a place where 'the glory of Jesus will shine forth in splendor beyond anything the astonished mind can conceive'.[7]

---

[7] Sermon 27.4

Moses Prophesies
Concerning Jesus Christ

I CANNOT CONCEAL from you something
that my soul conceived from the seed of what
was said yesterday, and has this very night
brought forth to birth. For we read in Scripture:

Lk 8:11

The seed is the word of God.† Yet no one need
marvel that it has all happened so quickly. Jesus
was here, and he gave his blessing. Come, and if
you find the harvest ripe, and reap so that *he*

Jn 4:36

who sows may rejoice with him who reaps!† As I
was saying, those words of Moses—*not a bone of*

Ex 12:46; Jn 19:36

his shall be broken†—seem to me to have given
rise to a rich harvest of meaning. For that great
man, faithful, as Scripture says, *in all that con-*

1 Sm 22:14

cerns God's house,† seems to me by the wonderful
artistry of the Holy Spirit, to have sung at one
and the same time a song of marriage to his
beloved and a song of mourning to the house of
Israel.

By bringing before the children of Israel the
figure of the paschal lamb, and by bringing
God's people out of the land of Egypt in his

Ex 12:27

blood,† he pointed straight at the only Son of
the Father, as if with a stabbing finger, and said:
See, here is the Lamb of God, here is he who takes

Jn 1:29
Ps 45:1

away the sins of the world.† Here is he for whom
my heart breaks into a song of praise,† so that at

the beginning of my book it is of him that I write.† He is that greatest and eternal 'beginning', in which God made heaven and earth;† he is the Word of the Father, for he spoke and all was made.† Whatever I have written, it is he whom I was writing about, telling and declaring all my works to the king.† Finally, when I bent in adoration and kept on repeating, *Lord, if I have found grace in your sight, show me your face,*† then it was his face that I longed to see with a longing past description.

Ps 40:10

Gen 1:1

Ps 33:9

Ps 45:1

Ex 33:13;
cf Gen 18:3

I have been lifted out of myself, but God has not let me down.† For I have seen the *day of the Lord*, I have seen it and been filled with joy.† I have seen the one I long for, I have seen the one I wait for, I have seen the light of my eyes, I have seen the king in his splendor† and the beautiful one in his beauty. I have seen him in his glory on the mountain, I have seen *him face to face, and yet my life has been preserved.*† On that day, not only was there a new light shining in my eyes, but even my ears, too, knew joy, pealing in thunderous rapture from the heavens! For the Father bore witness to his Son for me to hear, so that from that day forth, blessed have been my eyes, and blessed too my ears!†

Is 50:7

Jn 8:56

Is 33:17

Gen 32:30

Mt 13:16

After all this, how joyfully I came down from the mountain, how much more joyfully than once I came down from Mount Sinai! I came down with my face shining with a glory greater than I have ever known,† for on it was impressed the glory and splendor of the wonderful light that streams from the face of Jesus. So I returned to the true children of Israel, to those who rest upon Abraham's bosom waiting to see what I

Ex 34:29

Lk 2:10

saw. And I gave them tidings of great joy,[†] because I looked upon the glory of the Son of God.

See, his glory is at our very threshold! The
time has come for the Lamb to be led to the
slaughter. Already the children of Israel are
making plans to slay him, already every house
and family is arranging to consume him. Stand
firm, then, because tomorrow, in the blood of

Ex 12:27

this Lamb we shall escape from this captivity.[†]
Tomorrow is the true Passover, when Christ our
Passover will be sacrificed and we ourselves shall

1 Cor 5:7

celebrate it with him.[†]

Ex 12:5

The Lamb of God is certainly *without blemish*.[†] So this Lamb possesses perfect innocence,
because he is without blemish; perfect wisdom,
because he is male; perfect strength and universal grace, because he is a yearling. What if his
fleece were looked at by loving eyes and fingered
by pure hands! And his flesh, what if it should
be tasted and appreciated by a healthy palate,
though not by the sickly! What if his blood
should find a pure throat, which would savor it
for what it is! At any rate, this is the whitest and
softest fleece, the tenderest and richest flesh,
while his blood is blood of the finest grapes,

Dt 32:14

wine of the choicest stock.[†] So the fleece of this
Lamb is gentle lowliness; his flesh is tender
kindness; his blood is holy delight. His fleece is
truly a mantle, his flesh is truly food, and his

Jn 6:54

blood is truly drink.[†] Whoever covers himself
with this fleece, will not fear the coming of win-

Ps 147:17

ter cold,[†] or the shame of being naked. Whoever makes his meal on this flesh will not dread
hunger or disease. Whoever drinks this blood

Jn 6:54

will not thirst or grow sad for all eternity.[†]

This is the true keeping of the Passover: pi-
ously to eat this flesh and drink this blood, and
so become incorporated into this Lamb, and in
this way, actually to become the Lamb.

Sermon 31.1–3

THE TRUE PASSOVER OF CHRIST

AT THE END of the quotation these words
are added: *For it is the Passover,*† *that is, the Lord's*   Ex 12:12
passing. In the profoundest sense, the true keep-
ing of the Passover is this: first, to put on charity, which is to feed on the flesh of the Lamb;
and secondly, to incorporate others into Christ,
as far as grace makes possible. This is indeed a
good and life-saving Passover of the Savior,
from which arises medicine that will cure, from
which healing spreads abroad and the health of
salvation becomes ours.

Finally, there is a condition laid down for
eating the Lamb, a holy one and full of charity.
This says that, if those who have come to eat the
Lamb are too few, they are to join to themselves
the neighbor next to their house till they make up
the number of persons necessary.† The apostles   Ex 12:4
acted in accord with the charity of this holy
condition. They saw very clearly that Israel was
not able to encompass in its entirety the grace of

the glory of the Word-made-flesh, even if it all
flowed together as one to receive it. That is why
the apostles set out on their holy and justified
passage to the gentiles. Before that day the
house of the gentiles was very far distant, yet by
means of the 'cornerstone', it not only became

Ps 118:22 very close, but actually touched it.† In fact, it
became one with it.

On that day, therefore, there was a great and
solemn celebration of the Passover, when the
Lord 'passed over' from Israel to the gentiles.
Nevertheless, on this glorious day still to come,
there will truly be a grand and most festive
Passover, for then at long last, the Lord will
'pass over' from the gentiles to Israel and in the
same way, salvation will have to spread out from
Israel itself into all the corners of the world.

But vainglory and pride so often undermine
the highest virtues, and someone may suspect
that their stain may creep in here, where there is
the beauty of so much grace, and such perfection of virtue. To prevent this, at the very end,
there is this addition about the end of the Pass-

Ex 12:46; Jn 19:36 over: *Not a bone of his shall be broken.*† As they
make their meal on the Lamb, they will truly
have 'broken his bone' if they take a foolish delight in the joy of the grace they see within
them. Israel has broken a bone of the Lamb, if it
accepts God's mercy but forgets his justice, if it
does not tremble at the thought of his judgments because of its experience of the grace
which is within it, coming from and through
the Lamb. Besides, there would be damage, and
perhaps great danger to life, if a broken bone,
swallowed down with over-careless haste, should

stick in its throat when eating and afterwards there be no one to take it out.

So then, that there be nothing wanting to the celebration of this great Passover, all will join their voices into one to sing to you, O Lord of mercy and justice! Mercy and truth will go before your face,[†] linked closely together, so that the blessed people, *who know the joyful shout*,[†] may never fall away from that joyful shout, never falter in it , never take false pride in it. May the grace of that joy come to us, also, grace in his truth, and truth in his grace, through the gift of the spotless Lamb of God, Spouse of the Church, Our Lord Jesus Christ.

Ps 89:15

Ps 89:16

Sermon 32. 6–7

THE PATIENCE OF THE MARTYRS

HIS HAIR IS GRACEFUL AS A PALM-TREE.[†]   Sg 5:11

THE SECRETS of God's resting place are profound and inaccessible; the mysteries of the royal bower, being sweeter, are even more secret. It is the Lord's glory to conceal his Word, and he utters it only to those whom he loves and who love him. If we go humbly to the door of this door and knock with loving confidence, the doorkeeper who knows each one of us, will open to us.

Notice that hair, curls and locks all refer to the hair, but the terms mean different things. 'Hair' applies to the whole and to each separate hair. When it is rolled becomingly it is called 'curls'. When it is neatly combed and arranged with unpretentious care it is known as 'locks'. When the Spouse praised the bride, he commended her hair first and then her curls. The progress in love implies a growth in beauty and is an incentive to the love and praise of the Spouse. The bride in this occasion responded to the Spouse's praise by praising his hair, as we have seen.

First, 'hair'. When the Lord Jesus was preaching to his disciples about the constancy of martyrs, preparing them as mountains with his strength, girded with might,[†] we find him speaking like this, *The hairs of your head are all numbered.*[†] Again he said, *Not a hair of your head will perish.*[†] So great was the power of his words that they took new strength from this word from heaven,[†] especially when the Paraclete was sent by the Father in Jesus' name to bring to their minds these other things he had said to them.[†] The hairs on the heads of martyrs are the thoughts and desires of their hearts, firmly rooted in the love of Christ,[†] and joined in their countless numbers against the strength of this world, like a vast army.[†]

By enduring with imperturbable courage, they beautify and strengthen the heart. In the minds of the brave, how greatly these thoughts increase in depth and number when the blast of persecution threatens. Then Jesus is aroused from sleep. Then the arrows of prayer take on a

Ps 65:6

Lk 12:7

Lk 21:18

Ps 33:6

Jn 14:26

Eph 3:17

Rv 7:9

keener edge, and the fire of meditation flares up. At this time the exhortations of the evangelists and prophets are more frequently recalled, and God's eternal judgements thoughtfully remembered. What strengthens the heart more than all else is the memory of Our Lord's passion and the driving power of glory that will come upon us, an impulse that the passing sufferings of this present time render immense in its sublimity.† Rom 8:18

Hairs of this kind take their origin not only from the mind of the martyrs, but also from their head who is Christ. So they are numbered by him who gave them, and they do not perish. Anyone endowed with this hair will say, 'We have more on our side than they have'.† In spite 2K 6:16 of the wonderful strength of these hairs there is the danger that someone will take pride in his strength if he draws their root from somewhere else than from him of whom it is said, *The head of the man is Christ.*† But it is of Christ that the 1 Cor 11:3 martyrs cry out, *The Lord of hosts is with us, the God of Jacob is our stronghold.*† Be careful to cling Ps 46:7 to your Head and adorn this Head. Take thought only for his glory, and you will receive glory from him. It is he who creates these hairs whose strength is so great, he who counts them, he who washes them and arranges and tends them. He creates them by the promptings of the Holy Spirit, he counts them by increasing them through grace, he washes them through the sanctifying power of compunction, he arranges them by prudence, he tends them by the gracious gift of humility. Fix your thoughts on the loving kindness of the Creator, the generosity of the Giver, the tenderness of the Sanctifier, the watchful care of the Ruler, the providence of the guardian who keeps you safe.

Oh, how tepid we are! How careless of our thoughts! We have the promise that every good and holy thought has a claim to share one day in the eternal blessedness of his glory, so we should multiply these thoughts. By cleaving most firmly to their Head, the martyrs have attained an invincible strength beyond that of others, and neither things present nor things to come nor any creature whatsoever[†] can tear them away from their Head.

Rom 8:38;
1 Cor 3:22

Sermon 15.1-6

THE PALM OF VICTORY

PATIENCE, HUMILITY, GENTLENESS IN THE FACE OF SUFFERING

Sg 5:11   HIS HAIR IS GRACEFUL AS THE PALM-TREE.[†]

THE BRIDE COMPARES the Spouse's locks of hair to palm trees, because the palm is said to represent victory. The palm is given as a manifest mark of final victory to those who conquer in the struggle. This signifies the virtue of patience through which they joyfully triumphed in this life, or else the reward of patience, established still more joyfully in the glory of the life to come. This patience of the martyrs reigned supreme in the midst of their enemies. At the centre of their combats it went on its way, rejoicing like a conqueror, carrying the banners of its glory. Radiant in its trust, it exulted in its trials and gave thanks to God for all these things.† Patience is well called 'palm' or 'victory', because it conquers by the very means by which it seems conquered. Whatever the world thinks will damage it, it turns to gain. It draws help from tribulation, changes sorrow into joy, turns grief into a wealth of consolation.†

1 Tm 1:12

Jn 16:20

Our first martyr has an apt name, Stephen— which means 'crowned', for he was crowned in his glorification, and also crowned on earth in his patience. The martyrs boast of being crowned by the Lord while the impious weave them a crown of thorns, for in the power of God which is the suffering of Christ they are confident of reigning with him as kings. Since, in the hope of eternal joy and the joy of that hope amidst their afflictions, they receive in advance the pledge of eternal life, they reckon their sufferings as no more than a little trinket given them by the Holy Spirit; for 'the just man will flourish like the palm tree'.†

Ps 92:12

Not everyone can say with Paul, *We rejoice in our suffering*s.† Such a claim is the right of towering and lofty palms, which have advanced to their degree of height and glory according as they were blessed by God. They go *from strength to strength*,† and they grow from small palm sapling into lofty and graceful palms. They go forward to meet the Lord Jesus. The greatest joy comes from seeing the palm bear fruit and to *take hold of its*

Rom 5:3

Ps 84:7

Sg 7:8
fruit.† Hence the man who cuts off a palm branch is one who, without having enough patience to withstand all injuries, nevertheless tempers with the gentleness of long-suffering bodily discomforts and the trials of illness and adversity. He will take the cup without complaint.

Others patiently bear all troubles from whatever source. They know that Jesus draws the sea together; and that it is Jesus who gives the sea orders, who divided the waters when and how he pleased, and yet that it is Jesus who Mt 14:25 walks on the waves.† They believe that nothing is done by Jesus that is not in accordance with his name, nothing that is not loving and for our good; and in this confidence they send down ever deeper the roots of their intention. They Ps 92:13 become planted in the house of the Lord,† and they are planted together with Christ in the Rom 6:5 likeness of his death.† They should blossom in the hope of eternal glory, while patience itself turns sweet and: *A cheerful heart produces a* Prv 17:22 *blooming life.*† They have a foretaste of eternal joy which has an infinite joy of its own.

Persons like this know by experience what the first fruits of the spirit are like. They glory in their tribulations, regarding them as fruit which they are already picking. The way of God's witnesses and martyrs is at first very narrow. Afterwards it becomes broad and easy, when, soon, by means of the palm of patience, hope springs up from tribulation. Patience goes ahead of love to prepare the way, and then she rejoices like a Ps 19:5 giant to run her course.†

These towering trees should fear one thing: pride. They should not marvel at their own loftiness. Heavenly condemnation is the only thing such a graceful palm should hold in dread. This palm must be as lowly as it is lofty. Great in every way, it must humble itself in everything. If its humility does not match its height, the beauty of its holiness will be less than perfect. Let them be humble, and share the thoughts of the humble. Humility is needed for 'victory'.

In comparing the hair of the Son of Man to pure wool,† John means to imply the holy gentleness of patience shining forth in the sublime majesty of the Saint of saints. The meekness of patience, containing within itself the radiance of humility, is likewise indicated by the comparison with snow.† These two virtues are identical twins which the Lord places before us as what we must see in him and imitate: *Learn of me for I am meek and humble of heart.*† There will be no rest if submission lacks the pull of humility or humility is without the gentleness of submission. In all that pertains to the essence of virtue, it is the blackness of the raven that shows an instinctive abasement, showing a man to himself and to the world as contemptible; while the whiteness of snow is a lowly disposition and shows the heart what it is, and pleases the divine Majesty by its spontaneous subjection. Blackness and whiteness balance each other; that is to say, humility and gentleness should go together so that the heart is able to say, *I am black but beautiful, daughters of Jerusalem.*†

Rv 1:14

Rv 1:14

Mt 11:29

Sg 1:4

Sermon 15.7-10

Five Ways in which Christ
is Glorified

HIS HANDS ARE ROUNDED AND AS OF GOLD.†

IN A PREVIOUS SERMON I spoke of
Christ's left hand, which is the weakness he
took on himself for our sake. The time has now
come for the right hand to rise up and perfect
the work of our salvation. For we read: *His right*

Ps 98:1   *hand and his holy arm have brought salvation.*†
The glory of his right hand is praised by David
in three different ways in Psalm Ninety-eight;
likewise Isaiah calls it to arise by a threefold appeal: *Awake, put on strength, right arm of the*

Is 51:9   *Lord! Awake as in days of old.*† Let us look more
closely at these three types of glory.

The right hand of the Lord does valiantly,
raising Christ to life from the dead; *the right
hand of the Lord lifted me up*, lifting Christ up
above the heavens; *the right hand of the Lord does*

Ps 98:1   *valiantly*,† glorifying Christ in the faith of all
the nations by sending the Paraclete. There is
still one glorification of Christ lacking here,
though it is as great as all the rest. That is when
he will come in his glory, and in the glory of his
Father and his holy angels, to transform the
body of our lowliness into the body of his splen-

Phil 3:21   dor.† Then at last he will have put the finishing
touch to the work of our salvation.

These are the four titles Christ has to glory,
but before them, chief among them and greater
than all—in fact the basis of them all—is the
great condescension of the Word, beyond any

human power to describe or imagine. But it united that man to himself with the utmost graciousness and irresistible strength. When the Son called on his Father concerning this glory, with the words, *Father, glorify your Son*, he received the reply, *I have glorified him and I shall glorify him again.*† Again, when Christ was explaining at length to the crowd about his sheep, and promising to give them everlasting life, he finished his sermon with these words: *What my Father has given to me is greater than all these things, and no one is able to snatch it out of my Father's hand. The Father and I are one.*† Therefore the right hand of the Spouse is the glory of Jesus Christ. *He was predestinated Son of God in power*† and it was glory indeed that he received from his Father's hand in time, because of his holy union with the divine Word.

Jn 12:28

Jn 10:29

Rom 1:4

Corresponding to the five fingers on the right hand there are five kinds of glory.

The first is that the man Christ was taken up into a glorious union with the Word of God, and this may be called the thumb of his right hand, being more powerful than all the other fingers by reason of its strength and dignity.

The second is that, like the sun at morning, he burst forth on the third day from the sepulchre, though it was guarded with a stone and seals and a detachment of soldiers.† He brought the glory of his resurrection to all who would believe in him, and he changed the three days' sorrow of his new Bride into swift and everlasting joy. Speaking of the swift glorification of the Son of Man, he said, *If God is glorified in him, then God will glorify him in himself, and swiftly will he glorify him.*†

Mt 27:66

Jn 13:32

The third is that he is exalted in the splendor of the heavens, lifted up into the glory of the Father and established on the Father's throne of glory. All things in heaven and earth Ps 8:6 are under his feet.[†]

The fourth is that he distributes the gifts of grace according to his will. After Pentecost he poured out the Holy Spirit without restraint on all the earth, that he might glorify his name; and now today, according to the measure of his giving, as Scripture says,[†] he gives out those same Eph 4:7 waters in his fist.

The fifth is that every eye will see him on the glorious throne of his majesty when time has come to an end. So long hidden, his glory will shine forth in splendor beyond anything the astonished mind can conceive.

Sermon 27.3-4

The Heavenly Beauty
of Christ Our Lord

Sg 5:15 HIS APPEARANCE IS LIKE LEBANON,
CHOICE AS THE CEDARS.[†]

THE VOYAGE OF THE BRIDE is nearly done. Over the sea of her Beloved's praises, narrow but very deep, she has been borne by his

spirit's favoring gale, and now, prepared to furl
her sails, she rolls up all that can be said in one
brief and ingenuous saying, *His appearance is like
Lebanon.*† It is as if she were to say to the maid-   Sg 5:15
ens, 'How much longer shall I go winding the
sails round and round? I can never catch up with
his praise. He is greater than any praise, too high
for any mind to understand. I long for nothing
more than to celebrate him as he deserves, but I
fail completely. He eludes all my efforts, hiding
away in his sheer sublimity, and it is to those
who are with him in his heavenly kingdom that
he offers himself for praise and glory.'

In the highest heaven, then, is his glory,†   Lk 2:14
supremely radiant and sublime. There love
burns bright and understanding is vigorous.
There good will is ever eager and memory wide-
awake. There no anxiety distracts, no difficulty
presses, no fear disturbs, no hope seduces, but
everything works together to praise and to take
delight in the Son of God. There *day utters
speech to day,*† and I long to utter it to you, my   Ps 19:2
friends, but this is a matter too high for me and
beyond your capacities. Yet on that day of triumph in the height of heaven, when everyone is
both a *child of day*† and a 'light of day', day truly   1 Thes 5:5
utters speech to day, one person crying aloud to
another, *In the beginning was the Word,*† and *the*   Jn 1:1
Word was made flesh.†   Jn 1:14

There it will be possible to know the joy of
contemplating the appearance of my Beloved
with my own eyes, and of openly pointing him
out to sight. There his appearance is celebrated
with the delight that is his due,† because every-   Ps 147:1
thing converges on it, and the one tender desire

of every loving heart is to be made like him. In short, there the appearance of my Beloved diffuses itself throughout that whole sphere of light, pouring itself abroad without restraint, and thus wrests every eye impetuously to itself while it powerfully transforms every face into the likeness of its own brilliance.

So it is there that *his appearance is like Lebanon,*† because with him, there is a heavenly plantation of holy souls forming a true 'Lebanon'. The true Lebanon is closely planted with a great towering mass of cedars. Jesus, my Spouse, who is the true Solomon, built his house from them, and we read of it, *It is a great house that I desire to build.*† It was from this Lebanon that he came to us, as we find in the prophets: *God has come from Lebanon.*† Yes, from there he came to us, making himself *lower than the angels,*† and it was to heaven that he also returned, and his dwelling place is in its centre.

There is seen the most beautiful and blessed of women,† his Bride, who is in heaven, and who knows not a moment's pause in the blissful and satisfying enjoyment of her Spouse, because she has him at her good pleasure. There she has the right to say, *My Beloved is mine and I am his, who feeds among the lilies.*† Yet even she, while on earth, can scarcely do for half an hour what there she never ceases to do every hour.† For there at last is eternal life, there the full flood of those living waters which flowing from her Spouse came down to the remote reaches of these, our distant valleys. There is the well where they spring up in abundance, for there the Lord makes his dwelling so as to be enthroned as King for all eternity.†

Sg 5:15

2 Chr 2:5

Hab 3:3
Ps 5:8, Heb 2:7, 9

Lk 1:42

Sg 6:2

Rv 8:1

Ps 29:9

If something of his appearance shines in our hearts here below, it comes from the fullness of this Lebanon, for it is from that city which is above and is our mother[†] that *the appearance of* — Gal 4:16
his beauty shines.[†] Even if it now lies hidden — Ps 50:2
from our mortal eyes—for here we are walking *in darkness and in the shadow of death*[†]—yet — Is 9:2
when he comes once more from heaven, attended by blessed troops of angels, then all eyes will clearly see that *from Zion is the appearance of his beauty,*[†] because God will come in full sight. — Ps 50:2
In the past he had a look that the very angels found wonderful and lovely. He was, even then, the most beautiful of all the children of mankind,[†] more beautiful than the angels, but — Ps 45:3
then *cloud and darkness were round about*[†] his ap- — Ps 97:2
pearance. From the very moment of his conception, the appearance of Jesus aroused praise and wonder, glory and exultation. For the angels the light of his Godhead shone only the brighter from that ethereal and gleaming cloud, and from it the Father's voice thundered out to them more loudly, *This is my beloved Son in whom I am well pleased.*[†] — Mt 3:17

Sermon 34.1–4

VI

THE MYSTERY OF GOD'S LOVE

AN OVERVIEW

IN ONE PLACE John of Forde uses the expression *negotium amoris*, love's activity, to hint delicately that marital love is a symbol of the highest union; the union between the Word and the contemplative soul. This is more than a symbol. This union of love springs from a fundamental change in our being. It is the result of a seal that the Word of God has impressed on the soul. Jesus Christ himself is the 'only true and adequate Image of the Father'.[1] By gazing on this Image the soul becomes a reflection of or a likeness to the true Image, the ultimate source of love.

This teaching is founded on the mystery of essential love within the Blessed Trinity itself. It is worth lingering over this because it is basic to John's thought and reveals him as a great master of the spiritual life as well as being no mean theologian. He calls this essential love 'the richest vein of pure gold'.[2] In the previous sermon he had been discussing the Bride's love of God—the Bride being the Church. Compared with God's love for the Church, the love of the Church for God is as nothing. 'I am aware,' he says, 'of a vein of gold richer than the Church's love for God'. He confesses his total inadequacy in tackling the mystery. Nevertheless he makes the attempt. He begins his discussion of God's infinite love with this concise and lucid overture: 'It is incontrovertibly true that God's love with which he loves the Church compared with the love by which the Church

---

[1] Sermon 103.8, cf. Col 1:15
[2] Sermon 13.1

loves him is more precious, more weighty, more solid, more brightly shining.' Taking each of these qualities in turn he expands their meaning, always with the underlying premise that God's love must remain incomprehensible to us.

Sermons Eleven–Fourteen form a kind of treatise, culminating in a profound reflection on the inner mystery of the life of the Blessed Trinity. In them John reveals the true stature of his thought. They constitute a short but incisive treatise on love. I doubt whether there is a better or more typical example of his genius. God himself, he tells us, is ruled by his own law of Love. He has given us the twofold law: love of God and love of neighbor.[3] These are the two foundation stones on which the whole Gospel teaching is built. Yet they are also the same laws that God himself has practised from the beginning. They originate from the same law of God's love. The Father and the Son love each other with Infinite Love. In doing so they themselves fulfil the first commandment, since they thereby love God with their whole being, and moreover they love their neighbor as themselves.

Sermon Fourteen provides John with the opportunity of dwelling with love and devotion on each Person of the Blessed Trinity in turn. The Father is the principal source of all life and being. As the purest channel of living water, he loves his Son, who is God coequal to himself, with his whole 'heart' because he loves with his whole understanding and wisdom. He loves him with his whole 'soul' because with his whole will, goodness and loving kindness. He loves him with his whole 'strength' because with his whole justice, power and resolution'. John takes his cue here from Matthew 22:37: *You shall love the Lord your God with your whole heart, with your whole soul, and with your whole mind.* In transferring this commandment to the Blessed Trinity, he is, strictly speaking, using anthropomorphic language—as he would be the first to recognize. Yet, as we have no words to express the inner relationship within this Mystery, and as John was not geared to the negative

---

[3] Mt 22:37

theological language of Gregory of Nyssa, he is able to bring the mystery alive for us in a manner that sets aflame our faith, our devotion, and lets us glimpse for a moment some of the riches in the Trinity we have perhaps never before encountered.

John makes no attempt here to emulate the speculative thought of the scholastics. John of Forde rejects any mere speculation. He is content to reflect quietly on the relationship between the three Persons who are the Unity of Love, and find therein the centre for his own deepest intuitions on love. He invites us to dwell with him in this deep spiritual reflection and remain for a while in awe before the wonder of Infinite Love: 'From the beginning the Father loved the Son with all his wisdom, and through loving generation he brought it about that the Son himself should be all his Wisdom. He loved him with all his goodness, and in the same way he brought it about that he should also be all his Goodness. He loved him with all the endless awareness of his eternity, and so he truly brought it about that he, the Son, should be his eternal and changeless Only-begotten Son. In a word he gave himself wholly to the Son and loved him wholly with the whole of himself'.[4]

Among the authors of the twelfth century, John of Forde is notable for his teaching on the Holy Spirit, a teaching that permeates all his writing. At Pentecost the Holy Spirit hovered creatively over the apostles, just as he had hovered over the primeval waters of creation, to recreate the world to holiness. The Holy Spirit's name is 'Love'. This love is powerful and dynamic, not primarily sentimental. The Holy Spirit received 'Love' from the Father and the Son; rather he is the substantial Love of the Father and the Son. Love is his deepest name: 'For the Holy Spirit is Love itself, and he is the font of love springing up from both Father and Son'.[5] In himself the Holy Spirit is the Uncreated Spirit[6] because he is one with the Father and the Son

---

[4] Sermon 14.1-2
[5] Sermon 14.1
[6] Sermon 114.9

and coequal with them—all three Persons together being the one, single, uncreated source of love.[7]

John's important contribution to theology is to accentuate the role of the Holy Spirit in our lives since the time of Pentecost. At Pentecost the Holy Spirit came down on the apostles in flames of fire,[8] and at Christ's baptism under the form of a dove.[9] In the same way he comes down today on all of us to remain on the Church and on each of us with the same power and love. He does this in many ways. We may, however, distinguish with John a few ways that are more general in scope. Firstly, the Holy Spirit anoints us with the fullness of grace. This grace is divided, as it were, into seven great streams called 'the sevenfold gift of grace': 'the apostles were enriched most lavishly with the sevenfold gift of the Spirit. They were anointed with the oil of gladness above all their fellows'.[10] As Gift, the Holy Spirit is the proof and pledge of our own resurrection from death to life in Jesus: We eat and drink the food of resurrection. He makes our hearts burn within us as Jesus walks with us when we are engaged in reading the Holy Scriptures, and it is the Holy Spirit who opens them up for us.

Secondly, he is the Spirit of Truth who enlightens our understanding to grasp the deeper reality and meaning of life— by faith. In himself the Holy Spirit is the infinite reality who is God. When we have passed into the light of God 'the veils of symbols and sacraments will be removed and we shall see Truth in reality'. 'The naked Truth will show us his face'.[11] In this life the whole of creation is like a great book we have received from God. When we exercise the spirit of understanding given to us at confirmation we can open this book and read in it the goodness and wisdom of the Holy Spirit. It is under his guidance that we learn his power and greatness through the things he has made.[12]

---

[7] Sermon 14.1
[8] Acts 2:3
[9] Mt 3:16
[10] Sermon 43.1; cf. Ps 45:7, Heb 1:9
[11] Sermon 72.6
[12] Sermon 17.11

Indeed, the twentieth century has given us possibilities of perceiving God's creation in ways beyond the imagining of previous centuries.

Thirdly, above all he is the Spirit of Love: 'When love is already awakening to life through the unction of the Spirit, our eyes begin to see clearly'.[13] The gifts of wisdom and love are so closely linked in mediæval spirituality, and in life, that they become almost synonymous: 'What Saint Bernard experienced within himself through the spirit of love, he was able to express to others through the spirit of wisdom'.[14] The Spirit of Love, who is the Holy Spirit, speaks within the Bride, and she experiences ineffable words of love'.[15]

[13] Sermon 21.5
[14] Prologue, 4
[15] Sermon 95.5

Sg 5:11

HIS HEAD IS OF FINEST GOLD.†

WE HAVE BEEN CONSIDERING the 'vein of purest gold', i.e. the purest love of the bride for her Beloved. This is the kind of love the bride has for her Beloved in that blessed country where everyone lives in joy, because they live in total love. Yet this gold is only the finest of its kind. There is a vein of gold richer than this, compared to which this can hardly even call itself gold.

It is incontrovertible that the love of God by which he has loved his Church and goes on loving her, when compared with the love by which he in turn is loved by his Church, is much more precious, much more weighty, much more solid, and much more brightly shining. It is also prior and purer beyond all reckoning. It is first in dignity, but also first in origin and in eternity. First in dignity, because the One who loves is the Creator, and what is loved is the created. Prior in time because, by determining beforehand what he would love, he made it ready within himself so that it could love him back in its turn. Prior in eternity, because he so loved from eternity that he predestined what he had loved from eternity, and that very eternity of

Love is the cause of the predestination. *For those whom he foreknew, he predestined to be made conformable to the image of his Son.*† He loved us in the Church from the beginning, before all ages. This is the first and most powerful reason why we were called, why we were glorified.

Rom 8:29

O Love, in all truth astonishing and pre-eminent, which has taken possession of a heart of such great majesty and has filled him to over-flowing with such great tenderness and has been intrinsic in the Eternal God from all eternity! It is exceedingly lofty, extravagantly rich, wonderfully patient. From above comes the dignity of its majesty, from within the greatness of its sweetness, and before it stretches the everlast-ingness of its duration. In the womb of his eternal mercy, God's love has placed his elect in a certain order and arrangement, and when they are called it is in the same order that they immediately spring forth. This eternal love strongly guards those whom it has generated for heaven. It holds them tight to its heart in an indissoluble embrace so that no one can bring any charge against God's elect.† For if it is God who begets, who calls, who justifies, who can condemn?†

Rom 8:33

Rom 8:34

Some may feel anxious about sin. In reply comes the voice of a real Father, bursting out from the deepest vein of love: *Whoever is born of God does not sin.*† From the abundance of the heart the mouth has spoken,† but it is the heart of God, not of man. In the human heart there could never arise such great tenderness as to forgive the sinful child and attach no blame to him. Blessed the generation of those children; the greatest blessing is to have a Father so immeasurably ready to be

1 Jn 5:18

Mt 12:14

merciful, so overflowing with compassion! He cannot forget the children of his womb and cannot deny himself.[†] From all eternity the Love of God has been our mother, and while knowing beforehand that we were going to sin against him, even then he was thinking deep within himself thoughts of peace and not of affliction.[†] This deserves all our wonderment, yet far outstrips all our capacity for wonder. O the power of Love! O the great wonder of it in the Son who is God of God! God's love turned its whole thought to what it could use as medicine, to what was strongest in its power, most healthful in its wisdom, sweetest in its goodness. He repressed all his wrath and compressed it into his mercy, wholly pouring out his compassion upon us all. He took counsel with his wisdom about the most healing ointments, about giving suck to his little ones, holding them in his arms and giving them affectionate kisses.

From within the bosom of the Father's tenderness, the Only-begotten Son made answer, 'My Father, may it be as you desire. I too have pity on this multitude,[†] and I go to blot out all their sins with your love and my blood.' In the spacious womb of that eternal predestination Christ Jesus was predestined Son of God in power,[†] on whom the Father laid the sins of us all and on whom was laid the punishment of our peace.[†] Therefore the Only-begotten Son of the Father did penance before the Father for our transgressions. He set before the Father's judgement seat that cause of our reconciliation. The prophets speak of what will happen as though it were in the past. They imitate that eternal wisdom who accomplished what was in the future,

Cf. Is 49:15

Cf. Jer 29:11

Cf. Mk 8:2

Rom 1:4

Is 53:5

or rather, for whom there is no future and no past, but for whom everything is now and always present beneath the changeless gaze of eternity.

Sermon 13.1–3

THE MYSTERY OF LOVE IN THE TRINITY

The Law of Charity

THE PROMPTING OF LOVE itself urges me to speak a little of that noblest love: that of the Father for his Only-begotten Son. It urges me to make at least some stammering attempt. I am going to follow the hand that draws me, on condition that not for a moment should Love let go of the hand of the poor servant that follows it. It is an arduous climb up the slopes of this sublime mountain, and among the many stones it is easy to slip and fall.

We know that two commands of love have flowed out from the eternal fountain of love: love of God and of our neighbor.[†] God has shaped and chiseled them out of Mount Sinai with us in mind.[†] That mountain is the mount of Love, a rich and fertile mountain on which God takes delight to dwell.[†] God has dwelt there from the beginning and will dwell there for ever.

Mt 22:37 parallels

Ex 31:18

Ps 68:16

These two laws are eternal so they are old; they are loving so they are light. They are so eternal that their Author himself lives by these same laws and has done so from the beginning. *I know that the command of my Father is life everlasting,*† says Jesus. If love is life everlasting, then he who lives eternally lives by love because he is Love. From God's own Love these laws originate, and to see such great Majesty living by them renders them most lovely and compelling.

The greatest commandment is this: *You shall love the Lord your God with all your heart,* and so on;† and the second is very similar, *You shall love your neighbor as yourself.*† God has practised these two commandments from the beginning, for it was by these same laws that he loves his Only-begotten Son. He has wholly observed the law in all its wholeness. The Only Son of the Father too, from the beginning of eternity, agreed to these same laws with all his soul and all his strength. You have often heard the Father saying of his Son, *My heart has uttered a good Word,*† and when he finds a man after his own heart,† it is without any doubt his Only-begotten Son. He calls him also his Beloved of whom he says, *My soul is well pleased.*† Also the Father says to the Son, *Before the daystar I begot you.*†

Sermon 14.1–2

Jn 12:50

Mk 12:30, Mt 22:37
Mt 22:39

Ps 45:1
Acts 13:22

Mt 12:18

Ps 110:3

THE MYSTERY OF THE FATHER'S LOVE FOR THE SON

THE FATHER who is the deepest source of love and the purest channel of living water, loves God his Son with his whole heart, because with his whole reason, intelligence and wisdom. He loves him with his whole soul, because with his whole will, goodness, and loving-kindness. He loves him with his whole strength, because with his whole justice, power, and resolution. He loves him with his whole mind, because with his whole memory, eternity, and changelessness. But his neighbor, whom he loves as himself, is this very same Son, our neighbor too, neighbor to him through love and to us through compassion. By nature he is a neighbor to both, and this is why he was made the mediator between the two. No one but he was so well fitted to the task of accomplishing this union, because he came already joined to each side.

So from the beginning the Father loved his Son with all his wisdom, and through this loving generation, he brought it about that the Son himself should be all his Wisdom. He loved him with all his goodness and in the same way he brought it about that he should also be all his Goodness. He loved him too with all his strength and all his justice, and so established him as his holy right arm and the fullness of all his Justice.† He loved him with all the endless awareness of his eternity, and so he truly brought it about that he should be his eternal and changeless Only-begotten Son. In a word,

Ps 98:1

he gave himself wholly to his Son, and loved him wholly with the whole of himself.

THE ONLY-BEGOTTEN SON IN THE FATHER. So the whole of the Only-begotten Son is in the whole of the Father, occupying the heart of his Wisdom, filling the Spirit of his goodness, overflowing the depths of his Strength, satisfying the great womb of his Eternity. He is in the Father's heart, searching all the depths of his wisdom and knowledge.[†] He is in the Father's soul, exploring all his treasures of goodness and kindness. He is in the sanctuary of his justice, entering into all the abysses of judgement and the secret places of his verdicts. He is in his mind, the very same simple and changeless Being, and because of this, he is the Origin of all that is, holding it in the grasp of his Truth.

Rom 11:33

Last of all, if we maintain the bride's way of celebrating, then the reason why *his head is the finest gold* [†] is that the head of Christ, as Paul says, is certainly God,[†] and *God is love.*[†] In the truest sense, God is love, and the finest love, for he gives himself so wholly to the whole of his only Son that he reserves absolutely nothing to himself. There is nothing he possesses, nothing that he is, which he has not utterly handed over to his Son.

Sg 5:11
1 Cor 11:3
1 Jn 4:8

Let us pursue the comparison with gold, and also with this love, let us examine its qualities. This love is radiantly bright, especially as regards Wisdom, most precious as regards Goodness, very weighty as regards Power and Justice, and lastly immensely firm as regards its essential Eternity.

I do well to speak of Wisdom as light, as
the wise man says, *compared to light she is purer,*[†]   Ws 7:29
since she has the very brightness of eternal
light.[†] It is fitting too to speak of goodness as   Ws 7:26
being precious, because there is nothing more
valuable, nothing dearer. This is specially so for
us, for it was goodness that showed itself in pay-
ing the price of our redemption. Mass seems to
me an appropriate description of strength and
justice—and for the reason that mass, as energy,
can be twofold, upwards or downwards, and
strength and justice render to every man ac-
cording to his works:[†] to the one, what is above,   Cf. Mt 16:27
and to the other, what is below. With reason,
too, firmness is applied to eternity, because it is
changeless in its simplicity and exists in a mas-
sive internal harmony by the law of its own firm
solidity. Therefore God, the head of the Spouse,
is the finest charity, because utterly full of wisdom, of loving-kindness, of justice and power,
of everlasting changelessness.

Sermon 14.3–4

THE MYSTERY OF THE WORD'S LOVE
FOR THE FATHER

THE SPOUSE is the Only-begotten of the
Father, and he is loved by the Father as unique,
as coequal, as consubstantial. The Evangelist

indicates these aspects of love when he tells us, *In the beginning was the Word, and the Word was* Jn 1:1 *with God, and the Word was God.*† When he says, *In the beginning was the Word*, turn your mind to the unfathomable mystery of the love within God's heart. Think of its unimaginable sweetness, which no one knows or can know, except only the Father. It was of this that the Only-begotten spoke, *No-one knows the Son except the* Mt 11:27 *Father.*† When the evangelist adds, *The Word was with God*, think of how the Son is in every way equal to the Father. It is the great fault of blasphemy to think or say that the Son is lower than the Father, and the man who for any reason ranks the Father of majesty higher than his Only-begotten Son will be arraigned before him as a sinner. When the Evangelist concludes, *The Word was God*, turn your thoughts to the Son as consubstantial with the Father. There is certainly only one God; as Moses said: Dt 6:4 *Your God is one God,*† yet since the Word is God, he is just as truly God as is the Father. In receiving from the Father the essence of divinity, he receives also the power of having the same substance as he has himself. Here is clear proof of how unimaginably great is the overflowing love of the Father for the Son, and how sweet and strong is the passion of the font for its fountain of sweetness. The Father grants his Son to be in him as his most intimate self, as uniquely Beloved, as the Father's perfect likeness. He grants him to be before him as coequal in majesty, power and eternity.

Sermon 14.4

Jn 1:1

Mt 11:27

Dt 6:4

THE MYSTERY OF THE HOLY SPIRIT
AS LOVE ITSELF:

TRINITY IN UNITY

AS THE FATHER is the beginning with respect to his Son, so too the Son is the beginning with respect to the Holy Spirit, and just as the Holy Spirit proceeds from the Father, so likewise does he proceed from the Son. For the Holy Spirit is Love itself, and he is the font of Love springing up from both Father and Son. This is why he is said to be the Love of the Father and the Son, because he who is Love proceeds from both by their mutual will and their equal love. So we see how admirable and plenteous is the richness of love in the blessed Trinity, and what a great river it is of most sacred joy. From the fullness of this joy the Father utters the whole of himself to the Son, and in the same way the Son, together with the Father, utters the whole of himself to the Holy Spirit, so that these three are one single font of Love. The love of this unity will never slacken, for it is a unity of love that there holds blissful sway. There is, of course, nothing within the indivisible unity of the most holy Trinity which is not to be praised and reverenced in the highest degree, but it is no cause for wonder if love has a place of special privilege and power here at the very source and font of its own being. God has the power of making those who are joined to God one spirit with him.† In the strength and truth of this, then, it is not to be wondered at, if

1 Cor 6:17

> the Father and the Son and the Holy Spirit,
> each of whom is Love should be but one Love,
> the Love of a single essence and the essence of a
> single Love.
>
> *Sermon 14.4*

LOVE IS PRE-EMINENT

Examples of love in the world

EVEN HERE BELOW, love is everywhere
working to maintain its pre-eminence; we see
how it struggles to rule as king, whether as good
among the good or as evil among the evil. It naturally possesses the innate force of drawing
those whom it seizes towards a strong desire for
unity, and it draws with as much strength as
sweetness, and the sweeter it is the nearer to
unity. Every human bond serves the cause of
love, whether in the relationship of parents to
children, or children to parents, of husband to
wife or wife to husband, or in the various rela-
tionships that make up human society. Each and
every kind of love reveals some resemblance to
that true and everlasting Love if you look for it.

We can find examples in the creatures
around us, though they lose their value for us as
we grow used to them.* The Wisdom of God
played before his Father's face over the whole

* Cf. Augustine,
*Treatise on Saint
John's Gospel* 24.1
(PL 35:1595)

expanse of the earth,† and he plays before those
who learn to join in Wisdom's play by rejoicing
and feeling wonder.

Cf. Prv 8:31

Taking for example Jesus' own words, we
see how the hen yearns over her chickens,† how
tenderly and how often she warms them against
her breast, how repeatedly she gives birth. The
keener her affection, the harsher her voice; and
in a wonderful fashion, she yearns with affection for her young in proportion to her hoarse-
ness. She passes wholly into a state of love, and
shows this not only by her rasping voice, but by
fluffing out her feathers, by drooping her body,
by anxiously running to and fro, by constant
service, by sleepless watch, by brooding over her
chicks with selfless devotion.

Mt 23:37

Sheep too—so meek—in dealing with their
lambs put forth the full force of their affection.
They bleat tenderly, they provide sweet nourishment, they lead them about continually, they
defend them vigorously. Soon they mount horns
and they are armed with these for the safety of
their lambs, even at the cost of their own death.

WISDOM'S PLAY: UNION. You may call this a
game, but it is serious. It is God's own Wisdom
who is playing.† Let the Wisdom of God the
Father play and dance and leap before the ark of
the Lord† who from the heights of his love uses
the mirror of visible creation to send some brilliant rays of light down into our darkness. There
is no creature without a voice, none without a
tongue. In the innate desires of their instinctive
affections all things speak to us of the ineffable
mystery of eternal Love, if only we take the

Cf. Prv 8:30

2 Sam 6:16

trouble to notice. If not, they are dumb to us and we are deaf to them.

Mothers feel such intense love for their children that, no matter how they pour it out, it can hardly show itself in its fullness. Then there is that most beautiful of loves, the love of a husband and a wife, for it so unites them both that they become two in one flesh.† Finally we have that love that draws the rational soul to union with its Creator, so that anyone who is joined to God is one spirit with him.† What then will love not achieve in the very font from which it takes its origin?

Who will wonder if the fountain of love, at the very source of its being, springs forth with greater force, leaps up more joyously, froths and foams with more abandon, tastes sweeter, is more crystalline in purity, and more vigorous in strength? The marvel of love within the Blessed Trinity is to be clearly distinguished from all the other loves which it affects by this fact: by its wonderful and surpassing virtue, the essence of the Blessed Trinity is one, because everywhere, and those who love aright become one heart and soul.

In others, there is union; here, it is unity. In others, the effect takes place as long as they love aright. Here, it is a question not of effect, but of taking origin and flowing out and streaming forth from each one to each of the others, and from each of the others to each one. The Son loves the Father with a love absolutely equal to the love with which he himself is loved by the Father, meeting such and so great a Father as befits such and so great a Son with an inter-

Mt 19:5

1 Cor 6:17

change of love in all respects the same. Also the Holy Spirit, who is Love proceeding from both, hastens back with equal love to his beginning, the Father and his Only-begotten Son, from whom he flows as a living and never-failing font, and whom he embraces with the total Love that is himself.

PARTNERSHIP IN LOVE. Since love is twofold—not only a feeling of well-wishing, but a doing of good deeds—it delights that supreme and eternal Love to make even the creature able to receive him and to enter into a blessed partnership. This is the glory of love: to be lavish to the needy because of its own fullness, and to pour out from its richness on those who are without, seeing that its name is truly *as oil poured out.*† Hidden treasure and secret love, what use are these? Since the love of these Three for one another is so superabundant, they glorify each other with all their might. *Father, glorify your Son, so that your Son may glorify you.*† Of the Holy Spirit the Son says, '*He will glorify me when he comes*'.† God himself, who alone knows how deserving he is of every honor, owes befitting glory to his holy Name.

 All God's works have two ends in view: to share his love with his creatures and so make them blessedly happy; and then from his creature's happiness, to glorify his own name. Thus the one Man who saw reality perfectly, referred everything, and taught us also to refer everything, to the glory of God. When asked about the blindness of the man born blind, he answered that it was to make manifest the works

Sg 1:2

Jn 17:1

Jn 16:4

Jn 9:3

Jn 11:4

Rom 5:20

Rom 8:30

of God.† He attributed the reason for the death of Lazarus to the same end.† Saint Paul, talking of sin, sees all the reasons for it as interconnected, the full revealing of the mercy of God, the glorious shining forth of grace in its plenitude, the giving to believers of the promise of Jesus Christ.†

Whether we speak of the predestination of the saints or of God's love for the saints, the beginning and the end is the love of the Blessed Trinity giving its whole self to itself in love. It is certainly the beginning, for it is the perpetual cause, overflowing to them out of its own goodness. It is truly the end, for to its glory Love itself and all the effects of love are blissfully directed. In this end, the blessed Church of God's elect rests in the end that has no end, giving glory in the wonderful and incomprehensible love of the Blessed Trinity to its most joyful and indivisible unity, from whose gracious overflow the Church herself becomes deserving of love, predestination, justification and glory.†

Sermon 14.5–9

THE BRIDE'S LOVE FOR JESUS, AND FOR THE HEAVENLY CHURCH

ONE IS MY DOVE, ONE IS MY PERFECT ONE.[†]   Sg 6:8

WHO IS IT who ranks before all of the others? Surely the Spouse does not *run aimlessly or box like a man beating the ai*r,[†] so as to praise and extol so emphatically somebody who is nowhere to be found. No, no, unthinkable! She is there right enough, though hidden from us, she is there for the holy angels, she is there for her Beloved! Although there are few of her, compared with the number of queens and concubines, there is not just one of her, but several, and this we tenderly believe and hope with all our heart. Why should we, from our nothingness, limit the hand of the Most High? The Spouse asserts that she is 'one',[†] but not that she is alone.   1 Cor 9:26

          Sg 6:8

One is my dove, one is my perfect one.[†] She is the one who loves Jesus perfectly because she concentrates her whole occupation, her whole thought, her whole concern uniquely on her Beloved. This is not for her something optional, it is *the one thing necessary.*[†] At the very beginning, when love was just taking root, it was to some extent no more than an option, but persistent desire and repeated experiential knowledge has made it a necessity. For this reason Jesus absolved Mary from her sister's complaint.[†]   Sg 6:8

          Lk 10:42

          Lk 10:41

Yes, blessed above all women is she[†] who considers that she knows nothing except Christ Jesus,[†] and does one thing only: she forgets what   Cf. Lk 1:42

          1 Cor 2:2

Cf. Ph 3:13

is behind and stretches herself always to what lies ahead.[†] For, whatever is behind, however little it was, she recalls having sensed about Jesus, and so she pours out to him, from the depths of her heart, sighs like those of a dove, because of her imperfect love.

She sighs, because she has not yet come to a pure love for her Spouse, so uniquely lovable, so completely desirable. She sighs over his absence, sighs too over his presence. When he is absent, her sighing is not hidden from him.[†] Indeed, so little is it hidden that, from the depths of his sanctuary, from his resting place in the Father's bosom, she impetuously draws him down to her. But it is not importunity that wins the victory; it is love. Love is not importunate, though it is impetuous; it exerts a stronger pressure than importunity does, though more gently. It uses a gentle force, it draws sweetly, it exerts a pleasing pressure.

Cf. Ps 38:10

On the other hand, when her Spouse is present, she sighs no less, but sighs more sweetly. Obviously, she earnestly begs him to stay with her. She urges him to reveal to her the *marvels of his law;*[†] she questions him about the glory of his kingdom; she entreats him to let his face shine more brightly. While he is still with her, she anticipates his departure by asking him to visit her again without delay.

Ps 19:18

So wherever she looks, she has reason for sighing. She mourns with the weak, she is on fire with those who are made to fall,[†] she clothes herself in the feelings common to all humankind and enters into their experience, not considering what is her own but what is theirs.[†] This is her

2 Cor 11:29

Phil 2:4

true perfection: to know and sigh over her own imperfection, to sigh with those who sigh and to feel grief on behalf of those who do not sigh.† Rom 12:15

The only one of her mother.† I think that in Sg 6:8 these words the Spouse is specially indicating the love with which the bride is on fire for the heavenly Jerusalem which is her mother, and the mother of us all.† Yes, she loves her as a Gal 4:26 daughter loves her mother, as a nursling loves her nurse. She never forgets that she was formed in her womb and suckled on her milk. She feels grateful to her, because through her instruction she was taught the reliance of the faith, through her saving teaching she came to understand the right way to live, through the example of her love, she learned to love her Beloved, and through her merits and prayers she expects one day to see him fully. She knows that he alone exists who is eternally and change-lessly existent, and every rational soul only truly begins to exist when it starts to cleave, through love, to him who truly is of himself. So 'to be' really means 'to love', and that is why the apostle Jesus loved tells us, *He who does not love, abides in death.*† So the bride is to Jesus whatever she is 1 Jn 3:14 to the mother she reveres, she belongs more completely to them both as she is shared by them both.

Who can describe the maternal love of this mother for this daughter? Who can speak of the tender piety and love in her maternal breast, the love with which she yearns for her daughter, the gentleness with which she opens her bosom to her, inclines her ear, spreads her arms wide? Who is great enough to ponder the eager love

for her daughter's interests, running now to the
Father of the Word, now to the Word of the
Father, now to the loving Spirit of them both?
For her daughter's sake, her hands are ever ex-
tended, stretched out on high to the holy and
undivided Trinity. So the daughter has the same
special place in her mother's affections as she
has in the affections of her Spouse. That mother
takes her opinion from what she hears, forming
it from the expression of her heavenly Spouse
and taking the rule and measure of her love
from his eternal decrees. May her loving prayers
gain for us also the compassion of the Spouse,
the Father's Only Son.

Sermon 55.9–14

VII

THE GARDEN OF THE SOUL

AN OVERVIEW:
THE EXPERIENCE OF PRAYER

THE QUALITY OF CISTERCIAN life at the end of the twelfth century remained an impressive witness to the continuing sanctity of the monks. It is sometimes said that the 'golden age' was over. That is not the impression given by John of Forde, who was a first-hand observer of the monks who lived with him. Their undeniable holiness rested squarely on their whole-hearted commitment to prayer. He sees them in the early morning, after the night office, making their way to the altars in the church and kneeling there in private prayer with rapt devotion. They are distinguished, he says, by the 'austerity of life, their austerity of garb, the dignity of their silence, attendance at Vigils, their penance of self-control, and other such manifestations of holy service'.[1]

Pure prayer may be a gift, but it is a gift to be nourished and nurtured by the sincerity of one's life. Prayer is like a garden, if you will; it needs constant attention. *My beloved,* sings the Song, *has gone down into his garden.*[2] If you desire Jesus to visit your soul in time of prayer, you must surround yourself with the hedge of self-control, put a guard on the things you look at, keep your tongue from careless chatter, and be sparing in food, drink, and sleep. If the soil has been neglected, you will have hard work ahead: pulling up the weeds of evil inclinations, digging up roots with frequent compunction, planting the seeds of meekness and humility.

[1] Sermon 45.9
[2] Sg 6:1

You do not bring dung into the house, John says with a smile and a wrinkled nose, for it is not appropriate to do so. But the garden needs the dung of humble confession. This is the smelly compost that Jesus likes to see in his garden. Eventually, when the work is complete and the seeds grow and flourish, the garden becomes a place of flowers and herbs where the Lord can walk. 'This garden, when rich with blossoming herbs, breathing out the love of Jesus alone, is strongly scented enough even to draw him by the power of her fragrance, out of the Father's bosom.'[3]

Prayer that is sincere, loving, and continuous should inevitably result in harmony in the community. There will be the Christ-filled peace of brotherly union, a zeal for holiness that shows itself in pleasing gentleness, the kind of smile that indicates true humility. These signs of true prayer can be insidiously contradicted, however, by envy, tale-bearing, detraction, or bursts of anger—which John admits with regret that he has observed in some of the monks of his own community. To monks who have become steeped in this kind of behavior, the poison of slander begins to taste sweet. John comments, 'Our God is not a God of dissension, but a God of peace and love'.[4]

Some of the monks at Forde during John's abbacy had entered more deeply into prayer. For them prayer had had a transforming influence on their lives. Prayer had become for them a purifying way of life. Talking with them as their abbot, John had found Jesus was a fire within them that melted evil and united them totally with God. They could truly say with Saint Paul, *It is no longer I that live, but Christ lives in me.*[5] 'With the girdle of eager love and the cord of unbreakable peace, the fire in them united God to their soul and their soul to God'.[6]

If we ask what John means by this fire within them, we find at least something of the answer in their daily meditation. The

---

[3] Sermon 44.6
[4] 2 Cor 3:11
[5] Gal 2:20
[6] Sermon 7.6

words of the Gospel were constantly in their minds. The words
and works of the Lord Jesus filled their minds with sweetness.
Often while they meditated some spark of love and understanding would light up within them and they would feel the fire of
enlightenment. This must surely have happened frequently during the gospel readings at Mass and at Vigils, say, on Sundays.

John's own personal experience of prayer should reassure us.
He talks of it as 'a visit of the Lord'. 'I would ask you to listen patiently to what usually happens here within me, and I am sure in
much the same way within most of you'.[7] He begins his self-
revelation with the experience of 'the fear of the Lord', that is, a
sense of reverence due to the awareness of God's presence within
him. This is the beginning of the search for wisdom that is at the
heart of much of the writing at this period. John examines his
own conscience and finds there many dark corners he would pre-
fer to hide. But he cannot hide. It is as if the angels are standing
in front of him shining 'the light of Christ' into those dark places
and bringing them out into the full daylight. His own conscience
condemns him. He becomes aware that his sins, his evil
thoughts and desires—the things he has done and the things he
has failed to do—are rising up against him in the presence of
God and his angels. 'My Lord,' he says, 'unrolls the story of my
deeds, my thoughts, my desires and motives. He spares me nothing, and it is better so'.[8]

Tears of compunction are the result of this examination. He
is only too aware of the folly of his pride. There is no excuse. Yet
in his dejection he finds this consolation: he is reminded that the
cross of Christ is present and acting as a mediator on his behalf.
By faith he recalls that Christ died to give us life, and that the
grace of Christ's passion and death are always there to turn
God's wrath away from him.

As his prayer deepened another phase presented itself. After
tears and sorrow for sin follows the serenity of early morning: 'I

[7] Sermon 43.1
[8] Sermon 43.1

breathe again in the hope of forgiveness'. The heavy negative
feelings of guilt are replaced by an uplifting positive awareness of
peace and joy. He now feels himself borne upwards into the glorious presence of Christ's throne of love and loving kindness.
'From this throne I feel the Lord visiting me all the more often
as he realizes I need visitations of this kind more frequently.'[9]

The person at prayer does not necessarily swing between
feelings of desolation and joy. More often than not prayer remains on the stable level of pure faith where feelings play little
part. Perhaps this is what John means when he comments a little
anxiously: 'A cloud, not of light but of darkness has taken him
away from my eyes'.[10] It is a comment that anticipates the 'Cloud
of Unknowing' and the well-known Dark Night of Saint John of
the Cross. To some extent we should be prepared to remain
within this shadow until the light of eternity shines upon us.
What is this shadow? 'I think it is the protection, the cool, the
concealment with which he graciously overshadows that soul
that loves him, hiding her within the secret of his face'.[11] This
time of shadow is, for John of Forde, something actually desirable, because Christ's absence has a healing influence on us, his
delay gives us the opportunity of growing in patience.

Furthermore, when you are well prepared and when God
chooses to do so, he may raise you to a higher perception so that
you may merit to hear hidden words from him.[12] John treats this
experience with caution and circumspection. The impression he
gives is that, on the one hand, there are times of pure delight in
the Lord's presence, moments when a person can lose himself
completely. Probably he had some experience of this himself.
Listen to his own words:

> What am I when I am enjoying this invisible light? I
> have fled all transient things; I have melted mar-

---

[9] Sermon 43.4
[10] Acts 1:9
[11] Sermon 37.7
[12] Sermon 45.5

velously into my Spouse and my Source; I am sealed
again with the matrix from which my likeness came.
To sense his closeness, yes, this I can do; to speak of
it, impossible. Cleaving to my beloved I am oned
with him, conformed to him, absorbed into him so
that I have become one spirit with him'.[13]

Yet, on the other hand, even if he himself has been given such an
experience, he warns his monks against feelings of pride. There
is no point in welcoming Jesus into this garden of ours to admire
the flowers, if the place is still rotten with weeds of pride, malice,
frivolous talk.

This is not, of course, a problem for the person who is gen-
uinely seeking wisdom. The authenticity of the experience of
God can be assessed only by its fruits. If it truly has a divine origin, it will show itself principally in the twin fruits of reverence
and love. Reverential wonder shows itself when a person takes
care to avoid offending someone she admires deeply. There is a
high note of reverence that reaches the summit of wisdom which
becomes the target for all our efforts. John calls this experience
of God 'a visit'. A person who has been 'visited' like this is bound
to become more humble, more alert to shortcomings within herself, more compassionate towards others. Although John has a
great deal to say about 'reverential fear', his thought is always directed to the growth in love that is the chief fruit of this 'visit'.[14]
One of its primary characteristics is that the person becomes
more serene both in her inward disposition yet also visibly in her
outward conduct. John goes on to affirm that it 'adorns not only
the person's interior attitude but also her exterior deportment
with the reverence of gracious serenity'.[15]

The Jesus Prayer that was and is so popular among members
of the Greek Orthodox Churches was not as yet known in the

[13] Sermon 46.8
[14] Sermon 46.5
[15] Sermon 44.6

West in the twelfth century. This form of prayer is found as early as Saint John Climacus, who wrote in an often-cited passage, 'Let the remembrance of Jesus be present with each breath, and then you will know the value of *hesychia*', i.e. the silence of God.[16] Saint Aelred, the abbot of Rievaulx while John was still a child, advised his sister to pray frequently and to throw herself repeatedly at Jesus' feet by repeating his name very often with tears of compunction. You often find the lovely prayer, 'O sweet Lord' in his writings, and no doubt it was often on his lips during prayer. This prayer does not occur in John's writings, though he often uses a similar prayer 'O Lord God' very frequently (namely, forty-four times). The prayer that seems to be his particular favorite is 'O Lord Jesus' which occurs at least forty-six times in his sermons, and we may reasonably suppose that it was the usual short prayer he repeated during his times of prayerful quietness and at other times during the day. Another favorite prayer among the early Cistercians was 'O Good Jesus', but I have found it only six times in John's writings.

In John's thought, a person who has progressed so far as to become 'a bride of the Word' (to use his own chosen phrase) finds that a new type of serenity pervades her life. He sums this up in a fine passage in Sermon Twenty-eight:

> Ezekiel saw God's throne looking like a sapphire. Now the sapphire has the appearance of a serene heaven, and this signifies the serenity of mind possessed by those who contemplate the face of glory without ceasing and without ever becoming satiated with it'.[17]

It is here that prayer and wisdom and love fuse into a unity.

---

[16] John Climacus, The Ladder of Divine Ascent; Step 27:61
[17] Sermon 28.7

THE GARDEN OF THE LORD:
THE SOUL WHO LOVES GOD

THE LORD has called his bride by a whole array of titles: sister, friend, bride, dove, lovely one, and so on. Yet whoever is honored like this, may she never be tempted to the presumption of thinking herself better than others.

Be very careful, then, you who love Jesus or want to love him—oh, be very careful—to avoid the folly of thinking more highly of yourself than of others who share this same favor! Be certain that you will be put to the question about this. Take care, lest wickedness deceive itself, for he who questions you *is not mocked*.† If you want to progress in love, if you are concerned not to be lacking in it, your endeavor must never be to be lifted up about anything in yourself, but always to marvel at what is in other people. Put the kindest construction on others' charity, and keep close check on your own.

Gal 6:7

The bride explains that Jesus has gone down into his 'garden' i.e. to console with the gift of his presence any soul who embraces Jesus with a love like her own. She is right to call this soul 'a garden', because it is bordered with a hedge carefully enclosing it, fragrant with spices and springlike with flowers, all making it fit for the delights of love.

However much a garden-soul may be distinguished by grace, Jesus does not visit it often if the hedge of self-control is lacking, if a watchful guard over all the senses has not made a moat around it, if it is not sparing of speech and mortified in food and drink and sleep. It must take every precaution to safeguard the thoughts and desires of its heart, for from the heart *life proceeds.*†

Prv 4:23

So the bride looks round everywhere, searching for souls like this, on fire with the love of Jesus. She searches for them graciously and often, and this brings her to what she is looking for. She finds this treasure and then displays it to those who share the same grace as herself, saying, *My Beloved has gone down into his garden.*† She rejoices in this new bride of his. She brings to our attention whatever she may have heard about her, she breaks into praise spontaneously, under the inspiration of the Spirit of loving-kindness.

Sg 6:1

A CAREFUL SENSE OF RESPONSIBILITY. First, she praises a careful sense of responsibility, speaking of it as a garden,; then she recommends hard-work, modesty, and sweetness, an aromatic bed of herbs.

HARD WORK. First this plot is rank with the useless weeds of evil inclinations, growing spontaneously from our earth's wild abundance. So the bed must be thoroughly cleared with the spade of assiduous self-reproach and the hard labour of frequent compunction. The weeds must be rooted up with much sweat of the brow. Then, the soil must be well manured to make it fertile, and the Lord's bride must not think it beneath her to do this kind of servile work,† because her mind should be set on making his garden-beds fruitful. So she must strive, day and night, to be meek, through the exercise of humility.

Ps 81:6

HUMBLE CONFESSION. So we find that dung, which would offend the eyes of the Beloved if it were inside the house or court, has only to be spread on the seedbed to bring credit to the bride's industry and zeal. When we keep hidden within us all the filth of our dispositions, they grow fetid and disgusting, but let us once bring them to the light through humble confession and they are a fine preparation for a rich and fruitful harvest. In a wonderful way, the bride makes her evil into a source of pleasantness by putting her sins to good use. Through her constant application to hard work, her garden becomes well disposed for a harvest of holy seeds.

MODESTY. This garden—that is, the soul— marked out evenly on all sides, reveals the virtue of self-restraint, which is the outstanding beauty of any soul that loves God. Not only the interior of a person, but even her exterior bearing is adorned by a reverence that comes from gracious serenity. The grace of modesty is the uniform partition of the garden-soul whichever way one looks. It is not puffed up by success, it is not overwhelmed by adversity. It derives no happiness from applause, it does not wither when insulted. It is not aflame with impatience, nor does it give way to wantonness. It combines the scent of all the virtues into the one aroma of its breath.

No wonder the Lord goes gladly to see a garden like this, especially when all round its borders run humility's rampart and the mighty hedge of self-control. Nothing unclean enters

Rv 21:27

here.† Even if the tempter did creep in, he would find a strong woman who has girded her

Prv 31:17

loins with strength.† This garden, rich with blossoming herbs, breathing out the love of Jesus alone, is strong enough even to draw him by the great strength of her fragrance, out of the Father's bosom! The Lord, her Beloved, has gone down into his garden, which is the bride, to visit and admire close at hand those beds of love from which, far away in heaven, the scent had reached him. He has been aroused and he has woken, he has been drawn and he has come down; he has been forced, and he is here.

Sermon 44.1–6

WORK IN THE GARDEN

THE GARDEN. Is there anything in the garden which is not his? It was Jesus who dug it round, he who hedged it in, he who took a hoe to it, he who sowed and he who planted it, he who gave it the dew of his blessing, it was he

who made it grow.† He has seen to it that every-   1 Cor 3:6
thing it needs for its cultivation has its time and
method.

In all the work done in this garden, what
part is mine? I realize that my part is to consent
to what, of his own accord, he is doing; a willing
consent, but that very will is of his giving, his
guiding and keeping. Of myself I am doing
nothing because to be perfectly truthful I am
nothing.† He first dug round me, raising a bar-   1 Cor 13:2
ricade of spontaneous humility. He built a
hedge, enclosing me with pure reverence for
God, and a delicate chastity. He worked on me,
rooting up the depths of my heart and frequently turning over the buried secrets of my
soil. He used all that was shameful in me to en-
rich my dead clay and make it alive. He sowed
and planted graciously, inspiring me with holy
and fruitful thoughts. He provided the dew and
showers that the seasons demanded, frequently
bestowing on me the comfort of his holy presence. Finally, he brought all these things to their
conclusion, he gave the growth, and from the
growth the fruit. So that his grace may not
come to nothing in me, he never ceased to work
in me not only the desire and the ability, but
also the accomplishment of all these things, ever
ripening with his breath what he originally in-
spired. So the work of this garden, all of it and
every single part of it, is his, and so is the glory
of all this work.

MY LITTLE GARDEN AND GREAT GARDENS. For
what is this garden of mine, compared to those
great plantations of so many different spices in

paradise, that sublime place where Paul was privileged to hear mysterious secrets?† From that day on, that great contemplative broadened out his garden, to make it truly a paradise in which the Lord could deeply delight, a sanctuary in which those unutterable words he had heard would be enshrined. These words, which were not lawful for man to utter, were lawful for him to say to himself, were lawful for him to say to God, were lawful for him to hear, though he might not speak them.† Indeed, I think nothing in paradise is more unutterable than the words describing the inner love of God. We may take them on our lips. But only the Spouse can utter them. Love is so wholly unutterable that no-one can even describe it or know what it is, because of all the mysteries concealed within the Son, this is the greatest and deepest in paradise.

Paul once heard similar words, when first *the love of God was poured out* into his heart through the Holy Spirit who had been given to him.† But when he went to the very altar of the Lord of hosts,† he drew more fully into himself the fire of Christ's love from the furnace which is in Jerusalem. And he could come back to us with exultation, and cry, *Who can separate us from the love of Christ?*†

See, brothers, the abundance and luxuriance of that foliage so much admired by seculars: the austerity of life, austerity of garb, the dignity of silence, the vigils, the penance of self-control, and any other such things of holy service. But if these things are not enriched by a love of Christ in the heart, are they any more than the showy leaves of the fig tree?†

2 Cor 12:4

2 Cor 12:4

Rom 5:5

Ps 84:3

Rom 8:35

Mk 11:13

So, my brothers, remember that he come*s to pasture in the gardens,*† he looks to find fruit. It is fruit he looks for, not leaves. I mean the fruit of love which makes us love the living fountain which is himself, and love ourselves too within that fountain. Maybe the love of Jesus has not yet shone as brightly as it should in the hearts of some of us.

Sg 6:1

Sermon 45.1-9

FRUIT IN THE GARDEN

BUT WHAT ABOUT the love of eternal life, the peace of brotherly union, a zeal for holiness that is also gentle piety, a smile of humility and a holy meekness? These are the fruits of love. These are fruits, not just leaves.

On the other hand, anger, tale-bearing, envy, detraction—such as there are in some of you, and it grieves me to have to say so†—these things mean the destruction, not only of the fruit, but of the leaves as well. The dryness of heart that follows deliberately turns its ears away from the truth. But it turns itching ears and insolent tongue-wagging only in the direction of idle tales, scurrilous jests, and detractions.† A throat like this is a wide open grave† to which poisonous slanders taste like the sweetest foods. When people like this come together in unity,†

2 Tim 4:4

RB 43 and 65
Ps 5:10

1 Cor 11:20

it is to a very bloody and cruel banquet. They share a meal of their brothers' and fathers' flesh and mutually join in burying this flesh in the grave of their gullet.

My brothers, turn away from food like this; turn away with a shudder of revulsion and set yourselves to oppose it. Our God is not a God of dissension, but a God of peace and love.†

2 Cor 13:11

The Beloved is *pasturing in the gardens and gathering lilies*† when brotherly love is fragrant with holiness. This community breathes out a shared sweetness of the Holy Spirit. The Spouse assimilates them to himself—their head—, each one individually sharing in his Spirit; and by the union of holy love he makes them all one body.† The lilies may also be regarded as the radiant whiteness of chastity. The Spouse is in haste to gather this kind of lily in his gardens because without doubt there is someone who will *scatter them*.† It is a rare man who does not occasionally happen to be invaded and maltreated by the touch of sinfulness.† This is the reason for our daily sighs, this is why our eyes so frequently fill with tears, why a painful blush mantles our cheeks, because all too often the serenity of our pure whiteness, which is consecrated to our heavenly Spouse, has been dishonored by the grime of carnal thoughts and desires.

Sg 6:1

Rom 12:5

Lk 11:23

Ps 71:3

We must do our best, by the unspeakable power of loving tears, to restore to its first radiance whatever in these lilies has been withered by neglect. This may seem impossible to human power—to make battered lilies whole again—but it is not impossible for the Word of God, who is our Spouse. Not only can he gather lilies that have been scattered, but he can even make new again lilies that have been completely ruined.

O Lord my God, it is in your power, not only to gather what is scattered, but even to gather more than was originally lost. It is in your power to restore the fallen lilies, not just to a snowy whiteness, but to make them even whiter than snow. It is in your power, not only to give pardon to stains because of the virtue of repentance, but even to give those virtues the palm of victory. All this is in your power, you who live and reign with God the Father and the Holy Spirit, God, for ever and ever.

Sermon 45.7–9

ZEAL FOR PRAYER AND JUSTICE

YOUR TEETH ARE A FLOCK OF SHEEP.[†]   Sg 6:5

THE BRIDE'S ZEAL for justice may be compared to teeth. In the beatitudes, after compunction of tears, Christ extends the blessing to those who *hunger and thirst after justice.*[†] He is   Mt 5:6
setting the degrees and paths of his blessing in a regular series, so that they may go in an orderly progression *from strength to strength,*[†] moving   Ps 84:7
from grief of loving devotion to an eagerness for virtue. That is the zeal of teeth. Christ praises the zeal of his Beloved, and the *hunger and thirst*

with which she incessantly craves to achieve true perfection. Saint Paul too mentions seven fruits: carefulness, eagerness, indignation, fear, longing, zeal, revenge.† The zeal mentioned here is at its sharpest like the zeal of teeth.

2 Cor 7:11

Her zeal is also seen in her distaste for worldly anxieties. She thinks everything common and sour if it does not have, for her, the taste of the savor of heaven or her Beloved's love. She is zealous for the better gifts, especially for the best and most precious gift of all, which is love.† This is what she eats, this is what she hungers for every hour. She hungers for it even while she eats it, and when she has eaten, her hunger is still with her.† She thinks of all the gifts that have been given to her, how his beauty has been graciously bestowed on her. She finds no respite short of the full vision of her Beloved. The zeal of others also gives her the sharpest of spurs for her own zeal.

1 Cor 13:13

Sir 24:29

But that zeal is full of meekness and obedience. She has chosen the path of love. She is humble: her eagerness for a high place at the wedding feast makes her zealous in choosing the lowest.† She is gentle with all, and strives to be more humble than others in all she does. She wants to be like the rest of the flock. The soul that loves Jesus is very zealous for humility. But a burden has been laid upon her: the charge of other souls; and this means inescapable anxiety. She has become humbler, gentler, more prudent, more reverent, more fervent in love for her brothers and love for her Spouse: these are her 'teeth'.

Cf. Mt 22, Lk 14:10

You, too, my brothers, do you not learn from daily experience? I see with great joy how you rival one another in going up to the altar, *the sea of brass.*† Without delay, you hasten to the altar, and there you sacrifice your whole selves to the Lord your God.[1] This prayer of yours ascends to heaven, like incense.† This incense is kept safe by an angel who is there.† Wash your hands so that your prayer may spring up with greater purity and freedom. Be immersed frequently in the cleansing water of confession. At every washing there is a renewal of the noble image of God in you, sealed and signed. The two effects of this washing are cleanliness of righteousness, and zeal for virtue, i.e. purity and eagerness.

This washing is the confession of our sins to one another, and the daily confession of them to God. For the bride this means her gentle and humble sentiments. Mary Magdalene was washed by the forgiveness she received from the Lord. It has the power of forming us into a new creature. The bride takes care that her teeth are hungry for charity and fervent love. This is why she has the keenness of zeal and the gentleness of humility.

But I proclaim that our profession is humility; our outward behavior, our habit, our mutual encounter, our readiness to obey, all the marks of humility are like flocks of sheep. This must come from a desire for inward humility, that humility of heart taught by the Lamb of God. The

1 Chr 18:8

Ps 141:2

Rev 8:2

---

[1] John is likely thinking of the monks' zeal in prayer before the altar, no doubt having seen them often in the monastic church, fervent in prayer and devotion.

bride is anxious and careful about these things. She watches anxiously over her flock lest the Spouse should come and find her barren. She is rich with the fruit of charity and humility which give eternal pleasure to her Spouse.

Sermon 51.1–10

THE FRUIT OF CHASTITY AND THE VALLEY OF HUMILITY

THERE IS GOOD REASON for this holy and gentle soul to suspect that she has heard in the approval of the daughters of Zion a peal of thunder or else a trumpet blast. She regards these praises as if they are artful snares, and looks at their admiration with suspicion as if it were hidden espionage.

Sg 6:10

At any rate, she goes down to her orchard of almonds,[†] certainly examining every corner of it with vigilant scrutiny. She makes a scrutiny of her personal chastity. She knows well how passionately her Beloved values this virtue, for it was his choice to flower in and from the shoot of an almond-tree, Mary, that fairest and straight-

Is 11:1

est shoot that grew from Jesse's root.[†] The bride too is eager for this flower, in order that the flower of a chaste heart, the Lord Jesus, may blossom in her and from her. But she is always conscious, in her contented and humble examination, that she has been wedded to him in a manner completely different from that of the Virgin, so uniquely and pre-eminently chaste, who was taken up at the incarnation of God's Word by an incommunicable privilege.

Then she lifts up her eyes to all that blossoms in this garden: I am referring to the glorious modesty of the saints. Some of them were sanctified in their mother's womb,[†] guarding with the most delicate watchfulness the privilege that has been bestowed of them. Others were washed all over when they rose up from the waters of baptism,[†] and by the grace of the same Spirit that brought them back to life, they have kept intact the purity of that holy washing, given to them from heaven. She marvels at the sweetness of flowers like this that grow in the orchard, and at the fertility of the almonds and the towering gracefulness and straightness of the shoots.

Prominent among them are those who have risen up to the marriage bond, through the force of a resolute intention. They have declared war on their own passions, striving to overcome the frailty of their being human. They have girded themselves with weapons well suited to this kind of warfare: scarceness of food and drink; poor clothing; perseverance in watching, working and praying, and all the other exercises of a dedicated life, with which they labor to bring about in themselves the refinement of a winning gracefulness of behavior.

This gracefulness of his bride is so pleasing to the heavenly bridegroom that he delights to

Lk 1:15

Sg 6:6

hear her praises being sung. There is nothing in these holy souls, whether in their walk or appearance, their speech, or their actions, that is either suggestive or deceptive. Their only desire is to give pleasure to the One they seek to marry spiritually, and to be like rods of righteousness[†] in the hand of their God.[†]

When the bride ponders over the great orchard of her Spouse, she runs back to her own little garden and sees with shame and sorrow what she is lacking. Though she grieves at seeing her own defects, she rejoices in the progress of others since she is the Lord's bride, and love knows nothing of envy.[†] All the same she is careful to keep hold of just as much humiliation as is necessary to arm her conscience against any presumption that should suddenly assail her ears. Even if she is the bride she still has something to be ashamed of. She is no better than her fathers[†] who humbly admitted to having been given 'a sting of the flesh'[†] so that they might not take pride in the greatness of their spiritual favors.

O daughters of Jerusalem, when I consider the fruits of the valley, by which I mean the delicious produce of humility, borne by so many different trees in the orchard of my Spouse, and then turn to the produce of my own fruits, what heart do you think is left to me? I measure myself against those who have given posterity an everlasting memorial of their obedience and humility and respect for God, who have left to their heirs the clear imprint of their virtues. Humble in the sublimity of their virtues, sublime in the excellence of their humility; com-

Ps 45:6
Is 62:3

1 Cor 13:4

1 K 19:4
2 Cor 12:7

pared with these, my humility deserves no
praise at all. Much of my good health is due to
them, seeing it is the sweet scent of the obedience and humility of my Lord and Spouse that I
breathe into my nostrils.[†] They spur me on to
love, making me vividly aware, through their
perfume, their taste, their beauty, of the presence of my Beloved.

Job 27:3

These are the fruits of a true and holy valley,
the humility of the Most High God. It is truly a
valley, a valley pleasant and fertile, a green valley
brimming with light. It is not just a vale, but a
real valley, clearly a place made for friendly
companionship, for harmony, for sympathy.
Coming down from the shaded mountain of his
majesty, that majesty should himself become
like a valley to this vale of ours, by suffering our
pains and sympathizing with us, by giving us all
that is his, and accepting in return, all that is
ours. So, if there is any humility, obedience or
submission that does not have the taste of that
heavenly humility—i.e. does not derive its form
and motive from that source as from its own
true root—then the bride can only regard it as
fruit growing wild. The bride never rests, day
and night, from lifting up her heart in love to
her Spouse, at one time wondering at his eternal
wisdom and holiness and all the other *glory that
is his, as the only Son of the Father*;[†] and then
again glorifying the goodness, patience, and humility that made him stoop to being born of his
virgin Mother.

Jn 1:14

Sermon 61.3–8A

THIS BRIDE: ONLY A BEGINNER

I WENT DOWN TO SEE WHETHER THE VINES HAD BUDDED.†

AFTER EXAMINING HER FRUIT, the bride turns her eyes to looking at her vines, anxious to discover whether they have yet budded. Here we have a symbol of the practice of two kinds of charity. The bride never rests, day or night, from lifting up her heart in love to her Spouse, at one time wondering at his eternal wisdom and holiness and all the other *glory that is his, as the only Son of the Father,*† and then again glorifying the goodness, patience and humility that made him stoop to being born of his Virgin Mother. The bride concentrates carefully on these two kinds of vine, both of noble stock, devoting herself wholly to this task. She is confident that she will rejoice her Spouse's heart with their produce, and she hopes this will make him ready to grant her these wedding joys.

What does the bride mean when she wants to see whether the vines have budded? Her humility and her fervor appear in all their magnificence because she looks upon herself as a lover who has only just begun to love. By the 'budding vines' she means the tender, winsome beginnings of love. They show themselves when the words and works of the Lord Jesus fill the meditating mind with sweetness, when the bride's mouth parts with longing to draw in the Breath of God,† when her heart swells with sighs of love. It is then that everything that bears on the love of Christ is sought after eagerly, read about with relish, listened to joyfully, related with feelings of delight.

She turns her thoughts towards the charity of her forefathers, which was as fruitful as it was generous, and enabled them to say: *The love of God has been poured into our hearts, through the Holy Spirit who has been given to us.*† At that time, the love which was in Christ Jesus,† overwhelmed sin, and to her it seems that her own love has as yet borne no fruit.

Rom 5:5

Eph 3:19

The bride has every reason to call her vineyard sterile when she compares it to the richness of the vineyards which Christ makes blossom with eternal fruitfulness in the land he has promised us.† Even if she sees something growing on her vines, she will wonder whether it is really a flower with its promise of fruit, rather than foliage. Here we see her motherly solicitude, for she cherishes many children as if they were many seeds united within one body, as in the pomegranate.

Mt 5:5

She doubts whether her solicitude has yet begun to blossom. She hears a definite form and amount† of brotherly love laid down for her in the Law of her God. The form is: that as Christ loved her, so she must love her brothers.† The amount is: that she should give up all that she has, most freely,† and then give up her very self for her brother's salvation.† The form is: to watch sleeplessly over the safety of the souls whom Christ redeemed; the amount is: for their sake with Christ to lay down one's own soul.†

Eph 5:2

1 Jn 3:14

2 Cor 12:15

Rom 9:5

Jn 15:13

Sg 6:12
GOD'S CHARIOTS. The chariots of Aminadab†
stand for the whole of God's judgements. Round-
ness stands for his justice, their flying speed
for his wisdom, their power for his dauntless
strength, and their balanced proportions for his
impartiality. It is on these four 'wheels' that divine judgement rolls forward. They are terrifying to behold, as well as to hear. *The sound of*
Ps 77:18
God thunders in the wheel.† What normal person, pondering over the depths of God's judge-
Rom 11:33
ments,† would not tremble at the sight of them?

The daughters exult in the special graces
given to the bride, but she thinks always of the
depths of God's judgements. She sets herself to
be ready in advance with an imperviousness to
everything and everybody who praises and glo-
rifies her, so that she may be all the more pleasing to her Beloved, the less influenced she is by
human renown. She offers her spiritual life to
be judged by him alone to whom the Father has
Jn 5:22
rightly given all judgement,† who with the
Father and the Holy Spirit lives and reigns for
ever and ever.

Sermon 61.9–12

JOHN'S OWN EXPERIENCE
OF GOD'S PRESENCE AND ABSENCE

RATHER SHYLY and hesitatingly I am coming forward to pay the promise I made you yes-

terday. I am too well aware of how limited my ability is in this matter, and I should have thought it better to keep silence and conceal my lack of knowledge† rather than unveil it by my rash loquacity.

Sir 20:33

You are waiting to hear how the bride is enabled to detect where the Beloved has come from, and where, when he departs, he is going. I would ask you to listen patiently to what usually happens here within me, and, I am sure, in much the same way within most of you. I would not dare to claim any special experience in these matters superior to your own. I am quite certain that *there are some standing here*† who have been marvellously blessed by the Lord with the dew of heaven.

Mt 16:28

I shall begin in the spirit of fear, the beginning of wisdom†—that is, of love. Sometimes it is in this spirit that my Lord desires to visit me, and then he *bows the heavens* and comes down.† He sets up *his throne in judgement*,† and commands me to be brought before that dread tribunal where his angels stand on either side. He sets squarely before me my conscience, which I had thrust behind my back,† and he unrolls the story of my deeds, my thoughts, my desires, and motives. He spares me nothing. And it is better so. He touches my soul with effectual power; and with tears of compunction, the insane pride that has defied him melts away into smoke. While this lasts and I stand before so great a Judge, what spirit could be left in me, were I not able to bring the cross of Christ forward as my mediator, to claim his blood as my Redeemer? I can call on my behalf the price he paid when he

Prv 9:10

Ps 18:9
Ps 9:7

Is 38:17

died to give us life, to prevent him entering into judgement with his servant *in case he reduces me to nothing.*[†]

Ps 143:2

By God's mercy this cloud filling the whole of a man's soul should break into tears, and flashes of lightning lead on to rain [of tears], and then after a little while are followed by the serenity of early morning. I breathe again in the hope of forgiveness. For me justice is being changed into mercy, wrath into grace. With joy I call to mind that this is your throne from which you judge your poor in integrity[†]. All I read of this throne leads me to see it as *established in merciful love.*[†]

Is 11:4

Is 16:5

From this throne, I feel my Lord visits me all the more often as he realizes I need visitations of this kind more frequently. If between these visitations, anyone asks me, still numb from the feelings of devotion experienced a few days past, and complaining of my Lord's delay, where he has gone or turned aside, the only answer I can find is, *he has made darkness his hiding place.*[†] A cloud, not of light but of darkness, has taken him from my eyes,[†] and now that my love has grown so cold again, I feel I have good reason to fear that perhaps, after all, he has turned away from his servant in anger.[†] Finally I recall that he has returned to the judgement seat so as to visit me again from the same place.

Ps 18:11

Acts 1:9

Ps 27:10

But there are times when my Lord also comes to me to tell me more joyful things than, I for my own part, had expected or even hoped for. He tells me of the bliss of his incarnation, the love of his passion, the many ways in which he there abased himself to reveal his humility and meekness. When I ponder this well, chewing it over with an indescribable sensation of sweetness, I think to myself, 'He has called me to the marriage feast.† This thought makes everything a delight, everything a glory. All things become fragrant, and each single one of them has a delicate flavour. Yet, in all my happiness at being invited to the marriage feast, I do not forget what my Lord taught us. I take care not to choose for myself too exalted a position, fearing to make a blunder in the eyes of my host.† I have chosen to be abject,† to be the very last within the marriage hall, rather than to go outside even to the greatest of feasts.

As far as I am concerned, this solemn celebration of the marriage feast comes very rarely, and even then, it is over in a brief minute. I am forced to return to my own poor cottage, while the Spouse, as is right, ceremoniously keeps the solemnity all day with his friends and companions. I am desolate, lovingly turning over in my mind the crumbs and fragments that are left over from the marriage feast, and even those within a very little time vanish from my mind. At this point, if anyone were to ask me, all bereft of grace as I am, where my Lord has gone, I shall reply that he has departed to the place he came from, into his bridal chamber.† It is to there that he directs and invites my zeal and my love, and it is to there, where he so recently honoured me by showing himself, that I desire to follow and track him down as earnestly as I can.

Sermon 43.1–6

Mt 22:9

Lk 14:8
Ps 84:11

Ps 19:5

JOHN'S EXPERIENCE OF PRAYER

THERE ARE TIMES when—with a generosity that exceeds hope—he visits my sinful soul after a long period of waiting. He favors it with an unimaginable revelation of the love of the Father, who *so loved this world that he gave his Only-Son.*† So sweet is the mystery that it cannot be explained; but in his overflowing grace he reveals it, as it were, in a gentle whisper. I stand still, weighing up and trying to decide from where my Lord has come this time. Judging from what he is saying in my ear, I see and understand that he has stolen quietly from his Father's bosom, if a sinner may so speak, to tell us truly of his Father and explain what is within his bosom.†

After this blessing, the time comes when he decides not to stay with me any longer, and I have not enough strength of virtue to hold him back when he flees, or to call him again when he has slipped away. Reduced to all my former misery, I return to what I was in the beginning, that is, to my dust. So, with all the thanksgiving I can muster, I escort him when he leaves me for the place from which he came, and as far as he will let me, I conduct him on his way up to heaven to his Father once again. I praise him because he is so glorious, I rejoice because he has visited me, but I breathe a deep sigh because he has been taken away.

Sometimes a sweet intimation of love becomes audible to me, that love with which the Father loves the Son,† and the Son in turn the

Jn 3:16

Jn 1:18

Jn 3:35

Father, a love beyond words, even beyond heaven itself. It is more than audible, it is thundered at me, for whenever this chances to happen, *the God of Majesty has thundered.*[†] Then I stand transfixed, as if hearing a mighty thunder peal, and I droop my quivering little wings. I am astonished and overcome with awe that from so very far away, from the highest heavens,[†] the Father's Only-Son should have come to visit, on his dunghill, his little worm of a creature. '*How has this honor come to me*',[†] I cry, 'that my Lord has thought of me?'

But this does not apply to any soul whose ear the Lord has touched with his holy fingers and made it hear.[†] It can listen to Jesus as to a master.[†] The soul who has been anointed by Jesus now herself anoints Jesus sometimes[†] and follows the true Light, not in darkness now but in the full light of day.[†] I feel certain that any soul like this has learned for herself how to search wisely and never to make fruitless enquiries as to where either the Spirit or Jesus comes from or where they go.[†] Certainly, from what Jesus says or does, it is easy to guess, as pointed out above, what place he has come from, and to what place also he will retire.

I put my trust in the truth of what he says, that when he comes, his purpose is to make his abode with me.[†] Likewise when he goes, his purpose is nonetheless to prepare a reception for me in the place to which he has gone. For he says, *I go to prepare a place for you.*[†] Truth itself made this promise! How I thank him! My lot is in his hands,[†] and by his grace, it has fallen out for me most happily.[†] Through his goodness I

Ps 29:3

Ps 19:6

Lk 1:43

Mt 7:33
Jn 13:13
Jn 13:13

Jn 12:35

Jn 3:18

Jn 14:23

Jn 14:3

Ps 31:17
Ps 16:7

believe and hope that I am destined for the
many mansions which, in his Father's house, he
has built for his many mansion-dwellers.†

And so, both where Jesus comes from and
where he goes, yes, and even when he comes
and goes, can be deduced. But for this, the soul
must watch very intently, in the way I have
mentioned, and she must keep herself free from
all other concerns and devote herself completely
to this peaceful leisure, which is so demanding.
Each separate one of these goings and comings
results in a great reward. But, as both Elijah and
Elisha tell us, that servant who, when he comes,
actually sees him coming, is enriched with a
double portion of the Holy Spirit.† The Apostles,
too, who were privileged to watch and understand both when he went and where he went to,
as well as from where he will one day come, seeing him ascend to where he had been in the beginning,† these Apostles were enriched most
lavishly by the sevenfold gift of the Spirit. They
were anointed with the oil of gladness above all
their fellows.†

In saying all this I have been foolish,† because it is infinitely beyond my small capacity.
But love, I trust, is both the motive and the
theme of what I am writing, and that is strong
enough to win forgiveness for my extravagance.

Sermon 43.9–12

Jn 14:2

2 K 2:9

Acts 1:9

Ps 45:8

2 Cor 12:11

Seeking the Beloved Jesus:
Wounded with Weariness

Where did your beloved go? We will seek him with you.[†]

Sg 5:17

THOSE WHO ARE SEEKING GOD ask
this question of the person who has sought him
and found him. Notice, they do not say, 'We will
seek him for you'. No, what they say is, 'We will
seek him with you'. They are promising to be
partners in her search, not assistants, not servants. They are binding themselves to fellow-
ship, not to obedience. This is what the bride
intended; this is the very thing she has been
longing to hear: that they lay aside their occupations and their countless, clamorous cares, to
devote themselves henceforth solely to this one
concern. That is why she reveals to them the
wound of her weariness,[†] for it is her desire
that, through compassion for their mother, they
too should be wounded with the same sort of
desire. Her motive is plainly to form in them,
little by little through these loving incitements,
an understanding of this kind of love, until their
eagerness for holiness grows to such a pitch that
she may pierce them through with a very keen
wound of love. She teaches them to spurn all
empty, worldly consolation as if it were the
withered flower of the field, apples that have
rotted.[†] Instead she demands something of the
glory of the kingdom of God in their lives—as
if from flowers that do not fade[†]—and something of the justice of that same kingdom—as if

Sg 5:8

Is 11:2

Sir 14:18

Is 11:1-2

from apples that do not rot—something that breathes the scent of Jesus, that flower on whom rests the Spirit of God† and on which the angels in heaven feed. Such are the things she looks for in them to provide her with consolation in her longing for love.

When they have become used to these joys they are in a fit state to ask for more powerful graces. She puts more pressure on them, adjuring them solemnly to tell her Beloved how weak and faint they are.

All this, my friends, gives us the right to ponder—and indeed gives us the pleasure of realizing—the importance of talking about Jesus, the good it does to cleave to those who love him and *out of the abundance of their hearts*† speak about him. For if *faith comes by hearing,*† then surely, love does too. Wonders, in conjunction with faith, are powerful in arousing faith, and once love has been enkindled, words of love breathe strongly on the flames. There is a brightness about a word drawn from the vein of love, and love shows itself in eager, impassioned speech. I can say without fear of contradiction that there is no sign that has more power to draw me to love than the living voice of a soul that loves God. If I am deprived of his voice, then his very face draws me, or if he cannot come himself, then even the loving and sweet remembrance of what he is draws me on.

Muffle your ears, my brothers, against dangerous conversation and consequently use them to hear the Word of God.† 'Sanctify them in truth'† for the Word of God is Truth. Every time we listen to evil, it soils and poisons, it

Mt 12:34

Rom 10:17

Sir 28:28

Jn 17:17

makes the ear accustomed to trivialities. In the
end, it will make the ear deaf. So then 'open
wide your ears', open wide your mouth, 'and let
the King of glory enter in'.† Yes, let Jesus enter　　Ps 24:9
in. It is not his custom to enter unless the doors
are shut,† barred and bolted against vanity, for　　Cf. Jn 20:26
with that Truth cannot make his home. The
King of glory may consecrate the whole house
to himself and claim it as his own.

Speak out, say clearly where he is to be
sought. His ways are unsearchable because,
wherever his footsteps go, whether through the
sea of the mighty waters,† none dare ever recog-　　Ps 77:19
nize them. Yet we believe that, through his
Spirit, his path will be revealed to you.† For you,　　Rom 11:33
to search out his unsearchable ways is extremely
simple, for on you the traces of his coming and
going have been more firmly impressed. You
follow after your Elijah, wisely and watchfully,
wherever he goes, so that when you see him departing, you expect a greater outpouring of the
spirit.† We know that he departs from you now　　Cf. 2 K 2:9
to go away to heaven, and immediately he will
pour heavenly blessings down upon you. Then,
when he returns to you from heaven, it will be to
tell you something of the joy of celestial glory.

This is why we always see you as if you were
a bride awaiting her Spouse, w*hen he shall return
from his wedding feast.*† Your Spouse comes out　　Lk 12:36
of his wedding chamber† so as to tell you about　　Ps 19:5
the marriage feast which is everlastingly celebrated in heaven, and to share it generously
with you. He turns aside, but never for long; he
is always close at hand. For you said that after
two days, when he came knocking and you rose

Sg 5:5

Sg 5:6

Gal 4:19

Mt 11:25

to open to your Beloved and drew the bolt of your door, *he had turned and gone away.*[†] Then your prayers were partly answered, for he put his hand through the lattice and your body trembled at his touch;[†] your soul melted away when your Beloved spoke. So he went away, but not far, nor long to be away. He was delivered and returned to give himself to you. He went away from you for an hour, so that while he tarried, you might use the time to speak to us of him, and *form Christ within us.*[†] He went away from you, but only so as to offer us, in you, a greater fullness of himself, to let us enjoy his own self in this present life through you.

Your Spouse took care to hide himself from the wise and learned, but he offers himself to the little ones for them to know and delight in.[†]

Sermon 40.2–5

VIII

THE BRIDE OF THE WORD

AN OVERVIEW:
SPONSA VERBI

ONE OF THE THEMES John loves to dwell on is the spiritual person as *Sponsa Verbi,* bride of the Word. The expression is used by him to show just how resplendent is the love that such a person has for the Lord Jesus, not only in his human nature, but above all in his Divine Nature as the Word of the Father. In the bride of the Word love is total. Her whole being is transformed in love. We might recall the example of the Little Flower, Saint Thérèse of the Child Jesus, whose childlike love for God attracted the Catholic world in the 1920s and continues to do so to *this day.*

This should not in any way diminish the fact that for John, as for the whole tradition of scriptural exegesis before and after his time, the principal Bride, the *Sponsa Christi* of the Song, is the Church. We will come back to this in the next section. In a lovely passage later in his commentary, John of Forde combines the phrase *Sponsa Verbi* with a quotation from Saint Paul, a quotation that was used by all the great mystics of the Church to denote the wonder of the person whom God has chosen in a special way:

> The Bride of the Word was very rich in love, and delighted in every kind of happiness. She surrenders herself trustfully to the Father of the Spouse Jesus, because she was prepared by him for her union with his Only Son. But she offers herself, too, with total

confidence to the Son of God, her Beloved, because
he stooped to enter into this union with her. She recalls that she cleaves to Christ by virtue of his power
and his overshadowing and is made *one spirit with
him*.[1]

John is entranced with the beauty that he sees in the bride. In
Sermon Ninety-seven he comes back to the same thought, no
doubt expressing his own personal closeness. For him, the union
is so strong that his sermon overflows with dynamic words to
describe it: *'First, surrounding her in the circle of his embrace, it en-
closes her, and thus enclosed it binds her fast. As it binds, it tightens; as
it tightens, it draws; as it draws, it joins; as it joins it unites.'*[2] He
does not ascribe these sentiments to himself, since his humility
would not allow it, but the reader has the impression that he has
met souls who have known this in their prayer. I feel sure that he
was one of them. In the thirteenth century this 'mystical embrace' was to become a major theme in the writing of the mystics
of the Rhineland.

> Yes, this is how it happens, at any rate, to a soul that
> thirsts for the font of life. God breathes on her, and
> she is aroused by what we may call a most forcible
> bond of loving desire. Once aroused, she becomes en-
> chained, and she is drawn towards the delight of him
> who is within. So drawn, she clings joyously to Christ
> through love, and in her clinging, she knows the bliss
> of marriage and becomes one spirit with him.[3]

It is towards the end of his commentary that John allows his passionate love for Jesus to pour itself out in ardent talk of union
with the Word. Perhaps he had entered that state of the spiritual
life which Saint John of the Cross calls Transforming Union.

---

[1] Sermon 93.5, 1 Cor 6:17
[2] Sermon 97.8
[3] Sermon 97.8

One has the impression that John has become less restrained in his language, possibly because his own personal experience has been enriched with high mystical graces. I do not understand how the following burst of passionate feeling could be written by someone who had not experienced it himself. Again he quotes Saint Paul to enforce what he says:

> Already the sacred kiss of Jesus has been frequently and sweetly enjoyed, and the bride has been most graciously led into the King's banqueting hall.[4] Already she has clung in utter bliss to her married happiness, and now, held tightly within the embrace of his arms, there is nothing lacking except to become one spirit and one flesh with her spouse in the Holy Spirit.[5]

If the language used here were not unambiguously spiritual, and of a high order of mysticism, it could be mistaken for having an erotic implication. Clearly this is not the case, as any spiritual person will immediately perceive. Indeed, John of Forde had raised our thoughts to the loftiest plane when, in Sermon Fourteen, he reflected on the unity within the Trinity itself. Among the Three Persons there is, of course, an identity of *nature*. When John talks of the Holy Spirit as the bond of Love he has this lovely insight:

> From the fullness of the most sacred joy the Father utters the whole of himself to the Son, and in the same way the Son together with the Father utters the whole of himself to the Holy Spirit, so that these three are one single font of Love. . . . It is no cause for wonder if Love has a place of special privilege and power here at the very source and font of its own being.[6]

---

[4] Sg 2:4
[5] 1 Cor 6:17; Sermon 93.7
[6] Sermon 14.4

As a distinguished theologian, John, of course, places the unity in the Blessed Trinity on a completely different level. There is no question of the *Sponsa Verbi* having unity of nature with God. That unique and incomprehensible unity is possible only in the Source itself, as John tells us early in Sermon 7.2. No, she who is *Sponsa Verbi* cleaves to the Lord and becomes one *spirit* (not one *nature*) with him.

In the later sermons John becomes ever more ardent in his language of love. This may seem surprising, coming as it does from the pen of a man well advanced in years, but the ardor is entirely spiritual and wholly acceptable. Nevertheless, in the earlier sermons there is one passage that I cannot pass over without quoting more fully because its language is enchanting. He has been speaking about the virtues of humility, justice, love, charity—which are characteristic in the bride's personal life. But the Bride is still hoping for something more:

> Her hope is not disappointed. When the Lord sees her thus attired and so carefully following him and seeking his face, he thinks her worthy of the kiss of his mouth for which she has longed, and she becomes united with him and made one with him. Blissfully she enjoys her Spouse, judging herself to know but him alone, and clinging to him with whom she has become one spirit.[7]

John is so fond of praising the bride's spiritual beauty that you are led to believe he has some particular person in mind. He seems to have met such souls. He loves those words of praise in the Song, *How beautiful you are, my love, how beautiful!*[8] He is full of admiration. At the same time he brings in from Saint Paul another quotation which was recognized as expressing a high point in a mystic's life:

[7] Sermon 11.5
[8] Sg 4:1

The spouse, Jesus, blesses when he praises, and to be blessed by him means to have received some fresh grace from his mouth. So the Spouse bestows his blessing on his beloved calling her beautiful, confirming her still more in the beauty in which she is now pre-eminent, while at the same time decking her with the symbols of a greater beauty. For, as the Apostle says, *our inner nature is renewed from day to day in the perception of our true image, which is Christ, from brightness to brightness.*[9] The bride has reached the point of being allowed to contemplate the very beautiful face of her Spouse, Jesus, and to carry away very great brightness from that contemplation.[10]

Such a person, according to John, has been totally transformed within herself by the sight of the Lord Jesus. He looks for two ways in which this perfect image of God should express itself. He calls it a most happy union, making the bride of the Word become a mother in the spiritual life. In the first place she bears and brings forth the Word within herself by means of meditation and contemplation.[11] Secondly, at the same time she forms souls to Christ, since the true spiritual mother is eager to gain souls and make them grow in their love for Jesus: *He went away from you for an hour, so that while he tarried, you might use the time to speak to us of him, and form Christ within us.*[12]

John notes that in Psalm 44, which he greatly loves, Jesus is the fairest in form of the children of men. It is this word 'form', *forma* in Latin, in its many derivations, that has so much meaning for him. *Forma*, which is in reality the very essence of a thing, can be combined with other prepositions to yield such words as 'deform', 'inform', 'reform', 'transform', 'conform'. All of these carry great significance in the mystical tradition. Saint Bernard, for

[9] 2 Cor 3:18
[10] Sermon 47.4
[11] Sermon 71.6
[12] Gal 4:19; Sermon 40.5

example, in his 85th Sermon on the Canticle demonstrates how the soul which in its fallen 'form' has become 'deformed', receives the grace of God through Christ and thus becomes 'reformed', and then goes on to become 'transformed' in the mystical life of contemplation, and after many years of progress becomes totally 'conformed' to the Word in spiritual marriage.

In his primary beauty, Jesus is *the fairest in form of the children of men*, because the 'form' he has is the very nature of God united to the nature of man in the Person of the Word. Thus John concentrates on the praise of the highest 'form' or beauty in the Lord Jesus. He uses this favorite scriptural phrase from the psalms to indicate in a subtle way that the ultimate beauty of Jesus lies in his unity with the Infinite Word of God the Father: *'David placed this beauty at the forefront of his praises. "You are the fairest in your divine form above the children of men."'* John follows this with moving insight into the effect this has on a person whom the Lord has chosen to be admitted to the sight of this beauty. The word 'beauty' here falls so far short of the reality that John is trying to convey that it becomes utterly meaningless in comparison.

> In this appearance, my Lord Jesus has shown himself so beautiful in his surpassing form to all who have merited to be admitted to see him, to such an extent that from then on, those who have seen this appearance once, yearn with insatiable desire for this appearance again.[13]

John's emotion here as he gazes on this radiant whiteness of Jesus, charges his words with poetry:

> This lovely appearance of Jesus,
> like the appearance of Lebanon,
> makes firm and holds together
> all the Cedars you have planted,

---

[13] Sermon 35.1

irradiating and renewing them
in the whiteness of eternal Light
which is himself.

At the end of this marvelous sermon, of which I have only
been able to touch on the beginning and have left so much more
to be said, John comes back to the theme on that day when all
the saints are clothed in heaven *as a bridegroom adorned with a
garland, as a bride arrayed in her jewels.*[14] On that day, may we be
remembered as part of the beauty of his bride, by the Son of
God, *the fairest in form of the children of men,*[15] who with his
Father and the Holy Spirit, lives and reigns, God, for ever and
ever.

[14] Is 61:10
[15] Ps 45:3

Praise of the Bride for Her Humility; The Dawn of Her Love

I WOULD CONSIDER myself unfit to wonder at and praise the Lord's bride without first having been given sight of her. Oh, that someone would grant me to catch sight of such a soul, so that I might see her face to face. I would be blessed if I could see; my heart would glow with the very same fire of love she feels, and makes her soul break into flame and melt within her.

Let us contemplate one of these souls and wonder at her and exclaim: 'Who is this who can receive such praise from men and angels and God himself? Who is this whose holiness has so sudden and so luminous a beginning, so bright and so humble a progress, so splendid and ardent a perfection, so venerable and mellow a consummation?'

I have spoken too briefly, because the single night of this single soul grew to a brightness that illuminated the days of so many and the serenity of this single dawn arose to give light to the whole world. Why do I use the word 'arose'? No, that dawn did not merely 'arise' (*surrexit*), it 'rose up' (*consurrexit*). It rose up in all its strength, it rose up, the whole of it, totally, all together. It rose up and again it rose up as

Scripture has it: *Rise up, rise up!*† It rose up
shaking off all fear and sloth, in the Spirit of
freedom; it rose up, clothing itself in wisdom
and humility, in the Spirit of love—for the
preaching of the Gospel, in other words with
wisdom and knowledge to be a light to the
world, to the glory of God.

What can I say of those other souls who
resemble this one? In their zeal to be like perfect
apostles, they have held in contempt all that the
world has to offer the very beginning of a good
life. What great freedom and peace, dearest
brothers, are expressed in those words which
today, on the birthday of our father Benedict,[1]
are figuratively applied in praise of himself and
his blessed offspring. He seems to take it from
the lips of the Apostle and use it for himself and
his sons, saying to Jesus, *See, we have left all
things and followed you.*† This is an enormous act
of faith, my brothers, provided always that the
rest of the day advances in keeping with its rising dawn.

But every soul which is holy and reverent is
wise enough to remember that it was the Sun
that brought her into this morning brightness.
She never lets herself forget those words of the
apostle: *You were once darkness, but now, light in
the Lord.*† She will bless God and take his praise
upon her lips† because he has called her into his
wonderful light,† and this will be the serenity of
the dawn growing pale and silvery. Any soul
that Jesus brings into a state of such intense

Is 51:9

Mt 19:27

Eph 5:8
Ps 109:30
1 Pet 2:9

---

[1] Apparently this sermon was preached on the Feast of Saint
Benedict, 21 March, though the year is not known, possibly 1211.

happiness, where he is ready to impart to it the actual experience of his love and where Jesus blesses it from the very beginning of its conversion, looking at the soul and desiring its beauty,[†] such a soul is blessed indeed.

Now, if the Sun of justice rises for those who fear God,[†] how much more for those who love him! For those who fear, 'healing' will rise in God's wings,[†] but for the lovers, something more radiant and blessed, God's love. These wings carry up to the light those who love and are loved. The dawn of the soul that loves God rises, not so much every day, but all day, never tiring. For if one truly loves, then each hour seems like the dawn of fresh love. It was of love that Jesus said, *A new commandment I give you.*[†] There is a sense in which what is perpetually new is perpetually at the beginning. In fact, newness continually holds within itself its own beginning, so as to seem always at the point of starting, since it is wholly unaffected by decay or age.

But *blessed among women*[†] is the one who never finds idle slumber overtaking her. She rises up to her Sun, and will not endure being separated from him; she perpetually irradiates herself in his light, and she renews herself by continually contemplating him. Yet she is *fair as the moon.*[†] It is only in the night that the moon's beauty is remarkable. Can we say that the bride, too, has a night? She has indeed, but it is a very luminous night. It is so luminous that it is during the night that she goes to seek the one *her soul loves.*[†] Perhaps it is because she sought him in the night-time that she speaks of having sought him, rather than of having found him.[†]

Margin references:
Ps 45:10
Mal 4:2
Mal 4:2
Jn 13:34
Lk 1:42
Sg 6:9
Sg 3:1
Sg 3:1

She ponders over her personal failure, so that the more light there is in her pondering, the more clearly does her darkness manifest itself.

She also ponders over the light, being neither unaware of her borrowing it from the Sun, nor ungrateful. She has learnt to ascribe both kinds of light to him and to rely on him for the light by which she knows both him and herself. So to this Sun, the moon frequently returns to draw light from it for her own use, and the more she shows herself to the Sun, the less she seems in her own eyes. Yet the very circumstance that diminishes her is precisely what makes her able to receive enrichment from him. That Sun, always wholly full of his own light, never needs the light of others and never wastes his own, but *he resists the proud and gives grace to the humble.*[†]   Jas 4:6

Sermon 58.1–9

THE HUMILITY OF THE SERVANT

ALTHOUGH HUMILITY is certainly a daughter of the King, shining out among the others with incomparable beauty, she has been chosen for a special office.

Her lot is to clean the dust from the feet of the daughters to make them all pure,[†] to bathe   Is 4:4
the feet of the saints, to wash their garments, to

hold them out to the sunlight, and so to restore them radiantly white to those who hasten to the marriage of the bridegroom and the bride.

2 K 5

Humility makes Naaman lose his leprosy;[†] the Egyptian change his skin and the leopard

Jer 13:23

Rv 22:11

his spots;[†] the just become more just still, and the saints more sanctified.[†] Let us say something first about Jesus' humility. From the very beginning Jesus conducted himself with prudence and valor, surpassing all the servants of the king. At your going out from your mother's womb, O my Lord David [Jesus], you struck the proud, overthrew the giant [the devil], and

1 Sam 17:31-54

brought a mighty salvation to Israel.[†] You proceeded against him not in the power of your

Jer 21:5

arm[†] or in the greatness of your strength, but in our weakness which you took from the brook of our mortality. You tucked this weakness into your shepherd's purse, in the depths of your

Jn 10:11

charity, for you came as a good Shepherd[†] to feed your people, the flock you have inherited.

1 Sam 17:40, David preparing to fight Goliath.

You took five stones from this brook,[†] the five needs of this mortal body: hunger, thirst, nakedness, the need for shelter, feebleness of our sickly flesh. For our sake they were mercifully taken up by your Majesty, and it was through these weaknesses themselves that you so splendidly triumphed over the devil's pride. Since you were a little one, you made yourself like all little ones in weakness, except that you were a more ardent seeker after littleness. You chose to be born as a stranger and you desired to own and to inherit nothing in this world.

You had other stones, or weapons, too, no less bright than these. There was your obligation of service, the poverty of your parents with which you chose to contend, the meanness of the rags in which you deigned to be wrapped, the narrowness of the inn which could not take you in—little though you were, the abasement of the manger in which you chose to rest. Certainly these stones have little or no power in the hands of any other children, sons of Adam, and so Goliath despised them in the hands of the child too, as if they were childish weapons.† He knew nothing of this child's greatness, and how he had come with these stones to lay the proud low.

1 Sam 17:42

These things render those who are lowly glorious for the sake of Christ, calling us back to a measure of humility and lowliness. A little child, still sucking at his mother's breast, a tiny child, poor and dependent, a baby wrapped in swaddling clothes and immediately cast out from the home of his birth and flung into a manger for animals! It is this little child who suddenly shattered the brow of the proud Goliath with a stone, and snatched the sword from his hand.

O Lord my God, even if the lovers of this world pretend not to see it and the prince of this world takes no notice, you have now quite certainly taken your seat upon your throne and judged justly.† You have destroyed the pride of this world by many signs of humility in your coming. Even though you impose silence on yourself, Lord, there is still a terrible reality in the thunder of your silence. Great and powerful is the breath of your lips, with which you have rebuked the proud, the greedy and the ambitious, the lovers of ease, the seekers after subtleties.

Ps 9:4

Behold the entry of my God, my King, into
Ps 68:24   the sanctuary.[†] Let us enter even into the heart
of Jesus, since to that our good Master draws us:
Mt 11:29   *Learn of me for I am meek and humble of heart.*[†]

Sermon 9.1–5

HAPPY IS THE BRIDE
WHO KNOWS ONLY JESUS

Gen 6:3   IN SPEAKING TO ME, a person of flesh,[†]
the Holy Spirit sees fit to use words of flesh and
of fleshly desire, gently and graciously making
my desire wholesome, that he may clothe me in
his own desire. I embrace this loving condescension, I marvel at the wisdom, I give thanks for
the tender mercy which once *lowered his heav-*
Ps 18:9
Jn 1:14   *ens*[†] when *the Word was made flesh.*[†] Since I too
am flesh, it is now possible for me, even me, to
draw near to him who draws near to me. I long
Ps 2:4   to climb up to him *who lives in the heavens;*[†] and
so he has set up a ladder for me, made of words
like these, by which I can slowly and step-by-
step venture towards him. But I cannot climb
up safely to him unless that Lord Jesus supports
that ladder from above, holding it so that it does
not sway. I need him to send to me one of his
RB Ch. 7   angels who go up and down upon that ladder,[†]
so that in his hands I may be led as far along it
as he sees is possible for me.

The image of fleshly love given here is a
sign both of the mysteries of sacred pleasure and
of the fruit most chastely begotten. Certainly it
would be wrong to think that this heavenly and
spotless marriage was either less delightful or
lacking in fruitfulness. As far as *the heavens are
higher than the earth*† or rather, as much as *light
differs from darkness,*† to the same degree does
the pleasure that comes from heaven differ from
that which comes from the flesh, and the fruit
of light differ from the joys of darkness.†

Is 53:9

Qo 2:3

Eph 5:9

Poor flesh and blood, unworthy to taste this
sweetness, ignorant of a hunger for it! In our
hearts and minds what is bitter is sweet, and
what is sweet is bitter.† Truly happy, indeed
happiest of all women, is she who consecrates
all her desires to this holy delight, who strives to
remain unaware of all other sweetness because
of Jesus, and who wants to know nothing, but
only Jesus.† She knows well that in him is found
all sweetness, or to speak more truly, she has
herself most assuredly experienced in countless
ways that he is the well-spring of all delight.

Is 5:20

Mk 9:8

She rises, then, and walks about the *land
flowing with milk and honey,*† the land that is
Jesus himself. She walks about the length and
breadth of it, as much as heavenly grace allows
her. At one time the taste of her Spouse's sweetness comes from his kisses, at another it is in the
fragrance of his ointments. At one time she
knows the rapture of his embraces, at another
her joy is to be with him, speaking and convers-
ing, and yet again she has the privilege of contemplating his beauty. The Spouse affects her in
one way when he is present and she can enjoy

Dt 6:3

him, and in quite another when he is absent and she longs for him. Sometimes she is praised by him with the most indulgent love, and sometimes it is she who wonders and praises, when the very effort to do justice to her wonderful and praiseworthy Beloved leaves her speechless.

Who can count—or even distinguish—all the different ways of feeling joy, all the varieties of happiness, all the overflowing of bliss? A pleasure so noble and so manifold gives rise to spiritual offspring upon offspring, until the full measure of contentment has been reached.

The presence of Jesus is never sterile. Wherever he goes—provided only he comes in grace and not in anger—he brings a blessing so that *our earth yields its fruit.*† The Word of God never returns to him empty, but *it achieves what it was sent to do,*† and produces rich and wholly indescribable fruit. For, *who can describe the generation*† of the Word? Obviously no one. Either that generation by which he was begotten by the Father from before the ages, or that by which he was born of his mother at the end of the ages. But there is another generation too, in which, with supreme graciousness, he generates children of grace and in those children of grace, the gifts of grace, and no one's power can understand its manner or its effects.

Truly happy, indeed happiest of all women is she who consecrates all her desires to this holy delight, who strives to remain unaware of all other sweetness because of Jesus, and who wants to know nothing, but only Jesus. She knows well that in him is found all sweetness, or to speak more truly, she has herself most assuredly experi-

Ps 85:12

Is 55:11

Is 53:8

enced in countless ways that he is the well-spring of all delight.

Sermon 33.2–4

DRYNESS OF SPIRIT

HIS LIPS DISTILL THE FINEST MYRRH.[†] Sg 5:13

ANY SOUL THAT LONGS for the joys of love must not shrink back from its bitterness—like myrrh—if it desires to experience its sweetness. The lips of your beloved Jesus may be ready to kiss you, and in that kiss you may realize they are distilling bitter myrrh. Do not be so foolish as to reject it, do not offer a reluctant greeting to the grace that comes to you. You have submitted to the yoke of a strangely hothouse-sort of love, if you are happy only in its pleasures, and hasten away, all whining and squeamish, from the sorrows involved in the labor of love, which must of necessity present themselves to those who walk in love's ways. In short, listen to what is said by the Beloved to any soul having the fruit of love within its womb—or even just anxious to have it: *A woman has sorrow when she gives birth, for her hour has come.*[†] Jn 16:21

Anguish may lay hold of us as if we were about to give birth, but then we must be strengthened in the Holy Spirit, knowing that labor's pains herald a birth. The more overwhelming the suffering, the closer at hand is the reward; and when it reaches its peak, then suddenly all grief is blotted out as joy comes flooding in.

Yet the pangs of childbirth are not without their own benefits, even with all their pain. First of all, the loving heart sees its desolation as a rebuke, and is forced by necessity to think that the reason for it is its own unworthiness and lack of likeness to God. It feels compelled to say to itself: 'Why, I wonder, has my Lord not visited me with his accustomed grace? He came neither yesterday nor the day before. Where is the usual comfort of a deep, satisfying prayer? Where the rich holocaust of an outpouring of love? Where the overwhelming happiness of secret rejoicing? Where most of all, where is Jesus, in whose presence I once always lived, and now remember with such sorrow? Oh, what has happened? Why has famine taken the place of my happy plenty, mourning of joy, dryness of devotion and a thick cloud hiding the life-giving light? My unhappiness is crushing, as the prophet says, *the* Jer 6:4 *shadows of evening lengthen*,† and a lengthening, habitual night has cut off the light of divine consolation. I run after Jesus, calling and crying; I go after him, loudly pleading with him to come back to me, and as if I were like Pilate and he had some reason not to speak to me, he an- Mk 15:5 swers me not a word.† Surely he would not turn from me without reason, and surely the reason must be my own fault?

I have experienced how good he is. How Ps 119:65 frequently he has dealt kindly with his servant.†

He is still the same, though now he seems harsh to me, and I still believe, and hold with absolute certainty, that into the radiant brightness of his everlasting goodness no stain could ever come. Rather let me rage—and rightly so—against my own dullness of heart, my own sluggishness, my own bitterness. I have tasted wisdom so often, yet I find myself still so insipid. The Sun of justice has shone on me so often, yet I feel myself hard as baked clay. I seem to have come away from the sweetness of the heavenly manna with nothing but a mouth more bitter than ever.

On that day of glorious happiness when I sat down with the Lord Jesus at his supper and held in my hand some part of his own honeycomb,† do you think some sort of dying fly could have fallen onto the mouthful I was about to swallow? I mean something like ingratitude, pride, anger, or envy? How I fear that perhaps that loving eye saw me attacking the feast with far too little self-restraint, that my great delight in him was lacking in reverence, that I laid hands upon more than was fitting. *You have found honey*, says Solomon, *eat what is fitting for you, or you may overeat and lose the honey through being sick.*†

If I should want to justify myself, the poverty I feel at present and the hunger in which I have languished so many days already reprove me for my arrogance. Granted that I am not aware of anything against myself,† yet God has certainly found out the guilt of his servant.† So he hides his face from me,† and treats me as my foolishness deserves.† What shall I do then? I shall wait patiently for the Lord, until he notices

Lk 24:42

Prv 25:16

1 Cor 4:4
Gen 44:16
Is 8:17
Prv 26:4

Ps 40:1

me.† I shall place perfect confidence in the goodness that is his by nature, because he will always be alert to the cry of the poor man who abandons himself to him.† He will find time for me too, but only when he sees it is right, and that I need it. Meanwhile as far as is in me, I will endure my Lord's delay as if it were myrrh, a very bitter but very efficacious medicine for my wounds. I will put to death my members which are on this earth.† What kind of fragrance is more exquisitely adapted to this end than myrrh?

Ps 22:24

Col 3:5

Sermon 24.5–6

How Jesus Turns Aside
from His Bride and Then Returns

Sg 5:17

WHERE DID YOUR BELOVED GO?†

SOMETIMES Jesus did turn away from the crowd. We must note that these withdrawals of his give no grounds for mistrust. When the disciples were pulling hard at the oars, *he came to them, walking upon the sea. He made as if to pass by.*† They were astonished to see so unexpected a sight, and *cried out in fear.*† So the unexpectedness resulted in astonishment, the astonishment resulted in fear, the fear resulted in a shout, and

Mk 6:48
Mt 14:26

the shout resulted in their being listened to with compassion. Being listened to gave them confidence, and confidence in the end gave them the accustomed and longdesired presence of Jesus. For the children of grace, then, his turning aside was done not in anger but in grace. He kept away for a little while, but only so as to return to them more wonderfully and with greater grace.

For those who love Jesus, his goings away and his turnings aside are a preparation for greater grace. A 'turning aside' indicates a lapse of time that is brief and secret, one that will see a swift and unexpected return of the grace of his coming. When he was about to suffer and rise again, he said, *A little while and you will not see me, and again a little while and you will see me.*† He was encouraging them to wait patiently the *little while* of his absence, which was going to be more of a 'turning aside' than a departure or a journey. But there was a journey before him, too, one that he would soon be taking to his Father, when he would bid them farewell; and here also, he gave them wonderful encouragement. What he said was unbelievable, and the very hearing of it overwhelmed and crushed them, yet he promised with the strongest expression of sincerity that it would help: *I am telling you the truth; it is expedient for you that I should go away. If I do not go away, the Paraclete will not come to you, but if I go away, I shall send him to you.*†

Think now, I beg you, anyone who is listening to me, think of the joy and consolation that three days' 'turning away' was preparing for the little ones who waited. They were soon to have

Jn 16:16

Jn 16:7

the unexpected bliss of their Lord's resurrection. And then, think of the longer journey which he afterwards took to the Father, how that would produce even greater grace and a more generous outpouring of strength. All these 'turnings away' in which he frequently left them alone, from the day of his resurrection until the final day of his ascension, can we not think of them as 'red-hot coals'?† They were coals burning into ashes the worldly affection with which they so stubbornly clung to him, burning them with the new fire of holy love, which would gradually make them forget the taste of the world and experience new delights in the spiritual happiness that comes from Christ.

Ps 120:3

Every single time the Lord turned aside from them, he came back to them as something new and only then, for the first time, to be known and appreciated. So unprecedented, so overwhelming was the joy that faith could hardly encompass what was before their very eyes. The witness of every sense assured them with one voice that it was true, but the joy was so great that it forced them to doubt.

For the bride, the Spouse goes away first of all, and then, after that, he 'turns away'. In the early stages of his conversation and in the first flush of her joy, occasioned by his visits, the Beloved kept away longer and returned later and more infrequently; and the bride, discomforted by the disagreeable sensation of waiting, used to complain about the length of his absences, saying that her Beloved had removed himself too far. Now, however, she has won the privilege of enjoying his presence more often and in greater abundance. Now, whenever he withdraws, he merely 'turns aside', as though making a diversion without intending to make a longer delay. It is as though he were saying to the bride, *Again a little while and you will see me.*† Also, *Let not your heart be troubled, nor let it be afraid,*† for I am going and coming straight back to you. I am turning away, not going away; withdrawing for a little while, not departing. For a moment I turn away from you, but only to return to you at once with greater joy; you will rejoice all the more when after a little while I am given back. Look up, I shall turn aside to you like a river of peace, like a torrent of glory to inundate the daughter of Zion.†

Jn 16:16

Jn 14:27

Is 66:12

Sermon 42.1–6

ECSTASY AND UNION: BEYOND WORDS

I AM MY BELOVED'S AND HE IS MINE.†

Sg 6:2

[*This sermon begins with a eulogy of Saint Bernard of Clairvaux and his commentary on the Song.*]

THE LITERAL MEANING [of Scripture] carries about it some great mystery which is sealed. The bride has been describing her Beloved's attributes when the Spouse quietly made his appearance. He came to lay his healing hand upon her great illness—of which we spoke previously. So the bride, glowing in the fresh light streaming from her Spouse, and, as if seeing him for the first time, breaks forth into words of spontaneous and immense rejoicing, *I am my Beloved's, and my Beloved is mine!*†

Sg 6:2

Did even she fully understand what she said? Holy ecstasies like this produce a wonderful darkness of unknowing. What has happened is so wonderful, so unprecedented and beyond experience, that it brings with it what could be called 'an enveloping cloud of loving forgetfulness'. They completely lose sight of themselves and of what they seem to be engaged on. Simon Peter, when he saw for himself the face of Jesus shining with the brightness of the sun and his garments as radiantly white as snow,† cried out, thunderstruck with amazement, *Lord, it is good to be here!*† He was overwhelmed by a profound alienation of his faculties, because he was seeing something completely unexpected—in fact, until that time quite unheard of. As these things go too deep for the world to understand, what Peter said breaks out beyond what a human being can understand. In itself what he saw was so extraordinary, so that he could not find words apt for it.

Mt 9:2

Mt 17:4

Likewise with the Queen of Sheba: when she saw all the wisdom of Solomon, her breath failed her.† Is it any wonder that the true queen, the bride, after much weary panting and painful sighings of her soul, earned the grace to find, to look on, to hold and embrace to her heart's desire one so much loved, is it any wonder that her breath failed? And her words failed her too.

1 K 10:5

I am my Beloved's and my Beloved is mine.† Sg 6:2
Here there is nothing lacking in her bliss except
that her Beloved does not let himself be held
very long; and she groans over her incapacity as
yet for the total joy she desires. Having blissfully
obtained what she desired, she remembers to be
disciplined in her enjoyment of it, and, while
not forgetting the trials of the past, she gives
way to no anxiety about those still to come.

Indeed, since she knows that she has been
given in marriage to the wisest of men, who is
the very Wisdom of God the Father, she sings
more earnestly than ever of the dangers of los-
ing self control. This is especially true after he
had brought her into his banqueting hall. She
knows at once that she has to undergo the test
of whether, amidst her ecstasies of happiness,
she has learned to conduct herself with dignity.
The Spouse gave her this gift, and she had glo-
ried in it most greatly, earlier in the Song, *He set
love in order in me.*† Sg 2:4

This is the balanced judgement that comes
from true discretion. It keeps her balanced in
the middle, between two extremes—between
ecstatic joy and grief—so that she falls into neither danger. If it goes well with her, she is not
made over-confident, and if it goes ill, not over-
fearful. The bride of the Word should be the
kind of person who is not made drunk by being
given the full freedom of the banqueting hall,
nor one whom drinking makes garrulous.

The bride, in the very fulfillment of her desires is afraid of speaking, but is not allowed to
be silent. She feels a triumphant joy command-
ing her to speak, but her consciousness of what

she is compels her to hold her tongue. In fact, happiness and unhappiness share her between them and she will stay divided until her Beloved breaks down the *dividing wall*.† He will heal all the love-longing that her sick soul feels for him, when he reveals himself in his fullness. Shy fear curbed the ardent expression of love.

This fear is not a servant, but a most dear child of God.† He is coheir with love, and lives for ever inside the house.† So when the bride was in ecstasy, it hovered round her lips. It cut short what her words said; it intermingles with the joys she is experiencing, urgently repeating, 'Be careful not to go too far!'

The bride is now in possession of the embraces she has longed for, and says, *I am to my Beloved*.† She answers the young maidens, 'Why do you ask something that no words can tell? What am I when I enter completely into the enjoyment of light invisible, when I say farewell to all this world holds and am absorbed again by the God in whom I began, when I am imprinted with God's likeness in which I was made? Here on earth I am enabled to experience this, but I am utterly unable to speak about it. Cleaving indeed to my Beloved, I am united to him, conformed to him, I am lodged in his heart, made one spirit with him.† So he is the only one throughout this present life who knows what I am to him or he to me. Deep within his heart a new name is stored up for me, a name his own mouth has given me,† and he has inscribed it on his love, as on a stone. But he keeps his secret to himself, not even to me has he chosen to reveal it, until *he brings time to an*

Eph 2:14

Gal 4:7
Jn 8:35

Sg 6:2

1 Cor 6:17

Is 61:2

end,† that is, until the day we celebrate our wed- | Dan 12:2
ding ceremony. For my Beloved this time is a
time of silence, and for me and you it is a time
of waiting.'

You are not deceived in waiting for something so great, for you are like some delightful
garden, pasturing my Beloved and yours among
the lilies.† You both refresh him with your rev-   Sg 2:16
erent love and clothe him with your flowerlike
chastity. Beautiful indeed in those beautiful eyes
is the chaste generation that loves him, and he
has told us himself that to be with them is his
delight.†   Prv 8:31

Sermon 46.1–9

DEATH:
THE POWER OF CHRIST'S DEATH

O LORD JESUS, fount of life! From so many
deaths you draw me forth in the fullness of
your love. You lead me into your living and life-
giving light, not only bringing me over from
death to life, but also from life to life. You have
given me so many great and striking proofs of
the immense strength of your love. Now I, a son
of death, have passed into the adoption of your
sons. I open my mouth that I may turn to you
and draw from you the living Spirit—or rather,

I beg you, widen my mouth that I may yearn for you, O Fount of Life. Let me cleave passionately to you, and never let me be drawn away from you until you have given me to drink fully and be intoxicated by you, and until you have flowed

Is 66:12

down upon me like a river of peace.†

Now that I have been raised to life again by you, raised in so many ways, my own death provides me with very rich material for loving, which is why *my soul thirsts for you, and my flesh*

Ps 63:1

longs for you.† Under death's captivity, both soul and body groaned and were in labor even to this

Rom 8:22

very day,† but at the taste of your fullness, they drew to themselves the firstfruits of life. All the days of their life they will confess to you, Lord God, with one voice, that *your steadfast love is*

Ps 63:3

better than life.†

So your love is strong, Lord Jesus, *strong as*

Sg 8:6

my *death.*† Death greedily swallowed down my soul and my body, and with equal cruelty bestirred itself to absorb what it had swallowed and feed on it for eternity. But your love has come in advance to make mock of my death, and cry to it: *Death, I shall be your death.*†

Hos 13:14

Then, your love is as strong as your own death, and there is nothing in heaven or on earth stronger than that. What strength can be compared to that death that won the victory, not only over all death, but even over the prince of death himself? If I may dare to say so, your love and your death are in a certain way equivalent to each other, looking at each other on even terms, and are judged by the Holy Spirit to have the same amount of strength. To commend itself to its loved ones, your love made use of the strength of your death, while on the other hand, your death took its power from your love, desiring to destroy our death and renew mortals in life.

This is why your death is so powerful, so all-powerful, so strong, so invincible in the triumphs of the martyrs, so effective in washing away sin, so victorious in procuring salvation. It is because your love is as strong as death that it has made your death so intensely strong, far beyond all other forces. It follows that for all ages to come the might of your death is pre-eminent, Lord Jesus, since it found its immortal and life-giving strength in your love. This is why a wholly new light has arisen from heaven.† The loving remembrance of this death will be an impregnable shield and a pillar of light, inaccessible to their enemies. Finally, it is the gate to life, the only gate that gives access to the holy of holies, namely, the bliss of seeing God in heaven.

Ws 5:20

Sermon 105.7–8

CHRIST'S LOVE FOR HIS BRIDE

IN A PREVIOUS sermon,† we were thinking of the attitude of tenderness which makes God yearn like a father or a mother towards us, his children. Because of these two kinds of love, I

Sermon 28

am bound by a double debt: of love; and of honor, for I have been adopted in a double way. Seeing that he has made himself both Father and Mother to me,[†] he will also make me into his true child, through the spirit of adoption.[†] Now, if there is such tenderness of love in his heart, flowing out to his children, what must we think of the overflowing tenderness he must feel for his bride?

There is no more passionate relationship than that intimacy with which Spouse and the bride embrace one another. It takes precedence even over the love that unites children to their parents or parents to their children. It far outdistances it, as if gathering strength while parental love grows weak. So we are talking about that passionate tenderness which the Spouse feels for his bride, as is clear in every part of the Song.

The Spouse himself is quite unable to conceal this tenderness from the bride. Since he is a Spouse, he does not only know her as a Spouse, but he speaks to her as a Spouse, and acts towards her in all respects as befits a Spouse. He comes forth from his Father, and whatever he has heard from his Father, he whispers intimately to his beloved.[†] There is no concealment here. The veil has been taken away, and the bride approaches her Spouse in utter confidence. She is wholly free to gaze with unveiled countenance upon the glory of the Father's Only-begotten, and her whole desire is to be transformed into his likeness.[†] For his part, the Spouse refuses nothing she asks, and he leaves his beloved free to act towards him as lovingly as she wishes.

Dt 5:16

Rom 8:15

Jn 15:15

2 Cor 3:18

This is more than just granting her wishes: he surrenders himself to his bride to be spoken to, to let her breathe the scent of his fragrance, to be kissed and to be embraced, and finally to be held to her heart. For it is after experiencing all the joys for which, as we said above, she had prayed, that the bride cries out to the maidens, *I hold him, and I will not let him go.*[†] As far as the Spouse is concerned, everything gives way to the wishes of his bride, and it is his good pleasure that she should take her pleasure in him. How blessed the bosom which so great a lover was pleased to touch with his hand and lovingly to excite with his touch!

Sg 3:4

When the bride is touched like this, her whole being immediately trembles with joy. This is a fulfillment of those words of Jesus, when he promised to give his Spirit. He spoke of rivers of living water that would flow from the belly of the one he loved.[†] Now Jesus has been glorified, and he has shown himself within his bride's heart. That is why he has given her his Spirit in such abundance and why he has made the waters of his delight spring forth, as he promised, from her belly. That these rivers flow out from the body of Jesus into the body of his beloved can only be doubted by someone who is ungrateful for this favor, or has never experienced it.

Jn 7:38

These are the mysteries of the sacred marriage chamber, and they cannot be worthily dwelt on in any sermon of mine. None but the only Son of God can speak worthily of matters such as these. *May it be granted to us to know this experience and to understand what we hear, through the grace of Our Lord Jesus Christ.*

Sermon 29.1-3

The Bride:
Beautiful, Comely, the Face of God

YOU ARE BEAUTIFUL, MY LOVE.[†]

THE SPOUSE lavishes graces on his bride. Among this generation, the happiest of all is the one who has surrendered her soul to the grace that has gone before her, to be forever a whole burnt offering. She is never satisfied with what she has given, for she is always aware that it is not enough.

Every soul like this will be rightly thought worthy of having the name of 'bride' or 'loved one'. Among the number who are seeking and the throng who are running, she seeks with greater earnestness, she runs with greater speed. She follows him more tirelessly, she finds him more joyously, she holds him more tenaciously. What reward is there for this? The answer is: the Lord's blessing. After wrestling with the angel, Jacob wrested from him a blessing that was far from slight. In other words, the struggle of wrestling and refusing to admit defeat, brought him a share in the vision of God.[†]

Gen 32:24

With this blessing Jacob saw *God face to face and his life was preserved*.[†] The face that saw God

Gen 32:30

exteriorly gave a wonderful light to the interior face, so that he could see God interiorly, and he made great strides towards longing and hoping to contemplate the Light of God eternally.

The bride is no weaker than Jacob, but rather much stronger, having had more experience in wrestling. Not only that, but she shows much greater power in having to wrestle, not with some angel but with the Lord himself, whose name is *All-powerful*.† This glorious combat will end in extraordinary and memorable blessings for she has the fixed and settled determination not to let God go until he has blessed her.†

In the Song we hear these words of praise three times. The first time the praise is repeated there is a note of wonder, and attention is called to it. The second time, although it is the same expression, the note of wonder has grown into a sort of intense amazement. The third time, there is the same repetition but raised to the highest pitch of eulogy, for she is described as *all beautiful*.†

So the Spouse bestows his blessing on his beloved bride, calling her beautiful, decking her with the regalia of a new beauty. For as the Apostle says, *our inner nature is renewed from day to day*,† while it proceeds from brightness to brightness in the perception of our true image, which is Christ.† The increase in the bride's beauty brings with it an increase in humility, the one inviolable safeguard for anything beautiful.

Likewise she is called 'beloved' because she has been allowed to share in the secret thoughts of God the Father. This is the true definition of divine friendship, having its foundation in what is above and not in the things we mortals know. He says, *I have called you friends*,† that is, 'I have made you into friends. This is how I have done it: I have revealed to you the secrets of my Father's love, I have manifested the glory of God, I have unveiled to you the joys of heaven and led you to them through hope and desire.'

Ex 15:3

Gen 32:26

Sg 4:7

2 Cor 4:16

2 Cor 3:18

Jn 15:15

Moreover, now that she has been taken up into partnership by the Word of God, it could happen that the grace of such great beauty and friendship made her too majestic in the eyes of her associates, who have perhaps not progressed so far, or made her less accessible to them, or less kindly in manner.

Sg 6:3

She is *sweet and comely as Jerusalem,*† for this friend of God has learned to make herself resemble that entire city of saintly inhabitants. The Spouse is clearly referring to that beauty by which after gazing with her inner eye of contemplation she has tried to conform to the eternal beauty of the Spouse. Quite clearly, *all the glory of the King's daughter is from within.*†

Ps 45:14

Although she receives an indestructible loveliness from her close union with the Word, an increase of sweetness comes to her from her association with her fellow citizens. In her charming and holy intercourse with them she bestows grace on all, and yet she herself grows in grace from each single encounter. This beauty is also in her companions. The bride knows that the loveliness of her Spouse has many forms and has illuminated the face of every single one of them. With wonder, she has learned to see in each one of them her Spouse unchanged, and to do him reverence. In every face her Beloved shines out at her, her Beautiful One shows himself to her. She is crowned with an overwhelming glory of comeliness, longing as she does, not only to give pleasure to everyone, but to be pleasing in what she has received from them.

Sermon 47.1–7

IX

JOHN OF FORDE REJOICES WITH THE CHURCH

AN OVERVIEW

J UST HOW IMPORTANT is John of Forde's teaching on the Church has not as yet been appreciated. Although more than thirty of his sermons deal directly with the Church, it would not be far from the truth to say that, in fact, all his sermons are about the Church. Even when he is explicitly speaking in a sermon about the individual soul, he always implies that the person is a member of the Church. The principle on which the allegorical interpretation of Scripture (in this case the Song of Songs) is based is that the true meaning of the text can be found only when the text is applied to Christ and the Church. In christian theology Christ and the Church are not separate entities. The Church is the body of which Christ is the Head, and the relationship between them is a dynamic unity. Many of John's sermons conclude with a doxology in which Christ is *Sponsus ecclesiae,* the Spouse—or Bridegroom—of the Church. This must be considered as the most fundamental principle of his whole theology. When he refers to the Church as 'the first and principal Bride of Jesus',[1] he is laying down the overarching theme of his thought. The whole of his teaching concerning the Church could be summed up in the formula: 'the Bride of Christ which is the Church'.[2] In other words, the Church is the principal object of all the eulogies of this marriage song.[3]

---

[1] Sermon 56.3
[2] Sermons 20.7; 78.2; 104.12; 106.9
[3] Sermon 50.1

The encyclical *Lumen Gentium* of Vatican II looks back to the whole tradition for its formulation of the doctrine of the Church. In many ways John of Forde, by insisting on the unity of the Church with Christ, has anticipated that teaching and has even provided an insight that goes beyond it. He uses many of traditional scriptural symbols to illustrate the unique union between Christ and the Church. We can gain a clear idea of the richness of his thought from the interplay of these symbols. Here I can only briefly mention them.

One of the most important Old Testament symbols is found in Ezechiel 36:37-38:

> Thus says the Lord: This also I will let the house of Israel ask me to do for them: to increase their men like a flock. Like the holy flock, like the flock at Jerusalem during her appointed feasts, so shall the waste cities be full with flocks of men. Then they will know that I am the Lord.

This receives its definitive fulfillment in the Good Shepherd pericope of Chapter Ten of Saint John's Gospel. John of Forde develops the theme of the flock of sheep and the Shepherd in Sermon Six. The flock of God is the Church. Its members can be divided into three categories: the flock of men, i.e. those who have God's image in them, either by their fidelity to the grace of baptism or restored to them in the sacrament of reconciliation; the 'holy' flock of those who have left all things to follow Christ in poverty, chastity, and obedience—no doubt he is referring here to the religious state; there is another flock made up of God's great friends: all those who have reached the heavenly city—apostles, martyrs, saints, holy virgins. In reality there is only one flock and one Shepherd. Yet when Jesus calls himself 'the Good Shepherd' in Saint John's Gospel, he is asserting the unity of the Shepherd with his flock. Shepherd and flock make a unity. God is marvelous in the universal unity of all those who are 'in Christ'.

John takes up a traditional horticultural theme in many of his sermons. The Church, for example, may also be seen as a garden, fertile and full of trees, a garden on which the Holy Spirit rests. In Sermons Fifty-four to Fifty-seven he interprets the vine in the garden in a comprehensive sense as the whole Church which spreads its roots down the centuries from its first beginnings in Jerusalem until it now embraces the whole of humankind. In the early Church at Jerusalem the tiny saplings started to grow and flourish and soon, because of the preaching of the apostles and the blood of the martyrs, a great forest began to spread over the whole earth.

One of the most important symbols is that of the Church as the mystical Body of Christ. There are many facets to this relationship between Christ and the Church. The glory of Christ in his union with the whole Church and each member is seen in the early sermon:

> What could be more marvelous than that the Lord knitted the totality of the saints together in his Body. In two ways God is wonderful in his saints: he is wonderful in them taken as a whole, he is wonderful in each one of them.[4]

So the beauty of the whole person, Head and Body, pertains to each one of the members. This is the beauty that comes from Christ's union with his holy Body which is the Church. When the Father gave him this lovely Bride, the Church, in the union of marriage, he bestowed on Christ 'glory and great dignity'.[5] It was through the power of the cross that the Father gave his Son the throne at his right hand, and 'his whole Body, which we are, has been blessed, together with our Head and Spouse, with sure hope of glory'.[6]

---

[4] Sermon 5.2
[5] Sermon 36.6
[6] Sermon 86.10

John of Forde does not consider the Church primarily as an institution. For him, as for the earlier spiritual writers and fathers, the Church is first and foremost the Bride of Christ. In the traditional exegesis of Song of Songs the primary meaning of the word 'Bride' is the Church. John implies a deep bond of union and a new covenant: 'Talking of the love by which the Church is united to Christ her heavenly Spouse in the Holy Spirit, we should first of all see how this sermon should be applied to this Bride'.[7] John is here taking up Saint Paul's teaching: 'This is a great mystery; and I am speaking about Christ and the Church'.[8] The marriage took place, as *Lumen Gentium* was later to insist, when Christ united the Church to himself by dying on the cross and in his own blood he established a new and everlasting kingdom.

Even if John of Forde uses the expression 'people of God' only twice, he is close to the encyclical *Lumen Gentium* in referring frequently to the 'church of the nations' *(ecclesia gentium)*. The remarkable thing about the early Church was the speed at which it grew, first among the faithful Jews looking for the Messiah, and then rapidly among the people of the Roman Empire. Referring to this growth, John reflects on the light that started to shine during Christ's lifetime and continued to increase amazingly during the period of the early Church.[9] Calling it 'the church of the nations', he indicates that God's saving action is no longer limited to one nation. All nations are called into the unity of the Church. In that unity, there was no place, he says—idealizing those first beginnings—for anything that might be a scandal to charity, no quarrelling among those whose ideal was greater humility.[10] At first—again idealizing the early Church—he sees a wonderful union between Jews and Gentiles who were united together at that time in one faith. Medieval people thought that the 'Chosen Race' had cut themselves off from the

---

[7] Sermon 64.1
[8] Eph 5:22-23
[9] Sermon 56.6
[10] Sermon 17.9

source of grace by rejecting the universal invitation; yet John sees this as only a temporary stage. The loss of the Jews is the reconciliation of the world. On the last day, 'Joseph will comfort his brothers'.[11] The Church of the nations is the new Bride of Christ. At the beginning of the transcription of the Song of Songs made by Saint Stephen Harding early in the history of Citeaux, an illuminated letter 'O' witnesses to the same point: Christ is seated with this New Bride at his right hand, and at his left hand the Synagogue, rejected and brushed aside, indeed disfigured, seems to turn away. The call is now universal, not limited by race, color or state in society; rich and poor alike are called.

> The former bride made a way of life for me into Jesus' side, to the most intimate place in his heart. There I was formed from the side of my sleeping Lord; for he wished to sleep in death that I may be formed.[12]

These are high ideals and they demand a holy hierarchy in the governing structure of the visible Church. John of Forde had too much experience of bishops and prelates of his time to ignore the problems. He had been confessor to King John for several years and had come into contact with many members of the english hierarchy. He has some harsh things to say to those bishops and prelates who lived evil lives. He singles out for special rebuke those proud and rebellious men who rule badly in the Church.

No doubt there were also tireless and holy men who were zealous for the well-being of the Church and who built her up to a healthy life. Such were the apostles and their successors. No land or kingdom was enough for them. The salvation of the whole world was their aim, and they thirsted for it insatiably. Men like this, he says, are still within the Church today. Sometimes their function is to rebuke and correct. But they should do this with the tranquil love of God in their hearts. If done in this spirit their zeal brings health, strength and unity.

[11] Sermon 30.5
[12] Sermon 30.6

The martyrs, in their turn, are like a great army constituting the glorious raiment of the Church; for the love of the Catholic faith they fought as one in Christ, united in devotion even unto death. They consecrated themselves body and soul to the Lord Jesus and entered into a sacred marriage relationship with him. These martyrs, pre-eminent and illustrious, claim the highest place in the tree which is the Church. To fall in defense of Truth is a powerful foretaste of the glory that is to come.

The Interdict that Innocent III imposed on England in 1208 was a great test of John of Forde's loyalty to the pope. This dramatic penalty had a devastating effect on the life of the monks and the laity alike. Deprived of the sacraments and, possibly, of the Divine Office in choir, religious life in cistercian monasteries came virtually to a standstill. The Interdict was imposed primarily because the king refused to accept Stephen Langton as Archbishop of Canterbury in place of one of his own cronies. But it affected the religious and the laity far more than it affected the king. The Eucharist, the great sacrament of love, which is in many ways the very raison d'être of the Church, was strictly forbidden by the pope. Innocent III was the principal authority in the Church, under Christ. John did not question this. For him, as for the whole of european society—with the exception of heretics, Moslems and Jews—authority in the Church was inherited by the apostles and passed on to those who succeeded them down to the present time: 'They have been given this power and authority for God's glory and the protection of God's Bride; they should not twist it to gain their own personal honor and leave the Church naked'.[13] John was treading on eggshells here. He did not want to criticize the supreme authority of the Church: 'God forbid that any man should dare think that any action of theirs has been rash or over hasty'.[14] I take it that he has Innocent in mind here. Yet John sees the pope also as the mouthpiece of Christ: 'It is the mouth of the Lord that has spo-

[13] Sermon 49.8
[14] Sermon 41.3

ken, and the zeal of the Lord of hosts has done all these things'.[15]
Unity within the Church must stem from the principal authority
in the Church.

The primary purpose and mission of the Church is eschato-
logical, namely to lead all its members and the whole world to
the vision of God in heaven. The Church longs for the sight of
the face of God unveiled and for the transformation of all into
the image of the Only-begotten of the Father. John sees an even
greater significance in the union between Christ and the Church
when it is applied to the glory of the Church in heaven: 'The
fullness of glory is to be made one Body with this fullness, and to
be part of it is to possess it totally'.[16] Such is the ultimate
strength of Christ's love and its universality that it 'immerses
them in the ocean of eternal happiness in a blissful communion
where there are as many blessings as there are those to be
blessed'.[17]

---

[15] Sermon 41.3
[16] Sermon 78.4
[17] Sermon 105.6

In Praise of the Church

Sg 2:16

Sg 4:2, 6:6

1 Cor 9:19

Is 61:6

Sermon on the Church. Where praise is concerned the Church appropriates to herself the leading part, since she is the principal object of all the eulogies of this marriage song. Above all else, she claims as her own the glory and the title of Queen and Bride, so that she has the privilege, in a special way, of saying, *My beloved is mine and I am his.*†

The 'teeth of the bride'† symbolize vigorous men who are zealous for her well-being—apostles and preachers, who chew the food that builds up her life and health. The apostles and the preachers who emulate them have the same zeal for our salvation and go to the ends of the earth, marking themselves out for death if only they can win us for Christ.† No land or kingdom was enough for them: the salvation of the whole world was to be their food. About this, a great promise had been made to them, *You shall eat the wealth of the nations, and in their riches you shall glory.*† With insatiable avidity they crave such foods that they completely disregard any grading of food and think nothing is to be refused, if only they can satisfy their hunger.

'Teeth' are incisors, canines, or molars. These are arranged in the mouth of the Church.

Zeal: there is nothing more biting or voracious then these incisors. They are racked with a holy hunger for souls. They would be eaten by Christ and incorporated into Christ.† What could be more devouring than this, or rather what tooth could be more gentle?

Molars: these are the teeth of the Lord Jesus. He is the most zealous for the salvation of us all. He is the most ardent of all those who are zealous for the salvation of mankind, even to the point of being wholly dissatisfied unless, in a wonderful manner, he too in his turn should be eaten by us. He chews us and swallows us and passes us down into his own self, causing the same hunger within us. He longs to be eaten and swallowed and united with us, to become most intimately and profoundly a part of us. Hence those loving words of his, *Make your abode with me and I in you.*† So what is done in the sacrament of love, when we partake of the body and blood of Christ, is a clear indication of taking refreshment and sharing a meal. It is like a foretaste of the eternal banquet and communion.

'Teeth' also indicates that they are used to rebuke and correct. But God's anger is full of tranquil love. His correction can appear very sharp; his discipline springs from the compassionate eye of grace. So the bite of these teeth brings health, strength, and gives unity. By dividing they bring to consummation.

What toothache the Church suffers today from preachers who are a source of nothing but affliction and misery. They are zealous for wealth and rank and preferment—but not zealous for the things of God. God will break the

Rom 9:3

Jn 15:4

teeth in their mouths. Even though they are rotten to the root, they cling stubbornly on, and they resist any attempt to draw them out. When it comes to showing zeal for preferment, rank, endowment, and wealth, they have nothing less than elephant's tusks in comparison with the zeal of the ancient fathers, not to speak of a comparison with the great apostles. But when it comes to zeal for the things of Christ Jesus and the salvation of the souls for whom Christ died, they seem to become completely impotent to do any eating.

Sermon 50.2-6

THE CHURCH:
IN A BOND OF SACRED MARRIAGE

LIKE THE RIND OF THE POMEGRANATE ARE YOUR CHEEKS.[†]

Sg 6:6

THERE ARE DIFFERENT WAYS of praising which show great richness of praise. Since not a leaf falls from a tree without our Father's will,[†] still less would it be possible for any leaf to drop idly from this tree, the most powerful and fruitful of all the trees of the forest. Indeed it would be easier for heaven and earth to pass away than even one word among the words of

Mt 10:29

the Word, the Wisdom of God the Father. Rather, not one iota, not one dot, or any of his words can be spoken of as 'passing away'.[†]   Mt 5:18

The 'cheeks' of the Church are chaste souls. The Lord Jesus set his seal on the glory of purity. His was the voice they heard when they were called to the high state and prize of chastity. The old familiar ways of the world were not for them. They turned aside deliberately and, by a bond that nothing can untie, they consecrated their souls and bodies to that most beautiful 'dove', Jesus Christ, and entered into a sacred marriage relationship with him. Mindful of their secret and of the contract they have entered into with their heavenly Spouse, they avoid all public places and resolve to live in solitude, being above all things wary of anything that could endanger their innocence. They renounce the consolations of all things under heaven, having as their sole desire pleasing him to whom they have offered themselves. They live in solitude, waiting upon him. All too often he flies away to his heavenly solitude. The soul like this is happy in her solitude and pines away over the memory of her Spouse. It is fitting that he should say to her, *Your cheeks are beautiful.*[†]   Sg 1:9
He says, 'By loving me, by sighing for me, by imitating me, the charm of your cheeks has clothed itself in the beauty of my cheeks'.

The bride's cheeks are like broken pieces of pomegranate. The Church's virgin-martyrs have reached a still higher stage of chastity by being put to the test, by terrifying cruelty beyond the limits of human strength, almost beyond the limits of belief. Christ is their strength, their beauty, their crown. His is the prize of their lives. What can we call the great army of martyrs but 'a broken pomegranate'. The glorious union of the martyrs who, for love of the christian faith, fought as one, united in devotion even unto death. Divine strength kept them from faltering in their faith. The martyr is red with a most ardently burning charity, but also radiant white with the most joyful hope of eternal blessedness. The martyrs claim the highest place in the tree that is the Church. They are a pre-eminent and illustrious part of the Church. To fall in death in defense of their purity is a mighty foretaste of the glory that is to come. In spite of bitter pains, broken in body, they yet remain unbroken in spirit.

The secret heart of this temple, the Church of the saints, is the continence of those who follow the sublime path of chastity. So chaste and modest are they that they protect their chastity with modesty and with a godly veil of confession.

The Spouse praises the chastity of his Bride, the Church. The Church has peace from heaven and is careful to preserve her chastity, for it is in danger even when there is tranquil peace in the world. There lurks the invisible enemy, namely our fleshly appetites. Now, in times of peace, there is a sword of fire, more penetrating and more terrible. The Bride cloaks herself with modesty and a sort of bashfulness. This modesty is found in two ways: first, she avoids the movements of temptation, preventing them from raising their head; then, if they are already there, she reproves and subdues them. Modesty is excellent and leads to high glory. This rind of modesty is a good one, for it conceals all that is good except to God alone.

The modest soul hides her good deeds under her bashfulness and keeps them in a secret hiding place. These secret things remain her own, the good action destined to earn the glory of happiness. 'Secrets'. Some things are exterior, like vigils, labors, fasts, disciplines, and the like. But God sees the secrets of souls. What lies hidden is what gives refreshment. God praises what is lovely externally and what is charming internally, what has been done for all to see, and what has been done in private for her own happiness and the glory of her Spouse.

Sermon 52.2–9

BODY BEAUTIFUL, HEAD LOVELIER STILL

YOUR HEAD IS LIKE CARMEL.[†]   Sg 7:5

JESUS, the Spouse, began his catalogue of praise with the bride's feet and her sandals.[†] He ends triumphantly with praise of the Bride's head.[†] There can be no nobler interpretation of this than that given by the apostle Paul: *The head of a woman is her husband, the head of the husband is Christ, and the head of Christ is God.*[†] Since the Church is the Body of Christ, it is

Sg 7:1
See Sermon 64.

Sg 7:5

1 Cor 11:3

only right to consider the Head of the Church as Christ. This great description, made in her honor, applies to her because it belongs to each and every person in the great Body of the Church. And this is the highest point in the whole eulogy.

First and foremost this commentary is specially fitting for that foremost Bride of Christ, the Church.† So far, the Spouse has paid tribute to her various qualities according to her various gifts of grace; now he binds together all the members of the one Head which is himself. This Head he compares to Carmel, that is, to a mountain where there is pasture. It is a fertile mountain where both sheep and shepherds can find rich pasture, and there too lovers of solitude find a suitable place for contemplation. Under the guidance of the Holy Spirit both Elijah and Elisha withdrew from the world† and handed down the ideal of a solitary way of life to their sons and grandsons, which is what you are. That mountain is raised aloft above the peaks of all other mountains and is very rich in fertile soil, but it also spreads out spaciously on all sides. For this reason it is also known as 'the mountain of the Lord',† where every day the Heavenly Father builds his many mansions.

O Lord, God of might and power, who will climb that holy mountain?† Let me deserve to find some kind of place, however small, among the lowest members of this mighty Head. My place will not be unworthy of me. It is Wisdom who holds the measuring line here, and no inequality at all will be able to make Wisdom err from the true when he measures. I realize that I

St Gregory the Great, *Forty Gospel Homilies* (PL 76. 832)

1 K 18, 2 K 2

Ps 24:2

Ps 24:3

am nothing. But when I look at the greatness
and beauty of the Body in which I trust I belong, I can now venture to say that I am not
nothing. When I lift up my eyes to the towering
crest of this Body, I have at once grown enor-
mously great, and now I cannot contain my own
self. *I shall extol you, O God my King,*[†] for you
have taken me up into this glorious union with
your Body. The fullness of glory is to be made
one body with this fullness, and to be part of it
is to possess it all completely.

Ps 145:1

Happy is the Bride who hears her Spouse
speaking of the magnificence of her Head, so
that nothing may be lacking to the fullness of
her beauty. The meaning of Carmel is 'knowledge of circumcision'.[†] This means nothing unless it means knowledge of the Lord Jesus. For
to know the Lord Jesus is perfect understanding, a knowledge that only the pure in heart can
receive. Yes, he, Jesus, is the knowledge of the
humble, the knowledge of the blessed. Far from
that knowledge is all that is unclean, even if it
unrolls all that has been written of him, from
the beginning of the book right up to the end.
Blessed are the people who know the joyful shout.[†]
Only experience can grasp knowledge of this
kind, and only purity can deserve it. So anyone
who wants to have real knowledge of Jesus, and
to know the mystery of Carmel, must first be
circumcised with the spiritual circumcision of
the heart, where the glory and virtue come not
from men but from God alone.[†]

According to
Jerome, *Liber
nominum
hebraicorum;*
PL 23:1232

Ps 89:15

Rom 2:29

The true circumcision of the heart is to be
justified in Christ's grace. The more profoundly
anyone cleaves to justifying grace, the more

quickly he climbs Mount Carmel, and the more happily he dwells there. And Mount Carmel is Christ.

Sermon 78.1–5

BREAD OF LOVE. FISH OF PATIENCE. WINE OF JOY. FRUIT OF PRAISE

THERE IS an 'interior' tasting by which the Spouse distinguishes the various foods that sustain his human life, as well as the different tastes of these foods. Not everything tastes alike. Butter has one flavor, honey another. Bread differs from fish, and milk from wine, and so forth. As for bread and fish, although they were offered to Jesus after his resurrection,† nobody can deny that he also ate them before his resurrection, but differently. Before, he ate them in the sweat of his brow, since the near approach of his passion made him say to his Father in anguish, *Not what I will, but what you will*.† The very bread of Jesus, and also that of angels,† is to do the Father's will.† But in the days of his flesh when he was prone to suffering, that bread was mingled with ashes of repentance.† Clearly its taste was not the same as the bread of his resurrection, gleaming white, pure bread of the finest wheaten flour.

Jn 21:13

Mk 14:36
Ps 78:26
Jn 4:34

Ps 102:9

The fish of patience—which are tossed this way and that by the waves of the sea, finding life where all other living things find death—came to the shore of the resurrection to be in contact with Jesus. For Jesus, risen from the dead, stood on the shore;[†] and this fish tasted very different from [the fish eaten during] the days of his passion, when suffering produced patience.[†] Indeed, there are within him infinite riches of patience, yet every fish of this kind has something about it of the grilled fish of his resurrection,[†] a certain marvelous flavor of impassability and pure joy.

Jn 21:4

Rom 5:3

Jn 21:9

If you want to refresh Jesus with these foods, you must come to the point of saying with him, *My food is to do the will of my Father who is in heaven,*[†] and, *Gladly will I glory in my infirmities.*[†] You will show that you have risen with Christ and are *walking in newness of life,*[†] if you offer both these foods to Christ, while at the same time sitting down to eat with him.

Jn 4:34

2 Cor 12:9

Rom 6:4

Jesus promised that he would drink new wine with the apostles.[†] In speaking of 'new' he implied a reference to the 'old wine', making a distinction between the happiness and glow of love that belong to our present pilgrimage through *the valley of the shadow of death,*[†] and that rich and fertile love which the vine bears in the kingdom of God.

Mt 26:29

Ps 23:4

Yet, because it is this new wine—namely, the ineffable joy of the newness of life that comes from the resurrection—which he drinks with his disciples, they like little children are not as yet strong enough to bear the newness of this great joy. Therefore the Wisdom of God

Prv 9:2

mixes with his wine† a little milk of the kind of joy they can understand. He offers it first in the appearance of a stranger, and then in one they knew well, subduing the glory of his glorified body and accommodating it to their littleness.†

Lk 24:30

In the same way, he calls this diluting of his sweetness 'his milk'—namely, mother's milk, the milk of his breasts, just what is needed for building up his little ones. With wine like this the Bride rejoices the heart of her Spouse, as is clear, *Your throat is like the best wine.*† This wine too she gave to her Spouse to be blended with the milk of gentle humility and tempered sweetness, *He set love in order in me.*†

Sg 7:9

Sg 2:4

As the banquet ends, fruit is served, fresh and dried, and this I take as indicating the delights of praise and joyful thanksgiving. Both fresh and dried fruit are mentioned, commending recent kindness as well as happily recalling the favors of the past. The Bride is faithful to her Spouse; indeed, *the heart of her husband trusts in her,*† and she has learned never to let his present kindness obscure the memory of his past . . .

Prv 31:11

So the bride is right to call the Spouse's throat *most sweet*, seeing that it is blessed with the taste of all these different kinds of sweetness. For in butter, the benevolence of love enriches this heart; in honey, the sweetness of his inner glory sweetens it; in bread, love for his Father's will strengthens it; in fish, the gentleness of patience gladdens it; in milk, a sober simplicity consoles it; in fruit fresh and dried, it is filled to overflowing with the gift of sweet praise in all its forms. There are moreover other sweetnesses without number, beyond our reach,

and known only to that *most sweet throat*,[†] but it
is our hope that throughout all eternity they will
be blissfully revealed to us through him who is
the Spouse of the Church, Jesus Christ our
Lord.

Sg 5:16

Sermon 37.6–8

THE LOVE OF GOD FOR HIS CHURCH

Priority

HOW MARVELOUS and varied is the love
with which God loves his Church. This love
precedes the love that the Church has for the
Lord her God. It is higher in dignity, more intimate in sweetness, anterior in eternity. How can
these loves meet? The first comes up from such
a distance, flows out of such an intimacy, hastens so impetuously and swiftly from eternity. *I
came to meet them like a river of peace, like an
overflowing torrent of glory.*[†]

Is 66:12

God's love is indeed a river of peace streaming out in its greatness and flowing in with
gentle waters. At the same time it is a torrent,
rushing along with mighty force, and sweeping
everything away with it. The Church's love cannot make an adequate response to this love of
God. It can only stand like a dove with drooping

wings, now looking up to wonder at the majesty of this love, now gazing within to marvel at its goodness, and now looking back in amazement at its antiquity. It can only say in ecstasy of mind, '*Lord, who is like you,*[†] and what love is like yours?'

Ex 15:12

Purity

More than anything else, God's love is pre-eminent for its incomparable 'purity'. It is not purged by fire or by any other means. Nothing defiled can gain entrance to it.[†] Through the force of the immensity of its own natural purity, it has the power to purge away all that is impure. That it is free and spontaneous greatly enhances the charm of this purity. It flows out in abundance from the rich plenty of its own heart, so too it flows freely. It does not look for repayment, but rather lavishes itself in love, even with force and insistence.

Ws 7:25

The treasure of our love is hidden in the field of our heart[†] and lies buried in the depths. After great labor we can dig up a little of it, but it is earthy and impure. To be of any use it must first be smelted in a great fire. For this purification the fire of God's everlasting love is absolutely necessary. We must beg from the Father of lights some little spark from that great conflagration that consumes everything in heaven. Then we must lay sticks on it, and, lying flat on the ground, blow hard, do our utmost with sighs and longings. We must rouse it up in ourselves, until at last a steady little flame rises up from

Mt 13:44

this little fire, since we have at hand the huge and infinite forest of God's benefits created from all eternity and increasing every day into infinity.

So God's love has by its own nature the greatest purity. It has everything that is perfect in purity. It has no need of kindness from another, but rather lavishes abroad its own kindness.

Powerful and Strong

But the Love of God is not only sweet and loving in premeditation, it is also powerful and strong in activity. It is worth probing into its workings to see its power, its value, its weight, and its brightness and solidity.

POWER CONCEALED. First though, it is necessary for a reality of such deep deliberation and long-lasting silence to break into the open, and a mystery so well concealed will find it fitting to answer in a style in keeping with its magnificence. The Lord Jesus, when he lived among us, for a long time did not walk about in full view. For thirty years he purposely kept himself to himself. He was hidden and despised† and he made darkness his covering.† Afterwards, he broke the long-standing silence by opening his mouth and distilling the honey of his lips, and he broke for ever his peaceful retreat by opening his mouth and displaying the power of his marvelous deeds.

POWER REVEALED. God's love came to reveal to his Church the mystery silent from immemorial

Is 53:3
Ps 18:11

ages and hidden in God alone. He came out of
his marriage chamber† to preach on the house-
tops what had been whispered in the privacy of
the inner room.† Those eternal ages were for
our God like a time of contemplation and rest,
like a Sabbath. The day came for him to come
out into the open, and for contemplation to display itself in action. What had been for so long
in labor at last came forth. The womb of eternal
love was opened and it brought forth for us a
Saviour.† So the Wisdom of God has come
raising his voice in our streets,† preaching to the
world God's love. He cries aloud, *God so loved
the world as to give his Only-begotten Son.*†

Listen, O Church of God, listen and incline
your ear.† Consider the majesty of him who has
loved you, how he has loved you from all ages,
how undeserved this love has been, how great it
is. The one who loves you is exceedingly great,
and you, utterly unworthy of being loved, are
quite incapable of returning a love commensu-
rate with so high an honor. He does not seek
your love so as to be enriched by you. Your love
is a drop in a bucket. Even if it were a river, *all
the rivers flow into the sea and the sea is not made
greater!*† Have everlastingly in mind the everlasting years of that everlasting love,† because it
abounds for you from everlasting ages.

God has loved you from all eternity; love
him, then, now and forever. In him there was no
beginning to love, for you there must be no end-
ing. On your side is not a free gift, but the pay-
ment of the debt you owe. Yet this is not the
least part of his infinite graciousness and un-
forced love, in that all the debt you pay he takes

Ps 19:5
Mt 10:27
Is 45:8
Prv 1:20
Jn 3:16
Ps 45:10
Qo 1:7
Ps 76:6

as a kindness, receiving it as if it really were a free gift.

Listen how greatly you are loved: *God so loved the world as to give his Only-begotten Son.*[†] On this errand God has sent the one and only Son of his love, consubstantial with himself, to reveal his love towards us and incline us to accept it. O how sweet the messenger, and how sweet the message. He is the bearer of a deep mystery, and the angel of great counsel.[†] Run to embrace him! Hasten to kiss him! Bless in your heart the Blessed One who comes in the name of the Lord,[†] and bless him who sent him. From the goodness of his heart and the depths of his love, the Father uttered a good Word,[†] and the most certain proof of his great love is the sending forth of his Only-begotten Son. He sent him in order to give, he gave him in order to give himself and all that is his with him.

Sermon 13.4-6

Jn 3:16

Is 9:6 LXX

Mt 21:9

Ps 45:1

VALUE, WEIGHT, FIRMNESS, AND BRIGHTNESS OF THE CHURCH

VALUE: God's beloved, look more closely still at this love: its value, its weight, its solidity, and its brightness.

You have shown the value of your love in that you despised everything—and even your own soul so as to acquire it for yourself. But this is the value of God's love: he left the heavens and all his friends and neighbors who are not here below, and he came down to you, and he came to make you like himself, to seek you and to take up his abode with you.

How do earthly things compare with heavenly? To assert more firmly the truth of his love, the Son left his Father and the Father his Son. Of the Son it has been truly said: *A man will leave his father and mother and cleave to his wife* [the Church].† Of the Father and to the Father, we have the cry of the Son, *Why have you deserted me?*† This was a great cry. That cry was the thunder peal of infinite charity and unspeakable tenderness, so intent on recommending to us the Father's love that for our sake he showed himself forsaken and deserted. The value of that charity could never be more highly recommended than when it was made so clear, by the Father as well as the Son, how much it cost them.

You have been bought at a great price.† What are you, O man, to have been valued so highly and esteemed of such exceptional worth? Compared to what you cost, what is more precious? O wonderful exchange,† and a wonderful motive for the exchange! That majesty whom the heavens cannot contain endured being bought and sold at the cheapest price. That most abject thing, man, was purchased by God, and so there was an exchange of grandeur. Because of the inestimable value put upon him, he became inestimable. So, man, give a return of love to your purchaser and glorify him for your price.

Gen 2:24

Ps 22:1

1 Cor 6:20

From a Lauds Antiphon for the Epiphany

WEIGHT. To make quite sure of the weight of this love, let us weigh it, weight for weight. The weight of divine love against the weight of human sinfulness. Heavy indeed is the infinite mass of sinfulness. Yet this excessive load of huge stones is hanging round humanity's neck, dragging it down beneath the mighty waters.† The charity of God runs to meet his Church, now on the very point of sinking under, and in his hand he bears the scales of justice. So the Church with all its sinfulness is weighed in one pan, and on the other, directly opposite, Love lays itself to be weighed, having with it the God-man, his cross and his blood, and a very large bundle of myrrh† carefully gathered from the sufferings of Christ. In the presence of Love, all sinfulness disappeared in an instant like a cloud, and it showed on the scales as weighing nothing at all.† Because of its excessive weight, Love, together with the God-man, dipped right down to the depths, to where the Church was on the verge of going, and the Church through the power of the scales, rose up on high to where Christ had been about to go.

SOLIDITY OR FIRMNESS. You are truly just and merciful, O Lord. With very great love then God has taken thought for the Church, has redeemed it at the price of love, has lifted it up to heaven. He has bound it to himself for ever with the most indissoluble and firmest love. Beneath her head she has for softest pillow the left hand of her Spouse,† the everlasting memorial of all that he has endured on her account. Embracing her she has his right hand in all its holiness,†

Ex 15:20

Sg 1:13

Is 40:15

Sg 2:6

Sg 2:6

the eternal reminder of all the blessings he has shown her, especially in admitting her to the full fruition of the sweetness of union with him. The firmness of divine love binds closely together this holy covenant, and is itself the everlasting sweetness of the bond.

BRIGHTNESS. Who can describe, who can even gaze at, with sufficient wonder, the brightness of that glowing love? It moves always from brightness into brightness, and with love to strengthen and comfort the eyes, light is seen in light.† The love of the Church, with which it loves God, is surely also itself a light and a fire strongly flaming, but all this power to burn and shine it draws from that other Love. Eternally it draws from it what eternally it pours back into it, and so its love will never grow dim or faint. It sees in itself how great is God's Love, how ancient, how sublime, how generous, how spontaneous, how precious, how weighty, how firm, how radiant with light. It will see in that day how well the bride did to say, *The head of my Spouse is finest gold,*† and Paul, *the head of Christ is God,*† and John, *God is Love.*† Now you, who are the font of this Love, the Father of our Lord Jesus Christ, bless us gloriously with that love through the only Son of your Love, who lives and reigns with you, God, for ever and ever.

Sermon 13.7-10

2 Cor 3:18

Sg 5:11
1 Cor 11:3
1 Jn 4:8

THE CHURCH PRAISES

IT IS GOOD to confess to the Lord,[†] good to praise him, good to bless him. For the person who confesses has a very great reward, since the Son will also confess him before the Father.[†] The Bride, who is the Church knows this very well, and pours herself out in confessing, praising and blessing her Spouse. She confesses, praises and blesses him before the angels of God, and also and finally before the Father who is in heaven.[†] The Church does not seek her own glory, but yearns to save the souls of others. She has anchored her whole hope in the Father of the Word. She hopes that he will reveal himself to her, and she prays to his only Son, the only one who reveals him to whomever he chooses.[†] These words should be taken as referring to the early Church who is the mother of us all. The bride blesses the Spouse; and the Spouse blesses the bride. His blessing falls on all creatures. It is a great weight of blessing and it makes her holy.

    Turn your eyes away.[†] This may sound like a curse, but on the spiritual level it is the language of love, higher than that of the angels. It is like the words of Jesus: *If I do not go away, the Holy Spirit will not come to you.*[†]

    The bride, the Church, must drop her eyes so that when Jesus flies to the Father, her eyes may take wing also and fly by his side. They must delight in the sight of Christ their Lord become Spirit rather than in the flesh. It was good to be living close to Jesus in the flesh when

Ps 92:1

Mt 10:32

Mt 6:9

Mt 11:27

Sg 6:4

Jn 16:7

the whole glory of this world seemed like grass, but now something far higher is prepared for by her Spouse.

So far the words have been applied to the early Church, who is mother of all; what joy it is that the fullness of love should dwell within her.

THE SOUL PRAISES

BUT IF THE PHRASE is applied to any soul who has drunk deeply of the Spirit, she cannot satisfy her thirst until she stands before the face of God,† for it is he, the living stream, that can fill the thirsting soul. She is hastening to the fullness of charity. Having been trained by the Lord Jesus, she is handed over to the Holy Spirit so that he may teach her. For, as Jesus said to his first friends, *The Holy Spirit, whom the Father will send in my name, he it is who will teach you everything, and bring to your minds every-thing that I have said to you.*† He is the Spirit of Love, the fount of charity; it is he who creates new eyes for those who would see Jesus, by illuminating their minds and enkindling their hearts.

The new fullness of the Holy Spirit comes to us, and this requires stronger eyes. That is why we must turn our minds from a bodily consideration of Jesus and have new eyes to long for

Ps 42:2

Jn 15:26

the things of heaven and gaze on the spiritual realities that belong to Christ in heaven at the right hand of his Father.

By another interpretation: The words are an entreaty, not a command. Sometimes in Scripture the Lord invites us to resist him. The Spouse is speaking to his bride as a friend and makes a suggestion which he does not want her to obey since what he says implies the possibility of separation.

She is blessed in the deeper serenity of mind which has made her fit to see God here and now. The eye of the mind is more luminous still, because it is able to transform the soul that contemplates God into that same image and to carry it forward from brightness into brightness.† The eye of understanding follows the Spouse. He wants her to become like an eagle and to fly after him, to follow him even if he goes to heaven and there shuts himself up in his Father's bosom and stays, the Word in the beginning, even there, as far as she can, the Bride will cleave to her Beloved.

Never let it happen, Lord my God, that the gaze of my eyes be fixed anywhere but on my Head, so that I may cleave without intermission to you, my Beloved. These words are constantly in my mind: As the Lord lives, and as I live, I shall not let you alone,† but my eyes will always be on you.† *You must turn your eyes to me and mine to you, for I will never be able to look on you unless you first look on me, most Beautiful, most Powerful, most Sweet, only Son of the Father.*

2 Cor 3:18

Sg 6:3

2 K 4:30
Ps 25:14

Sermon 48.1–10

The Living Church:
Chastity, Patience,
and Love Among the Clergy

Sg 6:10

I WENT DOWN TO THE ORCHARD OF ALMONDS, TO LOOK AT THE FRUITS OF THE VALLEY, TO SEE WHETHER THE VINES HAD BUDDED, WHETHER THE POMEGRANATES WERE IN BLOOM.†

Ps 110:2

THE CHURCH HERSELF can be meant by the *orchard of almonds,* because the Lord has sent from Zion *his mighty shoot,*† the Lord Jesus, and that Zion is the church is admitted unhesitatingly by all. So it is the Church that is *the orchard of almonds,* a most pleasant and fertile orchard, teeming with trees that bud into the flowers on which the Spirit of the Lord finds repose. It is by the sanctifying power of the Holy Spirit that the flower of this holier way of life— at first a tender blossom that must change into the greater sweetness of the fruit—becomes eager to put to death *all in it that is earthly.* So it bears around in its body the cross of Christ, almost as if it were some sort of protective shield that will guard and defend the sweetness of sanctity's dazzling whiteness.

CHASTITY. Ordained priests in particular are obliged to both forms of holy living: to fight for chastity themselves; and to lead and train others in this same warfare. Yes, God's greatest treasure within the Church is clerical celibacy, which gives rise to the rich fruit of salutary example for the whole Church. If it loses its fertility, then

the power of the clergy could still be a rod of
fear, but it will not be a rod of guidance; it will
make nothing blossom and bear fruit for others
since it has not first shown in its own self the
miraculous sign of its own blossom and fruit.

FRUITS OF THE VALLEY. By fruits, the Spouse
signifies the humble of heart. This is delightful
to taste and to scent, and a source of great pleasure to that heavenly gardener. There is a lovely
taste, because these lowly ones have knowledge
of nothing earthly or fleshly, but only of the devotion of a humbled spirit. There is a lovely
scent, because they breathe forth the fragrance
of angelic obedience, or better, that of Christ
who, having gladly become for our sakes a free-
will sacrifice, offered himself to his Father as a
fragrant offering.† The Lord planted the para- Eph 5:2
dise in which he placed the first man with trees
that bore this fruit. For the rational spirit, made
in the image of its Creator, just that minute
called into being, the craftsmanship of everything around him forced upon his notice the
majesty of his Craftsman. Obviously, this spirit
learned to appreciate the majesty of his Creator
and the lowliness of his own position. The
whole of creation both seen and unseen† gave a Col 1:16
lesson in obedience, either by its example or by
being ready to serve him or at his side to help
him. So paradise was a whole world of delights
for man. It brought humble thoughts to his
mind and pressed upon him an awareness of
God's grandeur.

  But Christ, the new Adam,† the Spouse of 1 Cor 15:22
holy Church, who came to retrieve the long lost

joys of man, was the only one of Adam's seed who did not lend an ear to the serpent's hiss or stretch out his hand to the forbidden tree. He showed to the woman the fruit of the valley—that is, the fruit of humility—and he told her:

Mt 11:29 *Learn of me for I am meek and humble of heart.*† These fruits are fruits of salvation, fruits of life, fruits of happiness, and they spring from the fruit-bearing tree that is himself.

LOVE. After the fruits of the valley, the Spouse also looks for a rich yield from his vines, which is, I take to mean, nothing else than an abundant charity. This is the wine that gladdens both

Jdg 9:13 God and men,† that makes both God and men wholly intoxicated. This intoxication has stolen up on God himself, when, having received the cup from the soul that loves him, he falls into a heavy sleep on the cross, forgetting all the wrongs done him, overcome by this kind of 'wine'. It was out of the very great love with which he loved us that he poured out his soul in death and allowed himself to be numbered among the wicked.

It is these two kinds of charity—love of God and love of his brothers—that are the two vines he desires to see in bud, naturally expecting fruit to result from their flowers. The vine is in flower when our words reveal love, when we have a holy longing to love God or our brother or sister, when we pray devoutly to the Father of spirits, imploring love, when we listen devoutly to the Word whenever something about love happens to come to our hearing.

PATIENCE. After the budding vines, the next thing to be inspected is the pomegranates, the symbol of the royal virtue of patience. This is fittingly joined to love, which must of necessity be exercised in exercises of patience. Love is only true when at last it has become patient. It is impossible that patience should be found among us without the hammer of tribulations having worked on it. But equally, love that has not been tested by patience will be of little value, and patience which has not been shaped by love will be altogether shapeless and of no value at all.

So the Spouse looks to see if holy souls are breathing out patience, meditating on it and longing for it from the very depths of their heart. He looks to see if it breathes out, not from their own virtue which is nothing, but from him who is the God of patience and all comfort, since they wait for him with all the eagerness of sighs and groans and tears. It is idolatry to hope for any virtue except from the Lord God of virtues, from whom and in whom and through whom are all things.

Sermon 59.6–11

THE CHURCH'S ANXIETY ABOUT THE
EVILS OF CLERGY AND RELIGIOUS

Sg 6:10

I WENT DOWN TO THE ORCHARD OF ALMONDS
. . . MY SOUL DISTURBED ME, BECAUSE OF THE
CHARIOTS OF AMINADAB.†

I HAVE DISCUSSED how these verses befit
the Spouse; now let us see how God's grace
makes them also applicable to the Bride, who is
the Church. She herself, looking carefully in her
orchard, finds there matter to arouse grief rather
than approbation. If any earnest seeker after
truth were to enter today into the *orchard of almonds*—namely, into the life of those who have
taken a vow of chastity by accepting priestly or-
dination—and should diligently consider them,
would not such a man be very soon embarrassed
by his entry into the orchard? What has become
of all that the daughters of Zion found to
celebrate?

    In that enormous plant which, swollen with
honor and riches, has spread far and wide
throughout the land you will find very few

Is 11:1

shoots of the noble stock from Jesse's root.† You
will find a mere scattering of flowers upon

Is 11:2

whom rests the Spirit of Jesus.† Nearly every

Ex 7:12

shoot will have been turned into a serpent.†
Better to flee from the sight of them and avoid
their bite, unless at God's command you take
firmly in hand the task of loving correction. You
see that today God's Church is in the hands of
men such as these. They wield over the people a

Mic 7:14

rod of authority,† the power to control everything, at least insofar as it pertains to their own dignity and to the protection of their honor.

When you look closely at this rod, you find there no trace of the blossoms of Aaron's rod,† I mean the high priest, Christ. Churchmen of today possess Aaron's rod: they possess it in the lessons of the Gospel, in the creeds of their faith, in proclaiming their fidelity to it, in the sacred symbol of baptism, in the sacrament of the altar. This rod is as a witness against them, not as a wonder and an inspiration. Their concern is to make use of that shoot to give themselves the appearance of spiritual freedom, so that they may blossom into high office and bear the fruits of luxurious living.

Num 17:8

[*John of Forde now turns to the barren teaching and lives of those in authority in the Church in his time, and to the lack of fervor and zeal among those who have made religious vows.*]

LIKE A RIND OF POMEGRANATE, SO ARE YOUR CHEEKS, CONCEALING YOUR SECRETS.

The Bride's *cheeks* are modesty and patience, and they are there to shelter and protect the grains of faith entrusted to her from the trials that beset her on every side and to which she must of necessity almost constantly expose her *cheeks*. This is obviously a most difficult charge and a very heavy burden, for while she is forced to busy herself with external matters that summon her out to look after temporalities, all the time she desires far more to be occupied with those that call her to return within, directed heavenwards.

Sg 6:11

The chariots of Aminadab:† The wheels of fire represent the amazing speed, the very great acuteness, the unfathomable severity of God's judgements. God's judgements are spoken of as chariots because they move on four wheels: justice, prudence, fortitude, and temperance. Justice is eager for the glory of divine honor, for we know that the honor of God delights in right

Ps 99:4

judgement.† Prudence balances justice, so that zeal for distinguishing between motives and evaluating the intention has knowledge to control its fervor. Fortitude looks to the everlasting changelessness of God's judgements; and here the necessary balance is provided by temperance, and God compassionately tempers the severity of his sentence in the vessels of mercy that are called for.

I fear because of my own private *orchard of*

Sg 6:10

almonds.† I dread that when the Lord goes down into it, he will find fault with it for being barren. I fear that he will reject my fruits as rotten or bitter or unripe. But in this terror I have a great comfort that it is Aminadab—that is, Jesus—who is master of these chariots, and his very name speaks of meekness and tenderness. It is for this precise reason that judgement has been given by the Father to the Son of Man, so that men are solemnly brought before a Man for their judgement. From that human countenance they are to expect humanity and mercy to the honor and glory and splendor of the only Son of the Father.

Sermon 60.1–14

WISE TEACHERS;
EVIL RULERS IN THE CHURCH

Wise Teachers in the Church

BEWARE, we are given a completely new kind of serpent! They are strong with great wisdom. These men of grace wind their gracious way into the human heart—not on the seductive words of human wisdom, but rather they breathe out the doctrine of the Spirit in a gentle whisper of sound. This serpent-like prudence takes nothing away from the simplicity of the dove,[†] but, in the wonderful arrangement of divine wisdom, gives it an edge, while simplicity in turn gently tranquilizes its partners. They are simple as doves. They do not search for profit or for position and power by intrigue, or teach error by false leaven. What they preach is not themselves but Jesus Christ as Lord, with themselves as servants for Jesus' sake.[†] Paul says, *We were babes among you, like a nurse taking care of her little ones. We shared with you not only the Gospel of God, but also our own selves.*[†] Here we have the truly dove-like eye, a true dove. It looks only at Jesus, with a gaze wholly pure and simple, gazing at his bride in faithful and loving emulation.

Mt 10:16

2 Cor 4:5

1 Th 2:3-8

Evil Rulers and Pastors in the Church

How rare a bird is this in our land today![†] O Church of God, O dove of Jesus, his pure one,

Juvenal, *Satires*, 6

how different are the pastors and teachers you
know nowadays! Rarely do they look deeply at
you with the pure gaze of contemplation. These

Is 60:8

too *fly like clouds,*† towering menacingly above
your head, lofty in power, heavy with authority,
strong in their splendor. This does not come
from God. They are swollen with the lust for
power. Wherever the wind of ambition drives,
there they are borne with frantic haste. These
men are birds of prey rather than doves.

> [*John then launches into a diatribe against
> pastors who are greedy for power and privi-
> lege, who look only for pleasure and not for the
> good of God's people. Then he moves on to dis-
> cuss good pastors.*]

Good and Faithful Rulers in the Church

Let no one accuse me of speaking offensively of
all those who now bear authority. Even in these
days, the Lord has prepared no small lamp for

Ps 132:17

Is 61:9

his Christ;† and of that seed which the Lord has
blessed he has left no small remnant for us.† Let
us look, let us rejoice, with great admiration let
us cry aloud, *Who are these who fly like doves to*

Is 60:8

their windows?† These men are set high in the
sky; through the example of their sublime life,
and to all who dwell beneath them, they are a
shade from the heat by day, and a refuge and

Is 4:6

shelter from the storm and the rain.† They
tower aloft, but very humbly consider themselves lower than others, and fly back to their
windows—their time of prayer—like doves.
Even if they live in great mansions, they regard

all earthly greatness as cramped and tottering. Like a dove they meditate in the depths of their contemplation, considering all things as transient, and thus they put no value on them. With inexpressible groaning they yearn after the eternal tabernacles. In their mouth is ever a word of holy encouragement and tender consolation, like a branch of the olive. So that they may always have something from which to bring forth old and new,† a table is ever spread in their sight,† and on it are the loaves of offering.† Their dwelling is beside springs of water,† and from these springs of God, they draw grace for themselves, and also pour it out for us, through Jesus Christ our Lord.

Mt 13:52

Ps 23:5

Mt 12:4; Lev 24:5-9

Sg 5:12

Sermon 16.7–9

X

THE ANGELS:
THE FATHERS OF THE CHURCH

AN OVERVIEW

FINALLY, let us look briefly at two subjects which do not fall neatly into the structure of this book, but are close to the centre of John's thinking and were dear to his heart.

ANGELS. Firstly, the angels figure prominently in the Gospels at important moments in the life of Jesus: at the annunciation and at his birth; at his temptations in the desert, and in the garden of Gethsemane. They are also present in many places in both the Old Testament and the New Testament.

The angels have a highly significant place in John's spiritual journey, too. Just one quotation, out of more than a hundred others, should suffice to demonstrate this:

> The angel who was sent to minister to Tobias revealed to us the immense kindness and love of the whole host of heaven towards us. By the Lord's command this love waits, eager to assist us when we wish to set out and make progress. Their love is girded for service, going before us as our guide; it is the inseparable love of friendship, a trustworthy guardian, a delightful consolation. Their love is strong to help us, sweet to solace us, long-suffering to endure us, wise to advise us, powerful to heal us, sedulous to encourage us.[1]

These angelic beings, John insists, are always close to God, praising him and exulting in his presence, never turning away to

[1] Sermon 111.2

315

mar the beauty of their holiness. Theirs is for ever the joy of the Holy Spirit; and to all eternity they give voice to songs of jubilation and praise.

THE 'FATHERS'. Secondly, John rests his teaching firmly on the tradition of the Church. A careful study of his writings reveals that he was well versed in the classical latin writers—Virgil, Terence, Cicero, Callustus, Juvenal and yet others. His prose also shows the influence of the greek classics, though I cannot go more fully into this subject here. Yet his main sources, apart from Holy Scripture and the Holy Rule, are the renowned Latin Fathers of the Church, mainly Saint Augustine, Saint Ambrose, and Saint Gregory the Great—as he tells us explicitly in a passage quoted below.[2]

In this same passage he mentions and in many places he quotes from his immediate predecessors in the twelfth century, chiefly Saint Bernard of Clairvaux, on whom he relies for much of his thought, but also Gilbert of Hoyland who had written the sermons on the Song of Songs that preceded John's own commentary. Included on this list is Guerric of Igny whose lovely sermons are still a joy to read even today.[3] These three are Cistercian writers. We also find on this list Richard of Saint Victor whose work Benjamin Major is quoted in John's sermons Twenty-Five and Seventy-One, and probably in other places. He says of these men, 'Their fiery speech is evidence of the fire that burns in their hearts'.[4]

Abbot John draws on those who went before him, yet appropriates and expresses what he finds in his own unique way. He is therefore a wise teacher, for he breathes new insights into the tradition of the Church and finds striking ways of expression that evoke a deep and uplifting response in the minds and hearts of his listeners and, even after nine centuries, in his readers.

---

[2] Sermon 24.2; below, 'Fathers of the Church as Sources'
[3] Two volumes of Liturgical Sermons
[4] Sermon 24.2 (below)

THE VISION OF THE ANGELS

HIS APPEARANCE IS LIKE LEBANON, CHOICE AS
THE CEDARS.[†]   Sg 5:15

FOR THE ANGELS, from the very moment
of his conception, the appearance of Jesus
aroused praise and wonder, glory and exultation. Cloud and darkness in no way clouded the
sight of angels. For the angels the light of his
Godhead shone only the brighter from that
ethereal and gleaming cloud where the Father's
voice was heard, thundering out to them more
loudly, *This is my beloved Son, in whom I am well
pleased.*[†] This is the loftiness of the *cedars of*   Mt 3:17
Lebanon, this is the straightness, this is the
sweet fragrance.

This is the sublime justice of the angels,
namely, to contemplate God sublimely and
stretch out to him with all their strength. Then
this is their peace: that they mutually take delight
in the Lord with the most selfless love. In this
peace, their noble evenness leaves nothing
twisted or out of line with the evenness of up-
rightness, for *He makes peace in the sublime heights
of heaven.*[†] Finally, joy in the Holy Spirit, the   Job 25:2
fruit of justice and peace, is the fragrance of these
same trees. This is a scent most delicious to God
and to their own selves, and they never cease to
breathe it out from their own very beginning.

Never even for a moment have they dishonored the beauty of their holiness. Never from the beginning of their blessed state have they turned their eyes away from the face of the Father and his only Son, not for the slightest flicker. Joy in the Holy Spirit is believed to be the sweetness that belonged originally to them because in those blessed throats it gives birth for all eternity to songs of jubilation and praise.

With good reason, then, does the bride compare the appearance of her Beloved to the appearance of Lebanon, for the beauty of the Beloved keeps unimpaired the freshness it had at its birth, and therefore is all the more noble, for while the other is destined at some time to fade, his beauty from the moment of its first flowering came forth never to perish. This explains why the Spouse himself is called an angel by his Father. For being born of a virgin, he showed himself an angel not only in his charity and obedience, but also in his heavenly and untainted birth. So the bride compares him to the beautiful appearance of Lebanon.

For Lebanon is truly the virgin country of everlasting love, of unstained holiness, of purest delight.† It is named Lebanon, which means 'whiteness', for it happily preserved the whiteness of its holiness, not only without loss, but even with an increase of beauty. The whiteness of Lebanon—that is, the angels—emerged from the dark cloud of the fallen angels in all its white radiance, cleaving firmly and purely for evermore to the whiteness of that eternal Light† which is Christ.

Sir 24:20

Ws 7:26

Its beauty is renewed day by day by the continual contemplation of the face of Christ, or rather, it becomes progressively more white. It longs to transform its own appearance into his. These angels, these cedars, chose to take their stand in heaven, to live in a blissful integrity, each in turn cleaving purely and soberly to their unchangeable beginning, the Only Son of the Father. The strength of constant love keeps each of them looking with unwavering gaze at the living source of their light. Solely through the free gift of his goodness, he divides light from darkness, so that while darkness falls and fails, they themselves may become and remain *light in the Lord*.†   Eph 5:8

There is shadow even in that country of eternal brightness, for it contains a mountain. The mountain is 'shady' because the nearer it is to eternal light, the more certainly and profoundly it understands, as if under the symbol of shadows, the nature of its own state and inherent changeableness of substance. Its 'denseness' is the united companionship of blessed spirits, where love is all eager for the same thing, all active for the same good. To live each one for the sake of all, and all for the sake of each is to know a most pure and sweet enjoyment.

The Spouse of the Bride is the very wisdom of God, and it is said of him, *He is lovelier than the sun, and compared to the light he is found to be superior.*† Yet however incomparable his beauty,   Ws 7:29 it does not forbid a partial comparison where there is a certain likeness. And so the Bride holds out to the daughters of Jerusalem an utterly lucent mirror, full of grace, in which they may contemplate the appearance of her Beloved.

Sg 2:17

Jn 16:25

But even on this mirror the eyes of mortals cannot look long, because it is too bright. Only in shadow and in mystery is it possible, with side-long glances, *until day breaks and shadows flee.*† But of course, at the breath of that most joyous day, when the shadows of all mysteries have fled away, there will be no need of the mirror of comparisons. His very appearance will show itself quite openly, in fulfillment of the Spouse's own words, *I shall not then speak to you in parables, but I shall openly tell you of the Father.*†

May it be our privilege also to rejoice with his bride and in her, in the joy of that blessed 'telling', on the day when all will see the beauty of the Spouse of the Church, our Lord Jesus Christ.

Sermon 34.4-10

FATHERS OF THE CHURCH AS SOURCES

AFTER DEEP THOUGHT, you—and I together with you—will question on this matter those who have gone into this doctrine more fully and been more frequently anointed with the most holy kiss of Jesus. He has breathed on them and filled them with his Holy Spirit, so that they have understood how to speak in a way that pleases him. They hand down to us nothing that they have not first read in their own hearts, dictated from the mouth of Jesus, deeply incised with his finger, inscribed by the Spirit of the living God as if in ink.

Let us—our hearts filled with holy love—consider those companions of the bride:[1] Gregory,[2] Augustine,[3] Ambrose,[4] for example; and in our own day, those noble friends of the bride: Bernard,[5] Guerric,[6] Richard,[7] Gilbert,[8] and others like them. The unction of the Spirit first made these men its pupils, and then made them into teachers. It was in the marriage chamber that they learned to understand the marriage song, and only then did they become able to explain this sacred love to us. Even so, they could hardly expound in human words more than the slightest part of the great things they had learned in their hearts. Still, I receive them as angels of God, and I listen to them with my whole heart as to seraphim, a name that is said to mean those who both burn and set others on fire.

Their fiery speech is evidence of the fire that is in their hearts. When they talk of the love of the Spouse and Bride, it is not with stealthy dependence on the experience of others, but with open-handed sharing of their own experience.[†] With men like this the Spouse   See Bibliography

[1] All were prolific and widely influential spiritual theologians.
[2] Gregory the Great, Pope († 604)
[3] Bishop of Hippo († 430)
[4] Bishop of Milan († 397)
[5] Abbot of Clairvaux in Burgundy († 1153)
[6] Abbot of Igny in Champagne († 1157)
[7] Canon Regular of Saint Victor († 1173)
[8] Abbot of Swineshead / Hoyland, Lincolnshire († 1172)

Jn 3:11

speaks as to intimates. As he says, *We speak of what we know and we bear witness to what we have seen.*† They are the only ones blessed with a real understanding of what they say, for to have loved means to have understood.[1]

In this matter, it is they to whom we must turn for information. When the bride speaks of her Beloved's lips, it is quite likely she means men like these, since it is he himself who is found to have said to each single one of them, *If you separate the precious from what is worthless, you will be as my mouth.*†

Jer 15:19

Sermon 24.2

---

[1] Gregory the Great wrote 'Love itself is understanding.'

A SELECT BIBLIOGRAPHY

1. PATRISTIC AND MEDIEVAL COMMENTARIES ON THE SONG OF SONGS IN TRANSLATION

Anthologies

Denys Turner, *Eros and Allegory. Medieval Exegesis on the Song of Songs*. Kalamazoo: Cistercian Publications, 1995. Turner discusses the long tradition of Canticle exegesis and provides translations of commentaries from the seventh to the sixteenth century by Gregory the Great, Alcuin of York, Hugh of Saint Victor, William of Saint Thierry, Alan of Lille, Thomas of Perseigne, Thomas Gallus, Thomas Aquinas, Giles of Rome, Nicholas of Lyra, Denys the Carthusian, and John of the Cross.

Ambrose of Milan (Bishop, † 397)

See above, Anthologies

Bernard of Clairvaux (Cistercian Abbot, † 1153)

Bernard of Clairvaux: Sermons on the Song of Songs, 4 volumes. Translated by Kilian Walsh OCSO and Irene Edmonds. Spencer, Massachusetts-Kalamazoo, Michigan: Cistercian Publications, 1971-1980.

Gilbert of Hoyland [Swineshead] (Cistercian Abbot, † 1172)

Gilbert of Hoyland: Sermons on the Song of Songs, 3 volumes. Translated by Lawrence C. Braceland, SJ. Kalamazoo: Cistercian Publications, 1978-1979.

Gregory of Nyssa (Greek theologian and bishop, † c. 395)

Commentary on the Song of Songs, translated Casimir McCambley. Brookline, Massachusetts: Hellenic College Press, 1988.

John of Forde

John of Ford: Sermons on the Final Verses of the Song of Songs, 7 volumes. Translated by Wendy Mary Beckett. Kalamazoo: Cistercian Publications, 1977-1984.

Origen (Alexandrian exegete, † *c.* 251)

The Song of Songs: Commentary and Homilies. Translated R. P. Lawson. Westminster, Md., Newman Press, 1957

William of Saint Thierry (Cistercian, † 1148)

William of Saint Thierry: Exposition on the Song of Songs. Translated by M. Columba Hart OSB. Spencer, Massachusetts–Kalamazoo, Michigan: Cistercian Publications, 1970.

2. UNTRANSLATED PATRISTIC AND MEDIEVAL COMMENTARIES ON THE SONG OF SONGS

Anselm of Laon (?) (early twelfth-century scholar), *Enarratio in Canticum canticorum.* J.-P. Migne, Patrologia Latina, 162. [Hereafter PL]

Bede the Venerable (eighth-century english monk), *In Canticum canticorum, Libri VI*, in *Bedae Venerabilis Opera 2: Opera Exegetica.* Edited David Hurst OSB. Corpus Christianorum, Series Latina. Turnhout: Brepols. 1983.

Geoffrey of Auxerre (twelfth-century Cistercian), *Expositio in Cantica canticorum*, Edizione Critica a cura di Ferruccio Gastaldelli, 1. Rome, 1974.

Honorius Augustodunensis (twelfth-century Benedictine), *Expositio in Canticum canticorum.* 172:347-496.

Jean Gerson (Chancellor of the University of Paris, † 1429), *Super Canticum canticorum*, in M. Glorieux, ed., Jean Gerson: Oeuvres Complètes, volume 3. Paris 1971.

Procopius of Gaza (late fourth–early fifth-century exegete), *In Cantica canticorum*, J.-P. Migne, Patrologia Graeca 87(2): 1545-1780. [hereafter PG]

Richard of Saint Victor (twelfth-century canon regular of Saint Victor), *In Canticum canticorum expositio.* PL 196:405-524.

Theodoret of Cyrrhus (fifth-century bishop and theologian), *Explanatio in Canticum Canticorum*. PG 81:27-214.

3. SECONDARY WORKS ON MEDIEVAL CANTICLE EXEGESIS

Astell, A. W., *The Song of Songs in the Middle Ages*. Ithaca, New York: Cornell University Press, 1991.

Bell, David N., 'The Commentary on the Song of Songs of Thomas the Cistercian and His Conception of the Image of God'. *Citeaux: Commentarii Cistercienses* 28 (1977) 5-25.

Clark, Elizabeth A., 'The Uses of the Song of Songs: Origen and the Later Fathers', *Ascetic Piety and Women's Faith: Essays on Late Antique Christianity*. Lewiston, New York: Mellen, 1986.

Flint, Valerie, 'The Commentaries of Honorius Augustodunensis on the Song of Songs', *Revue Bénédictine* 84 (1974) 196-211.

Matter, Ann E., *The Voice of My Beloved: The Song of Songs in Western Mediæval Christianity*. Philadelphia: University of Pennsylvania Press, 1990.

Rowley, H. H., 'The Interpretation of the Song of Songs', *Journal of Theological Studies* 38 (1937) 337-363.

4. TEXTS OF JOHN OF FORDE'S SERMONS

The critical Latin edition of John's Commentary on the Song of Songs: *Iohannis de Forda Super Extremam Partem Cantici Canticorum Sermones CXX*, edd. Edmund Mikkers and Hilary Costello, Corpus Christianorum Continuatio Medievalis 17-18. Turnhout: Brepols, 1970.

John of Ford: A Sermon for Palm Sunday: 'Un sermon inédit de Jean de Ford', ed. Anonymously (C. H. Talbot), *Collectanea Ordinis Cisterciensium Reformatorum* 7 (1940-1945) 36-45.

5. STUDIES ON JOHN OF FORDE. A SELECTED BIBLIOGRAPHY

Aitken, Beverley, 'John of Forde: Twelfth-Century Guide for Twentieth-Century Monks', *A Gathering of Friends. The Learning and Spirituality of John of Forde*. Edd. Hilary Costello and Christopher Holdsworth. Kalamazoo: Cistercian Publications, 1996. Pages 189-198.

Costello, Hilary, 'The Idea of the Church in the Sermons of John of Ford', *Citeaux* 21 (1970) 236-264.

————. 'John of Ford', *Cistercian Studies [Quarterly]* 13 (1978) 46-67.

————. 'John of Ford and the Quest for Wisdom', *Citeaux* 23 (1972) 141-159.

————. 'The Secret of God in John of Ford', *Hallel* 11 (1983) 80-89.

———— and Christopher Holdsworth. *A Gathering of Friends. The Learning and Spirituality of John of Forde.* Kalamazoo: Cistercian Publications, 1996.

Holdsworth, Christopher. *'Another Stage . . . a different world': Ideas and People around Exeter in the Twelfth Century.* University of Exeter Press, 1979.

————. 'The Cistercians in Devon', *Studies in Medieval History presented to R. Allen Brown*, edd. Christopher Harper-Bill, Christopher Holdsworth, and Janet L. Nelson. Woodbridge, 1989. Pages 179-192.

————. 'John of Ford', *Citeaux* 21 (1970) 105-110.

————. 'John of Ford and the Interdict', *English Historical Review* 78 (1963) 705-714.

McCorkell, Edward. 'Herald of the Holy Spirit: John of Ford's Sermons on the Song of Songs', *Cistercian Studies [Quarterly]* 20 (1985) 303-313.

Mikkers, Edmund. 'The Christology of John of Ford', *Cistercian Ideas and Reality*, ed. John R. Sommerfeldt. Kalamazoo, 1978. Pages 220-244.

————. 'Image and Likeness: The Doctrine of John of Ford', *One Yet Two*, ed. M. Basil Pennington. Kalamazoo, 1976. Pages 352-356.

————. 'Jean de Ford', *Dictionnaire de Spiritualité* 8 (1999), columns 516-527.

————. 'Les sermons inédits de Jean de Ford sur le Cantique', *Collectanea Ordinis Cisterciensum Reformatorum, Ref.* 5 (1938) 250-261.

Oxenham, Elizabeth, 'The Return of the Jews at the End of Time in the Sermons of John of Forde *On the Song of Songs*', in Costello-Holdsworth, *A Gathering of Friends.* Pages 117-130.

————. 'Under the Apple Tree': A Comparative Exegesis of Song of Songs 2:3 in the Sermons by Bernard of Clairvaux and John of Ford', *Bernardus Magister*, ed. John R. Sommerfeldt. Kalamazoo, 1992. Pages 277-286.

INDEX